The Merrimack

BOOKS BY *Raymond P. Holden*

CHANCE HAS A WHIP

BELIEVE THE HEART

ABRAHAM LINCOLN: THE POLITICIAN
   AND THE MAN

FAMOUS SCIENTIFIC EXPEDITIONS

GRANITE AND ALABASTER *(Verse)*

NATURAL HISTORY *(Verse)*

THE ARROW AT THE HEEL *(Verse)*

SELECTED POEMS

THE MERRIMACK

Rivers of America

EDITED BY

Carl Carmer

AS PLANNED AND STARTED BY

Constance Lindsay Skinner

ASSOCIATE EDITOR
JEAN CRAWFORD

ART EDITOR
BENJAMIN FEDER

The Merrimack

BY

Raymond P. Holden

ILLUSTRATED BY

Aaron Kessler

RINEHART & CO., INC.
NEW YORK • TORONTO

Grateful acknowledgment is made to the following publishers for permission to reprint excerpts from their works:

Henry Holt and Company, Incorporated, New York, N. Y., for permission to reprint an excerpt from "West-Running Brook," Copyright, 1928, by Henry Holt and Company, Inc.; Copyright, 1956, by Robert Frost.

Little, Brown and Company, Boston, Mass., for permission to reprint excerpts from *Thirty Years*, by John P. Marquand, Copyright, 1954, by John P. Marquand.

PUBLISHED SIMULTANEOUSLY IN CANADA BY

CLARKE, IRWIN & COMPANY, LTD., TORONTO

COPYRIGHT © 1958 BY RAYMOND P. HOLDEN

ILLUSTRATIONS COPYRIGHT © 1958 BY RINEHART & COMPANY, INC.

PRINTED IN THE UNITED STATES OF AMERICA

For Barbara—and another river

Preface

Anyone who attempts to produce a portrait of so complex a subject as a river should, I think, be forgiven if he takes the liberty of mingling a certain amount of montage with his colors. A textbook of anatomy is not a portrait of a man. A guidebook is not a portrait of a living river. Some of the elements of river portraiture must even be worked into the picture with the help of mirrors. Each mile of channel and shore, each tributary, each village and city of the river valley is as important as each cell of a living body. Yet the painter must discover how to suggest their presence, as the presence of vital cells is evident in cheek and eye, without drawing each one in detail. He must, at the risk of incurring the displeasure of those who might have managed differently, decide what to put in and what to leave out in order to produce the total effect which to him is the river which he portrays. I have tried to present the Merrimack in all of its features and dimensions, as I see and feel it. The details which are not drawn in are not absent from my vision or from my feeling. Like cells of the human body they would bleed if injured. Without them the body could not flourish.

Here is the portrait, at best a reproduction, of a living river.

Raymond P. Holden
North Newport, New Hampshire
February 1958

Contents

The Merrimack

1 The River as an Identity

....

How are we to think of a river? Even the greatest of
streams, were they to be drained of their water, would not appear from very far above the earth to have made much of a
mark upon its sphere. There are, of course, exceptions, such
as the Colorado, whose canyon might be visible from the
moon, yet the Colorado is far from the greatest of rivers and
the majority have not entrenched themselves very deeply.

In human history, however, rivers are of enormous importance, having an effect upon men and their ways which
cannot but be visible from great distances in time, if not in
space. Tigris, Nile, Ganges, Yangtze, Jordan, Tiber, Thames
and a thousand others, large and small, will always be apprehensible no matter where man stands.

Among these is one of which I wish to speak. It is no
ancient river, either in terms of its association with man or
in terms of its own history. Many rivers are older than man
but there is little doubt that this one, as we know it today, is
not. Many rivers cannot be seen in their entire length at once
no matter how high the eye may mount above them. This
one can be. I have seen it myself, from source to sea, from an
altitude of no more than ten thousand feet. Yet looking at
the Merrimack River from the high vantage point of human
thought it is impossible for me or any man to see all of the
channels into which its influence has flowed.

How are we to think of a river? If we think of it, without mankind, in its place in primitive nature, it is little more than a drainage ditch, a rather simple device for enabling the law of gravity, as applied to water, to operate. It has, of itself, neither beauty nor use, since both use and beauty are of man's devising.

What a river is, then, is not merely the downward stream of water particles, laden with dissolved minerals and suspended organic substances, which carries back to the sea the moisture which the sea gave to the land for treatment. It is rather the parallel, the induced flow of life from a watered region outward, through dimensions too numerous and unrelated for mapping.

True, there are facts. Yet what are the facts of a face which has the lighted look of eyes and the sound of speaking breath? What are the facts of a river? Where is it located? How much land does it drain? What is the elevation above the sea, and the distance from the sea, of its source? How much water does it carry? How many people does it serve and how does it serve them? How did it get its name?

There are such facts pertinent to the Merrimack and they will be stated, yet they are not greatly contributory to an understanding of what the river is. Nothing is quite so simple as a mere statement of fact appears to make it. A boy who lived at the junction of the Pemigewasset and Winnipesaukee rivers near Franklin, in Merrimack County, New Hampshire, said, when asked by his teacher where the Merrimack rose, "Right behind my father's barn!" He stated a fact which, without others to go with it, might as well, like most facts, have been a fancy. The accident of name does not bound a river.

The name "Merrimack" is the white man's version of a

combination of Indian sounds signifying place of strong (or swift) water. The real source, whether the waters which spring from it have at their rising the name which they bear when they reach the sea, is the source which is farthest distant from the sea. The Merrimack rises under the chin of the Old Man of the Mountain, in the town of Franconia, eighty-five miles from Franklin. It rises on the slopes west of the Crawford Notch and in a score of high valleys from Lafayette and the Twins, Carrigain and Kancamagus, to Moosilauke in Warren. It rises in the hills about Winnipesaukee and Lake Wentworth close to the Maine border. Yet it is not known as the Merrimack until its waters, gathered in the Pemigewasset and the Winnipesaukee, reach the region of that boy's father's barn in Franklin, barely a hundred miles from the sea.

THE RIVER ON THE LAND

To understand how the Merrimack River can have been and can continue to be what it is to New England and the nation it is first necessary to know what and where it is. The easiest way of giving a background for the story to those to whom the river is only a name will be to describe its setting and its neighbors.

Between the southwestward curve of the New England shoreline and the St. Lawrence River, which empties the Great Lakes into the Atlantic Ocean between Labrador and Nova Scotia, is a region of mountains, in northern New York, Vermont, New Hampshire and Maine, from which the rain and snow which fall upon them drain, for the most part, southward through rivers of greater importance than length. These, without mentioning their tributaries, are from west to

east, the Hudson, the Connecticut, the Merrimack, the Piscataqua, the Saco, the Androscoggin and the Kennebec.

The Hudson, with the help of its tributary Mohawk,
carries the waters of the Adirondacks and a part of the Green
Mountains to the Atlantic in New York harbor. The Con-
necticut, dividing Vermont from New Hampshire, drains
both the Green and the White Mountains into Long Island
Sound. The Merrimack gathers the waters of nearly half of
New Hampshire and a large section of eastern Massachusetts,
entering the sea at the old and elegant city of Newburyport.
Some twenty miles northeast of Newburyport, at Portsmouth,
New Hampshire, the Piscataqua discharges the collected wa-
ters of the Salmon Falls, Oyster and Cocheco rivers into New
Hampshire's only harbor. Farther east, the Saco, which rises
on the eastern and southeastern slopes of the Presidential
Range, flows into the Atlantic past the twin mill towns of
Biddeford and Saco in Maine. The Androscoggin, rising in
the most northerly highlands of New Hampshire, carrying
part of the drainage of the northeastern slopes of the White
Mountains, joins the Kennebec near Bath, Maine, and there
pours through a fjordlike estuary into the sea.

The Merrimack is not the largest of these rivers and it
cannot be considered to be more important historically than
the Hudson or the Connecticut, but in its relationship to the
culture and economy of New England, which during the first
half of the nineteenth century, at least, were the dominant
culture and economy of the nation, it is unique. Perhaps
there can be no better way of coming to an appreciation of
the truth of this statement and of the story which I have to
tell than to follow it from sea-salt mouth to mountain source.

Twenty miles southwest of Portsmouth, New Hampshire, and the mouth of the Piscataqua, three miles south
of the Massachusetts-New Hampshire boundary and about

forty miles northeast of Boston, a gap in the sand dunes between Salisbury and Plum Island—a gap which but for a man-
made jetty stretching out from it into the sea would be almost
unnoticeable—marks the spot where the Merrimack gives to
the Atlantic the drainage of some five thousand square miles
of New England soil. Traveling up the river, under the
bridges of Newburyport past the mouth of the Powwow
which separates Amesbury from Salisbury, the swift, smooth
flood of the river runs between rounded hills flecked with
patches of wood and open fields dotted with dwellings and
farms. Seventeen miles west of the sea at Newburyport is the
first abrupt descent in the river's course, the falls above Porter's Island about which the shoe-making city of Haverhill
and the town of Bradford are gathered. From Haverhill the
river winds west and sometimes almost south through eight
miles of rolling farmland to another fall about which, on both
sides of the stream, has grown up the textile city of Lawrence,
now struggling to free itself from the effect of too much reliance upon the unreliable. Still farther upstream, to the southwest, another series of falls, among them the Pawtucket Falls
of the pioneers, is almost obliterated by canals and channels
beneath the mill buildings of the determined city of Lowell,
struggling, like Lawrence, to maintain in the face of shifts
and collapses in the textile industry its life-giving industrial
character. Through the center of the city of Lowell, almost
unrecognizable as the tranquil "Meadow River" which Thoreau and Emerson and a handful of minute men made famous,
the Concord River gropes for the Merrimack and finds it. Just
upstream from Pawtucket Falls, almost invisible now, were
the locks by means of which the Old Middlesex Canal, dead
and gone for more than a hundred years, brought Boston
commerce to the Merrimack. West of Lowell, beyond Wica-
sauke Island and Chelmsford, the river's course finally turns

northward through the high and wooded hills of Tyngsboro, beyond which it crosses the line into New Hampshire, a line of demarcation which was in dispute for more than one hundred years. On the right bank as you move upstream is the town of Hudson, known before 1830 as Nottingham and Nottingham West, whose chief modern distinction comes from a strange quirk in the river's economy. Here at Benson's Wild Animal Farm, whose name is a distinct understatement, is New England's most interesting zoo, to which wild creatures are brought direct from the jungles of Asia, Africa and South America and trained before being distributed to other zoos and circuses.

On the west bank of the river, at its junction with the northward-flowing Nashua River which has brought with it the soils of Lancaster and Groton, Massachusetts, is the city of Nashua, the most important relic of ancient Dunstable, now like the cities of the lower river struggling to adjust itself to the wounds to which the rapacity of men and their inability to see far enough into the future have laid it open. Nashua, which took such hope successively from canal, railroad and textiles only to see them all fail her, is still a New England city of character and dignity, building a new economy on the ruins of the old, as it did after the great fire which almost destroyed the city in 1930.

A little way upriver from the city of Nashua, beyond stretches of placid water bordered by sand and pine, between Thornton's Ferry and Reed's Ferry in the town of Merrimack, whose names recall the era when bridges were nonexistent, the Souhegan River, carrying the waters of Baboosick Brook, enters from the west. The Souhegan rises in Ashburnham, Massachusetts, on the slopes of Watatic Mountain and flows northeast through New Ipswich, Wilton and Milford, old towns which have retained, as a New England town should when pressed, more of their character than their prosperity. East of Milford the Souhegan is joined by a small brook with a large name—Quohquinapassakassanahog—at the upper end of which lies the tiny village of Amherst, where Daniel Webster made his first active appearance in a courtroom and where, six years later, in 1811, Horace Greeley, Lincoln's gadfly and founder of the *New York Tribune,* was born.

From Reed's Ferry to Goff's Falls in the town of Bedford is perfect pine country, sandy and gently undulating, once cut almost bare but now largely re-covered with green forest. It was along this stretch of the river that Thoreau, during his week afloat in the Merrimack, saw how the sand—once the covering mat of tree-roots and forest mold is broken by destructive tillage or too heavy grazing—can well up almost like water and turn acres of the countryside into a desert waste. Here, close to a spot where Thoreau and his brother camped for the night, is John Goffe's mill, on Bowman's Brook, an old mill built by Colonel John Goffe, Indian fighter and hunter, in 1744, and recently restored by his descendant George Woodbury.

The Piscataquog River, not to be confused with Portsmouth's Piscataqua, joins the main stream of the Merrimack just below Amoskeag Falls, drawing its water from a large bow of sparsely settled land from North Lyndeborough through Francestown and Deering to North Weare, overlooked by Crotched Mountain and the twin Uncanoonucks.

Above the turbulent and long-troublesome Amoskeag Falls, whose conquest by canal was one of the first steps in the taming of the upper river, rise the great mill buildings of the Amoskeag Manufacturing Company, once the largest cotton-mill concentration in the world and now both a memory and a living manufacturing center, having been taken over by a number of new and varied industries to keep Manchester,

once threatened with extinction, as told elsewhere in this book, a healthy, thriving city.

From Manchester past Martin's Ferry to Hooksett, where another cross-country dike of upthrust rock creates another fall, the river seems more agricultural than commercial, swift without being turbulent, like the strong muscle hidden in a quiet arm, bordered by forest and field, reflecting hills of increasing height and suggesting by the character of the clouds reflected on its surface an exciting nearness to the greater mountains of the north. From the Pinnacle, just above Hooksett, between the new New Hampshire turnpike and the river, you can see, as Thoreau did when he climbed it 119 years ago, the vast blue bulk and serrated ridges of the mountains a hundred miles away in which the Merrimack has its most distant source and which are responsible for its power.

Between Hooksett and Concord, New Hampshire's capital city, are more interruptions of the river's tranquillity in Garven's and Turkey Falls in the town of Bow. In the same area, on the east bank a short distance apart, the Soucook and Suncook rivers, draining the region of transition from peneplain to upland, gather the waters of the eastern towns of Allenstown, Epsom, Pittsfield, Barnstead, Strafford, Farmington, Loudon and Gilmanton, waters no longer sandy and slow but beginning to be milky white torrents cobbled with boulders.

Concord is about midway between the mouth and the source of the Merrimack and here, as if uncertain how to reach the sea, there are unmistakable signs that the river has wavered in its course. Ponds in the glacial drift of the valley east of the capital's Main Street, cut off from the flowing river, mark parts of the channel of an ancient meander. Concord's commercial activities, which, though many and varied, have not given it the aspect of a manufacturing town, make, as far as the city proper is concerned, no use of the river's power. A few miles north of the city the deep, smooth stream is broken by another swift descent in Sewall's Falls, and a little farther upstream the Merrimack's largest tributary, the Contoocook—which rises far to the south in the highlands of the Monadnock region almost at the Massachusetts border and which is the only river in New England whose entire flow is northward—pours into the main stem of the Merrimack system.

NORTH FLOWING BRANCH

The Contoocook, which is probably known to few people outside of New Hampshire, is one of the most beautiful of inland rivers, and it has preserved in its valley the image and atmosphere of an earlier New England than that which we know today. From Peterborough to the Merrimack there is little that is unlovely. Peterborough was one of the early textile centers, the home of the first library in the United States to be supported by tax-raised funds, and is perhaps best known today as the indirect result of its choice by one of the greatest of American composers as a retreat in which to do his composing. Had Edward MacDowell lived beyond his early forties he would in all probability have taken rank as the nation's greatest musical genius. Unhappily he did not, but his widow created by hard work and the help of friends a memorial worthy of his genius—a colony, on the site of his woodland studio, known as the MacDowell Colony, to which creative artists in need of a place to work in peace and quiet may come and find it. Many are the poets, dramatists, novelists and musicians who have produced enduring work in this Merrimack Valley sanctuary.

It was on the Contoocook, at Hillsborough, that New Hampshire's only President of the United States, Franklin Pierce, was born. On a hill high above a bend in the north-bound stream near Henniker there stands the home—built in 1760 and done in the style of the fine houses of Portsmouth and Newburyport—of a fabulous character known as Ocean Born Mary. This house was one of two built by the brothers of Mary Wilson Wallace, whose birth at sea in 1720, when her mother was en route from Ireland to Boston, saved her ship from destruction by pirates. The pirate Captain who boarded the ship gave up his idea of making the passengers abandon it when he saw the newborn babe, and instead presented a bolt of brocaded cloth to the terrified mother and asked that she give her daughter the name Mary and have the material made into a dress to be worn by Mary at her wedding. A piece of the dress has been preserved. Mary herself—ever after known as Ocean Born Mary—was preserved for ninety-four years, dying in Henniker in 1814. The house is still standing on its wild hill above the Contoocook, and though it has not taken on a coat of paint it has in recent years acquired a number of colorful embellishments for its legend.

At the junction of the Contoocook and the Merrimack, the village of Penacook, partly in Concord, and partly in the adjoining town of Boscawen (usually pronounced something like Boskwin), makes use of the water power of the reinforced river. Beyond Penacook is the Daniel Webster country, including Salisbury, Franklin, Northfield and Canterbury. In a part of Salisbury which is now included in Franklin, New Hampshire's greatest statesman was born and spent the impressionable years of his youth, years which were, as I shall point out in a later chapter, of vital importance to the nation.

In Franklin the Merrimack, as such, is born, for here come together the collected waters of its two main sources, the Pemigewasset and the Winnipesaukee, the former an indistinguishable continuation of the lower river and the latter adding such a volume of water to the system that it is more than a mere tributary. When Dr. Philip Carrigain of Concord made his great map of New Hampshire in 1816, he gave the name Merrimack to the stream which more recent maps list as the Pemigewasset. Merrimack it is, though of such different aspect as to justify a separate name.

THE EARTH BENEATH

I have suggested that the Merrimack is not a very old river. Not old as rivers go. Not so old as man, who has lived even in North America for somewhere between twenty and thirty thousand years. The Merrimack cannot have flowed in its present course for much more than ten thousand. As we pause here at the junction of the Pemigewasset and the Winnipesaukee, it is not difficult to see why this must be so, to understand why the heart of New England must have been, when man was beginning to triumph over his environment along the Tigris and produce the molecule of civilization, little more than a barren waste of broken rock and sand and primitive plants. It is certainly a fact that the region now comprised by the Merrimack Valley must have been drained in pre-glacial times and that a river did the draining. Yet it cannot, in its lower reaches at least, have been the Merrimack. There are traces of an old river channel under the city of Lowell, to the south of the present stream, and it is not impossible that the waters of upland central New Hampshire drained to the southward, perhaps into the convenient basin of Massachusetts Bay in the neighborhood of Boston.

To get at the real history of the land through which the Merrimack flows it would be necessary to go back three hundred million years, perhaps four hundred million, when the sediments which formed New Hampshire rock were being deposited by the shallow seas which spread over New England and remained over it for perhaps a million years. It is enough to say that the surface of the earth was not at that early date any more stable than it is now. Sometimes it humped itself and poured the seas away and then subsided to let the water return and deposit more sediment.

In the Devonian period, about three hundred million years ago, great changes in the earth's crust took place, folding and squeezing the horizontal layers of sediment until they resembled the flutings of an accordion. Naturally the layers of sediment which had hardened into rock broke and slipped over one another or fell away leaving great faults. The pressures involved in these alterations changed the sedimentary rocks into what are known as metamorphic rocks. Crystals began to appear. Molten rock from deeper in the earth flooded up through cracks and provided the heat which produced further changes and left New Hampshire full of slow-cooled igneous rock which we call granite.

Two hundred million years ago, in late Paleozoic time, New Hampshire became a permanent land area whose elevation shifted but never enough to let in the sea again. It was sometimes mountain, sometimes plain. In this period it may be said, perhaps, that the raw material of the Merrimack Valley was formed, but it was still too unstable for erosion to wear out a permanent watercourse.

Some time between five hundred thousand and a million years ago the land took a relatively stable form and the downflow of water set to work cutting recognizable valleys. Yet it was not until about one hundred thousand years ago that the sculptor, ice, began to put the finishing touches on the uplands of New Hampshire. The mountains were by this time high enough and the climate cold and moist enough to support local glaciers which, long before the coming of the great ice sheet, carved their signatures on the mountain walls.

Some time between fifty thousand and one hundred fifty thousand years ago, and probably more than once, the mountain glaciers of New Hampshire grew and intensified their work. Between forty thousand and sixty thousand years ago a vast sheet of ice which had gathered in eastern Canada and Labrador began to spread southward until, finally reaching and absorbing the mountain glaciers of northern New England, it continued onward to the sea. Twenty thousand years ago this great glacier, influenced by a changing climate, began to wither away, retreating northward but leaving accumulations of ice in vast basins among the worn-down hills. Between fourteen and ten thousand years ago most of the permanent ice in New England had disappeared.

The recession of the glacier had not been a rapid one. It was not a case of ice and snow in March and bare ground and springing green in April. It was a slow, if thunderous, retreat with a wild rush of roaring waters emerging from the ice front in spring and summer, a continuous snapping and roaring of crackling pinnacles and toppling cliffs, and in winter an artillery bombardment of regelation. The mountainous front of the ice receded and readvanced, totaling perhaps no more than a liberation from its weight of two hundred feet of ground in any year and covering those two hundred feet with silt and gravel and boulders.

By 10,000 or perhaps 9000 B.C. most of New England was uncovered but with many large remnant masses of ice discharging huge volumes of water which had no choice but to follow the lowest ground toward the sea, scouring out, by means of the fine particles of glacier-ground stone with which it was laden, the beginnings of valleys as we know them, held back sometimes by prominences of the land which, relieved of the great weight of the old glacier, rose up tilting downward toward the mountains in the north.

As more of the remnant glaciers melted away, the river channels grew more durable and gradually established themselves, cascading over ledges of rock which could not be cut through, bending around piles of material left by the ice in the shape of moraines and eskers.

AS THE EAGLE SEES IT

The best picture of what has resulted from this ancient process, here in the upper river, is to be had from the air, since you cannot follow two streams at once on the ground. At Franklin the Pemigewasset swings slightly to the northwest for a dozen miles through a rapidly sloping area of wooded hills and meadow intervals, climbing at the rate of

ten or eleven feet to the mile toward Bristol. Through Bristol
to the Pemigewasset runs the tumultuous Newfound River,
carrying the waters of the beautiful Newfound Lake which
mirrors Mt. Cardigan, in a descent of over two hundred feet
in less than three miles. Above Bristol the river swings sharply
east toward New Hampton, named by Jonathan Moulton
after his native village, the third New Hampshire town to
be settled. The New Hampton Academy, originally a Baptist
theological school but now a college preparatory school for
boys, with a long list of distinguished graduates, was founded
here in 1821.

At New Hampton the Pemigewasset River is little more
than ten miles from the point at which the Winnipesaukee
River leaves its parent lake, the largest in New Hampshire.
If you were in an airplane at a point midway between New
Hampton and The Weirs, circling slowly, you would see to
the northeast, east and southeast a shining wilderness of
island-dotted water, the Lakes Region of New Hampshire,
with Squam Lake draining into the Pemigewasset below Ashland and huge Winnipesaukee pouring its flood through Win-
nisquam and the Winnipesaukee River to the junction with
the Pemigewasset at Franklin. To the north and northwest
lies the blue-shadowed and cloud-tufted bulk of the great
mountains, cut by the deep, arrow-straight cleft through
which the white Pemigewasset descends fourteen hundred
feet in forty miles from Profile Lake to Ashland. In the distant
northeast, over the four-thousand-foot bulk of Sandwich
Dome, is a vast area of forest and mountain, entirely unin-
habited save by occasional lumbering crews, known as the
Pemigewasset Wilderness, now a part of the White Mountain
National Forest and so preserved both as a wild reserve of
natural though not untouched forest and a source and control

for the important East Branch of the Pemigewasset, which joins the main Pemigewasset stream below the lumber town of Lincoln at North Woodstock.

Only campers, loggers and mountain climbers know the streams, the forest trails and high summits of this region. Along the main north-south branch of the Pemigewasset, however, are scenes familiar to millions of visitors from all over the country. The Old Man of the Mountain, jutting his granite chin out into space fifteen hundred feet above Profile Lake, is one of the most famous of all natural phenomena; and the Flume, a deep cleft in the natural rock formed by the washing away of the material which was once forced into it while the side wall rocks remained untouched, has been a tourist attraction for more than a century. At North Woodstock, from the west, tumbles through a series of rocky caverns between Mt. Kinsman and Mt. Moosilauke the icy water of Lost River. All about, north, west and east, is forest which, though most of it has been cut over more than once, is today much as it was three hundred years ago.

FOREST, FLESH OF THE WATERS

The so-called "primeval" forest, in the sense of a forest changeless since the beginning of time, certainly never existed in New England or anywhere else, for there were forces acting to bring about forest change long before man brought his ingenuity to bear upon the problem. The New England forest, which covered practically 95 per cent of New England, was, when the first Europeans saw it, probably one which had gone through many changes caused by climate, wind, flood, fire and insects—none of which was invented by man, though he has managed to intensify the impact of all of them—and had reached a state of equilibrium.

Even before the white man came to this region we know as New England, even, for that matter, before the Indian came to it, there would have been patches where the great forest was broken. Fire, started perhaps by lightning, burning over hundreds of acres, destroying the consumable forest mold, would clear a space which might take a century to heal. Wind and ice storm could level great tracts and under the resulting tangle choke off forest growth for years. Blight of scale and winged insects could maim many square miles of trees in a season and leave them dying and weak, unable to withstand storm or winter.

There can have been no time when a trip up the Merrimack Valley, had there been anyone to make such a trip, would not have brought to view clearings resulting from such disasters. Yet they must have been more localized than the clearings which appeared in the eighteenth and nineteenth centuries when man, greedy for a living from the land, had really organized his ability to devastate.

In spite of the changes wrought by man and nature in the Merrimack Valley, its less than two hundred miles lead today from the present to the past, from the sea to the mountains. About the headwaters of the river, in the mountains of Franconia and the Pemigewasset Wilderness, are conditions of forest and upland which cannot be very different from those of eight or ten thousand years ago, while in the peneplain below, where the cities lie, nothing is as it was even three hundred years ago.

2 Men Look upon the Flowing

....

We do not know at what point in time men's ears first heard the sound of the waters of the Merrimack system, a sound, in the upper reaches of the river at least, of many notes that are almost a part of the forest, kin to the soughing of the pine boughs and the sweeping rustle of maple, beech and birch.

The great forest which slowly succeeded the ice in New England was, however, like an area of low pressure drawing living things toward it from the west and south. The pressure was never very great, for man had not yet learned to associate his inchoate ideas of agriculture with regions which did not immediately suggest the practice of it. The continent was large and never crowded and the pressure upon man from behind was never much greater than the pull of the emptiness before him.

The Merrimack Valley, like the rest of New England, was of course inhabited, in a sense, before the white man reached it. Man had come to the region at a fairly early date, trying out the climate of the lands which, following the recession of the glacier, the sun had made useful to him. The Indians who first moved up the river valleys and through the northeastern forest, however, seemed not to learn from the land much more than how to survive. They adapted themselves to the conditions which they found and, as primitive people will, devised tabus and fetishes which served, in a measure, as modern game laws serve us. Yet they never were really masters of their domain. They had a few permanent settlements, preferring to wander with the seasons, now planting crops of corn, beans, squash and pumpkins in the clearings and river intervals, now hunting and fishing. They had New England to themselves for centuries but they changed it little. They never learned man's fearful and wonderful secret of adding, for good or ill, a new dimension to the world, the dimension of the mind and its works.

The native people of the Merrimack Valley formed a small section of the great northeastern linguistic group known as Algonkian. They were a group of families organized on a tribal basis but without any apparent political organization and probably without any recognized full-time chieftain, although organization for attack or defense always seemed to find a leader agreed upon—a man such as Passaconaway, whose name is perpetuated by both a village and a four-thousand-foot mountain. Passaconaway was the head, off and on during his lifetime, of the Penacook Confederacy, a kind of Merrimack Valley treaty organization which looked after the safety of the valley tribes, the Nashuas, the Souhegans, the Amoskeags, the Penacooks and the Winnipesaukees. These, like all the other Indians of the Northeast, had when the first Englishmen came among them suffered from an enemy from which no chieftain could protect them. The smallpox killed all but perhaps a thousand of them before 1630.

It was Passaconaway, shrewd and willing to be friendly, who led the Indians of the region when the first white man came and it was the newcomers' somewhat fantastic descriptions of him which set the pattern for much of our ensuing misconception of the Indians. There was among the early adventurers in New England a strong inheritance from the Middle Ages, not so long past, of belief in the magical qualities of the unfamiliar. So, to the New England settler, Passaconaway, the primitive man who could live and be unafraid without the white man's pabulum for body or spirit, became a man of magic "who could make the water burne, the rocks move, the trees dance, metamorphise himself into a flaming man. He will do more; for in winter, when there are no green leaves to be got, he will burne an old one to ashes, and putting those into water, produce a new green leaf, which you shall not only see, but substantially handle and carry away; and make of a dead snake's skin a living snake, both to be seen, felt, and heard."

Poor Passaconaway! For all his reputed witchcraft he could not turn a leaden prospect into a golden one. He died exhorting his people, begging them to surrender themselves peacefully to the white man, something which they could not quite learn to do, and which the white man ended by making impossible.

Many of the early settlers have written about the Indians but few understood them and most reported what they saw in terms which are impossible to accept. Their myths and legends, made much of in the nineteenth century, are so confused and clouded with civilized romanticism that no Indian would recognize them.

The Indians were, however, as will be seen, at first friendly and of much help to the pioneers. Later, for more reasons than one, they were cruelly hostile. They came to exert upon the colonists a pressure quite out of proportion to their numbers.

RIVER OF MYSTERY

It is probable that white men set foot in New England a thousand or more years ago, five or six hundred years before Columbus. There is some slight evidence on this point which will be mentioned in a later chapter; more evidence will undoubtedly be uncovered as time goes on. There is, however, no easily accepted proof of European settlement in the Merrimack Valley, or for that matter in New England as a whole, before the beginning of the seventeenth century. European knowledge of New England begins for all practical purposes something more than a century earlier than that, with the voyage to the northeastern coast of North America of John Cabot of Bristol, England, in 1497. Cabot visited and apparently mapped Newfoundland and the region immediately about the Gulf of St. Lawrence, although his original maps are now lost.

It may seem strange that in an age of exploration and discovery, such a notable landfall, more directly connected with North America than Columbus's, was not followed immediately by voyages southward, feeling their way along the New England coast. It may seem equally strange that looking back upon that period we find that there appears to be no mention of Cabot's voyages (he apparently made a follow-up voyage in 1498) for more than twenty years after they took place.

In the fifteenth and sixteenth centuries, however, there was much personal rivalry and political chicanery in the world of exploration, and no matter what they discovered explorers could drop out of sight, with their discoveries, overnight if there were shifts of favor and influence at home.

Apparently John Cabot suffered from some such shift, for although it was he who was later recognized as the founder of the English claim to North America he disappeared from history shortly after—perhaps during—his second voyage.

If he did, as he intended to do, sail on his second voyage southward from the Gulf of St. Lawrence, he must have coasted along past Maine and New Hampshire and perhaps Massachusetts, but we have no way of telling that he did.

A man named David Ingram, no great admiral rich with gold braid, lace and plume, but a simple sailor with some of the characteristics of a soldier, may have been the first Englishman to set foot in the Merrimack Valley, which the French wandered across many times in the latter half of the sixteenth century. Ingram was, according to his narrative which was printed by Hakluyt in 1589, marooned by Captain John Hawkins somewhere on the Gulf of Mexico with nearly one hundred other voyagers whom the Captain found it inconvenient if not impossible to feed. Many of these went west and found their way to Mexico. Ingram and two others traveled by Indian trails all the way to the St. John's River, which roughly separates Maine from New Brunswick. There he found a French ship which took him to France.

At the time of Ingram's remarkable journey, which there can be little doubt that he made, writers of fiction and of non-fiction were not two distinct breeds, as they happily are for the most part today, but were combined in one. This fact, which accounts for Ingram's mention of elephants, cities of silver and crystal and other wonders, accounts also for the inattention which historians have shown toward this marooned sailor and his amazing story.

Ingram must have been a man as resourceful as he was imaginative, for except for his companions no other man of his day is known to have made such an overland journey through the northern country. Although he does not identify the Merrimack in his narrative, there can be little doubt that he crossed it and that he was the first Englishman to set eyes upon it.

Thirty-four years later Bartholomew Gosnold, another Englishman, reached the coast of Maine in the vicinity of Casco Bay and sailed southward until he reached Cape Cod, apparently like many of his contemporaries without seeing the Merrimack.

This seventeenth-century habit of coasting along in the Gulf of Maine without noticing one of New England's greatest rivers deserves some comment.

If a mariner in a seventeenth-century vessel not too obedient to her helm were to sail south from the Maine coast keeping the shore in sight, he would come upon a group of rocky islets. These were unnamed until they became known as Smith's Islands after Captain John. Today they are known as the Isles of Shoals. It would be reasonable to suppose that a good sailor on an uncharted coast would keep outside such islands and steer perhaps due south. If he did he would, seeing Cape Ann ahead of him, keep his southerly course and end up in Massachusetts Bay, having missed the Merrimack entirely. Even those who, like Martin Pring in 1603 and Champlain in 1604 and 1605, visited the Piscataqua River, off the mouth of which the Isles of Shoals lie, seem to have traveled between the Piscataqua and Cape Cod without noticing the Merrimack, a far more impressive stream but partly hidden from the sea by the great sandy dunes of Plum Island.

There is a tale that the Sieur de Monts saw the mouth of the Merrimack in 1604 and told Champlain what he had seen but there is no evidence that Champlain actually visited it.

Champlain says in his account of the voyage which he began on June 15, 1604:

> Steering south to get away from the land that we might
> anchor, after sailing about two leagues (about five miles)
> we perceived a cape on the mainland to the south, one
> quarter southeast of us, at a distance of some six leagues
> (roughly fifteen miles.) Two leagues to the east we saw
> three or four rather high islands, and to the westward a
> large bay. The coast of this bay, ranging around to the
> cape, extends inland from the place where we were about
> four leagues (ten miles.)

The "rather high islands" are probably the Isles of
Shoals, the cape on the mainland no doubt Cape Ann and
the "large bay" the circular indentation of the coast between
Cape Neddick, near York Harbor, Maine, and Cape Ann in
Massachusetts.

In Champlain's account of his coastal voyage of June
18, 1605, he refers to the same region. Picture the man
standing on his quarter-deck as his ship lay off Cape Ann. In
his ponderous puss-in-boots costume, his salt-stained leather
legs braced against the roll of the ship, his body massive in
wine-stained wool and flounces of tobacco-reeking linen, in
gentlemanly excitement questioning the sagamores brought
from shore in his creaky skiff by the Sieur de Monts, they
standing by in apprehensive friendliness, their deerskin-
wrapped nakedness glistening under loops of moose teeth and
bear claws, smelling of the wild, of woodsmoke and of pitch.

The great Frenchman gave each sagamore a knife and a
biscuit:

> After that, I made them understand as well as I could
> that they should show me how the coast tended. After I
> had drawn for them with a charcoal the bay and island
> cape where we were, they pictured for me with the same
> charcoal another bay which they represented as very
> large. Here they placed six pebbles at equal intervals,
> giving me thereby to understand that each of these marks

represented that number of chiefs and tribes. Next they represented within the said bay a river which we had passed, which is very long and has shoals. We found here quantities of vines on which the green grapes were a little larger than peas, and also many nut-trees, the nuts on which were no larger than musket balls. . . . This place is in latitude 43° and some minutes.

The Indians also told Champlain with somewhat misleading enthusiasm that all along the coast they cultivated gardens and grew food stuffs.

The Frenchman must have been a trifle off in his reckoning. If the Isles of Shoals were five miles to the east, Cape Ann fifteen miles to the south and the deepest part of the bay some twelve miles to the west, he could not have been in latitude forty-three but must have been some minutes to the south of that line. Yet it is probable that the river "which is very long and has shoals" was the Merrimack. There is no evidence that Champlain sailed into it or landed at its mouth. Indeed it is more than unlikely that he did.

The mouth of the Merrimack was at that time filled by a sandbar over which there was no more than seven feet of water at low tide. Unless the sea was perfectly calm without breakers or swells, which it never is, a vessel would have been in great peril crossing that bar even at high tide, when there would be some fifteen feet of water in the passage. The rollers of even a calm sea, with no land between Plum Island and Portugal to diminish them, dashing over the bar and sucking back, would, even at high tide, alternately expose and flood the sand. Indeed the town records of Old Newbury seem to indicate that no ocean-going vessel ever crossed the Newburyport bar until 1646 when Captain Aquila Chase sailed in.

Captain John Smith passed by the Merrimack's mouth

on his way to the Piscataqua in 1614 and returned to England to ask his sovereign to give New England its name. Captain John did not mention any river between Cape Cod and the Piscataqua except in his *Description of New England* where he refers to that great river of Massachusetts which the natives said extended "many daies journey into the entralles of that country." This might have been the estuary of the Mystic and the Charles in Boston Harbor, indicated on his map.

Plum Island must indeed have been good camouflage for the mouth of the Merrimack which, one might suppose, had it been conspicuous and navigable, would have been seized upon as a possible answer to the not-yet-silenced prayer for a passage to India and China. For whatever reason, the Merrimack was seldom even mentioned by any of the earliest explorers.

Yet exploring and fishing expeditions on Cape Cod and near the Piscataqua became more numerous during the second decade of the seventeenth century and it would have been strange if the great river had remained undiscovered either by

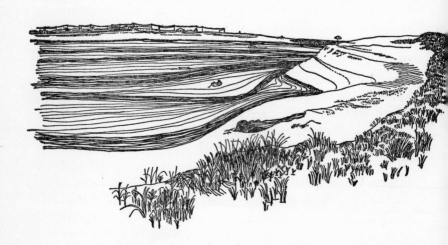

sea or land. In 1621 John Mason, former governor of New-foundland, who had never seen New England, petitioned for and received a grant from the Council for New England of Plymouth (England). This grant purported to convey a large if nebulous tract of land, known for some reason as Mariana, which extended "from the river of Naumkeag, (Salem, Massachusetts) round Cape Anne, to the river Merrimack; and up each of those rivers to the farthest head thereof; then to cross over from the head of the one to the head of the other; with all the islands lying within three miles of the coast." This grant would have caused an almost fourth-dimensional problem in surveying had it ever been surveyed. The problem was somewhat complicated by another grant made in the following year, 1622, to John Mason and Sir Ferdinando Gorges jointly, which covered all the lands between the rivers Merrimack and Saga-dehock (the modern Kennebec) extending back to the great lakes and river of Canada. This new territorial grant was known as Laconia. It provided for the establishment of a settlement at the mouth of the river Piscataqua, not for the security of religious freedom but for the purpose of fishing and trading in furs.

In 1623 two well-equipped groups of settlers arrived at the Piscataqua. The first, under David Thompson, took up their residence at the very entrance to the river on Odiorne's Point in Rye, where the settlers built a house and a salt works. The second party under two London fishmongers, Edward and William Hilton, went eight miles up the river and set up their fishing gear at a place which they called Northam, now Dover. There is little room for disagreement as to which settlement was actually the first in what is now New Hampshire but, as Thompson's beachhead failed to hold Thompson for more than a few years and most of his granted acres came ultimately into the possession of the Hiltons, the Dover establishment seems the more impressive of the two.

The name "Merrimack" was obviously applied, in the grants to Mason and Gorges, to a river already known and named. Yet there is no record of the first use of the Indian word. It is probable that the Indians, in giving information to the earliest white visitors, pointed out the stream by name. The river therefore was undoubtedly known as the Merrimack before the first European saw it. As the Merrimack it flowed calmly through its course of almost two hundred miles, lying upon the land like a map of the nervous system of the region which it drained, while eager, ambitious, cruel and impassioned men sailed by it on the seas or argued and wrangled in the councils of England over the unknown flesh of its bones.

Among those who engaged in the latter activity were Mason and Gorges, who, possibly thinking to make assurance doubly sure, as a lawyer will use in a deed every synonym known to his kind in order to be sure to hit upon the right and binding word, kept applying for, and obtaining, new grants.

Perhaps the preoccupation of the English with wars, great and small, during the first quarter of the seventeenth century helped to keep Mason and Gorges from developing and profiting from their great New England estates. By 1629 the European situation began to look better and Mason, who had some reason to doubt the effectiveness and durability of his grants, applied for still another charter. He received one, on a grand scale, as vague and redundant as the earlier ones. The new charter, which paid no attention to what had previously been granted, gave to Captain Mason all the land "from the middle of the Pascataqua river and up the same to the farthest head thereof, and from thence northwestward until sixty miles from the mouth of the harbor were finished; also through Merrimack River, to the farthest head thereof, and so forward up into the land westward, until sixty miles were finished; and from thence to cross over land to the end of the sixty miles accounted from Pascataqua river; together with all the islands within five leagues of the coast."

The inability of this description to apply to the land it intended to describe was the source of trouble for everyone concerned for more than a century. What is important about this perplexing document is that it mentioned that Captain Mason intended to call his domain New Hampshire.

It was later contended that early in 1629 John Wheelwright and a few others had purchased from the Indians a tract of land comprising a large part of that in the Mason patent. Wheelwright was not actually in New England before 1636 and so could hardly have paid for his title in person, as he was supposed to have done, in coats, skirts and kettles, things which the Indians considered a valuable consideration and a fair exchange for the use of the land. Use of land, not ownership, is all that Indians of that day could have believed there was to sell.

It might be argued that, since the Wheelwright purchase was said to have been made six months before Mason's "New Hampshire" grant was made, word of the transaction had reached England and that Mason, in applying for a regrant of what he must have believed had already been granted to him, was trying to nullify the sale to Wheelwright by the Indians at a later date. It is more likely that the Wheelwright deed of 1629 was a hoax arranged to trouble the Masonians. If it was, it is certain that Wheelwright had nothing to do with it. Be that as it may, the Mason charter of 1629 and other grants made subsequent to it which need not be described here, had only a temporary effect upon the settlement of the region to which it gave a permanent name.

STILL UNTOUCHED

If a man had been able, in 1629, to fly high above the
Merrimack and look down upon it, he would have seen it
serene, shining and sure, cutting through the forest and interval of a disputed land upon which no trace of the dispute
nor of its makers was visible to the naked eye. He would have
seen nothing but a vast stretch of deep green forest in which
even the hills were lost, the lighter green of meadows in the
bows and bends of the river's course and the blue and sun-
shimmer of ponds small and large. Far down near the wide
mouth of the river where it bends eastward toward the sea,
spreading out in salty shallows the glacial sand and silt of the
uplands, he would have seen nothing but sunlight, water-
shine, the scallop rise and fall of surf and seabirds over the
running tongue of the tide.

Perhaps below him he might have noticed, spreading
over the river like a moving net, a vast dark flock of wild
pigeons heading for some new forest to strip it of beechnuts,
chestnuts and acorns. Perhaps he might have caught sight of
an occasional wisp of smoke from an Indian bivouac; perhaps,
if he looked long enough, of an Indian bark canoe or dugout
working its way toward the fishing grounds at the river's
mouth. But he would have seen in all the Merrimack's length,
as it traversed so surely the lands parceled out by civilized man
with such magniloquent uncertainty, no trace of civilized
man's habitation.

In 1629, when New Hampshire got its name, the settlements at Dover and Portsmouth were not so separate from
those on Massachusetts Bay as the unsettled condition of the
Merrimack River which flowed between them would seem to
indicate. There was communication, probably largely though

not entirely by sea, between the two groups, a communication which had unpleasant consequences.

The New Hampshire colonists were impelled and sustained more by commercial than by spiritual considerations, a circumstance which should not be held against them. They were not irreligious, but they were Anglicans whose faith was not quite so personal as that of the Plymouth people. It was not uncommon for men from Massachusetts, who found the Puritan rigors of the South Shore too harsh for them, to migrate toward the freer if not exactly cushioned life of the Piscataqua. Yet even with this accretion the colony at Portsmouth grew very slowly. The colonists, with little help and little increase from abroad, were absorbed with their own struggles and had no time for exploration and expansion. They were on good terms with the Indians, as indeed they needed to be, but they were vigilant and hard-working.

In 1628 the Dover settlers heard reports that Indians were hunting in the woods with muskets, something unheard of up to that time. The Plymouth people had been very careful to keep the natives from acquiring weapons like their own.

One Thomas Morton, an Englishman described by some historians as a "rake," had visited Massachusetts Bay in 1622 and gone back to England with a scornful distaste for the colonists of Plymouth. He returned in 1625 and set up a colony of his own which he called Merrymount, near what is now Braintree. This was close enough to Plymouth to give the tight-lipped elders of that place a feeling that hell fire was approaching them.

The Plymouth folk, whatever their shortcomings, were probably more suited to the role of founding fathers than, whatever might be said in their favor, were the people of Merrymount. Yet Morton was probably not as bad as he was painted. His transplanting to New England of the old English conception of May Day, with its half-pagan revelry about the symbolic pole, could not possibly have seemed good to those who had subscribed to the Mayflower Compact, though we today might feel that a little Maypole revelry might have been good for those earnest and frightened souls. Morton was not content to show his neighbors why his conception of the conduct of life differed from theirs. He made the seriously antisocial mistake of selling firearms and liquor to the Indians. Undoubtedly he was not the only one who did so. The French in Maine and Canada certainly did. Morton was perhaps the first and it is possible that his heedless act was one of the inciting sparks applied to the tinder of Indian resentment and animosity, sparks fanned into flame as time went on, for political reasons, by the French particularly and by the English also. Certain it is that in the second decade of European settlement in Massachusetts Bay and the Gulf of Maine, interracial fear was added to the difficulties of the colonists and had a considerable effect upon the rate and the extent of settlement.

It was not until nearly fifteen years after the arrival of the *Mayflower* in Massachusetts Bay that the shores of the Merrimack saw their first permanent European habitation.

3 First Trickle of a Human Flood

··

When the first European settlers took up their station near the Merrimack, they did not reach their destination directly from the sea. All the early arrivals at the colony at the mouth of the river came up from Ipswich way, through the bight between Great Neck and Plum Island and up the Plum Island Sound—which then carried more Merrimack water than it does now—to the Quascacunquen, now the Parker River. Here the first Newbury settlement, other than the camps of transient fishermen, was established in the early summer of 1635.

In that year something which seems strange to us today became obvious to those who had come to the plantations of Massachusetts Bay. With three thousand miles of wilderness before them the colonists found themselves crowded and endangered, as if their beachhead were under fire from the forested inland hills. The fire to which they were exposed was not that of a hostile army nor of an aroused band of savages. It was the deadly sniping of time, which we might have supposed would have been their ally. Their cattle, sheep, horses, goats and hogs needed grazing land and hay and grain fields and they could not wait while the heavy forest was rolled back. A village would be established, as at Ipswich, but after the original settlers had dug themselves in, built a meeting house and dwellings and cleared a common for their stock, other arrivals would threaten their safety by requiring more productive land than could be made ready between spring and winter. The newcomers had to go home or be asked to move on.

Ipswich, which had been settled in 1633 and become a town in 1634, found itself within two years in this inhospitable position. In 1633 and 1634 thirty ships arrived, bearing something like three thousand immigrants and their cattle. Some went to Cambridge, Salem, Watertown and Boston. Some remained at Ipswich, which began to bulge at the seams. Among these was the Reverend Thomas Parker, who with a company of some forty persons embarked as soon as the going was good in spring for the still unsettled country up inside Plum Island to the north. Parker and his company landed on the north shore of the river now known by Thomas Parker's name, some two and a half miles south of the Merrimack River and the present city of Newburyport.

The founders of Newbury, once they had themselves and their goods ashore, gathered together under a tree and formed their church.

During the first summer the Newbury settlers had their hands and minds full, building houses—a meeting house, a parsonage, dwellings and, by September, a tavern. They worried about the Indians who, having found the Europeans less filled with brotherly love than they had hoped to find them, were becoming increasingly unruly. They worried about the application of their religious ideas to their daily life. They worried about each other and about their dogs and cattle. They worried about ships which did not come and about ships which did. They made solemn rules about such things as personal adornment, of which the following is a sample:

No person after one month shall make or sell any bone lace or other lace to be worne on any garment upon pain

of five shillings the yard for every yard so made or sold,
or set on, provided that binding or small edging laces
may be used on garments or linen.

No. The pioneers of Newbury did not spend all their
time hewing wood and drawing water, tending their flocks and
their fields. They fined people for not going to town meeting
and they fined others for talking too much when they did go.
They could not bear to see the cross demeaned by appearing
in the English ensign, so they cut the crosses out and when
reprimanded for doing so put all the flags they had aside and
would not use them. When Thomas Milward, a seafaring
man who came to join the community, called them traitors
and rebels for not displaying the King's flag, they had him
arrested and hauled into court where he was released only
after making written apology.

The first settlers of Newbury were spiritually closer to
the Pilgrims of Plymouth than they were to the Anglicans of
Dover and Portsmouth. They apparently subscribed to the
dogmas of the council of ministers which met in Cambridge
(then Newtown) and published a list of eighty erroneous
opinions which were held to be damnable. It should be said
that even a devout dogmatist in any church today would have
a hard time making head or tail of three quarters of these
errors, yet the Newbury people permitted the Massachusetts
General Court to banish, disfranchise or take the right to
bear arms away from their fellows, some prominent citizens
among them, who entertained erroneous opinions.

Here they were, a handful of harassed colonists with
little chance of doing all that had to be done before winter
set in, beset by wolves and Indians, not knowing what to
expect of the sea, the soil or the weather over both, confused
by new arrivals with no place to go, compelled to do military
service, to keep their fences tight, to keep up their badly

made roads, to pay taxes to the colony with money which they did not have, to cut out with their own hands the lumber for their houses and barns, to make their own clothes and furniture, to provide for the day when they might have nothing— a day which all new settlements in the New World had to face—to cope with hurricanes and even earthquakes, which seem to have been frequent. Small wonder that the mystery of the great river a few miles away failed to draw them, that they seldom ventured into the forest to the north. Small wonder, too, that, depressed and exasperated by the lack of room in the narrow strip of meadow and marsh between the forest and the sea, and harassed, as we shall see, by other considerations, they split up in a few years, some remaining where they were and others moving to a new location, this time on the Merrimack near where a ferry of sorts had already been established for the accommodation of those who wished to visit the rising settlements of New Hampshire.

In April of 1637, the Pequot War in Rhode Island having reached a serious point, a company was raised in the northern towns to help put down the Pequot Indians, who in the previous year had killed two Europeans, John Oldham and a Captain Stone, both of whom would have been, and in fact were, considered by the strictest Puritans to be undesirable characters.

Eight men from Newbury joined with sixty-one from Ipswich, Salem and Boston to march to Rhode Island but decided when part way through the forest that they could not proceed until they had settled, in terms of what has been described as the "vexatious legalism" of their church, whether they were proceeding against the Indians under a covenant of grace, which would have aligned them with the rebels Anne Hutchinson and John Wheelwright, or under a covenant of works, which would have aligned them with the strict Puritans. The church of Massachusetts, as distinguished from that of the "antinomian" exiles of Rhode Island and Connecticut, could not have tolerated an expedition which did not know whether it was acting under God's inspirational command or doing a good deed for the sake of the favor with which such action would be regarded by the elders of the church.

These devout soldiers not only put theological hair splitting before the performance of the task of their punitive expedition. They were so vindictive against anyone who expressed an opinion at variance with that of their church's dogma that they are said to have discharged one of their officers for entertaining opinions which the Cambridge conference had classed as errors.

They feared the anger of their God more than they feared the ferocity of the Indians, for no Indian flinging his axe or leaning his musket against a tree to fire at them could be as real as the Deity who thundered forth in meeting in the not-always-understandable but threatening voice of their pastor.

The Newbury men had left home to avoid having to conform to the practices of the accepted Church of England as exemplified by the increasing power of Archbishop Laud, whose actions and motives, if not his beliefs, were strangely like their own. Yet they had been in the New World only a few years before they devised a new religious intolerance, the lash of which was felt by such persons as Roger Williams, Anne Hutchinson and John Wheelwright for not quite identical reasons.

GOD'S MEN AGAINST THE WILDERNESS

We shall probably never know why the vastness, the wild beauty and—despite Indians, hardship and wild beasts—the freedom and proffered tranquillity of the New England environment did not soften their Calvinistic passion for conformity. Perhaps the terrors with which they must often have been confronted seemed, without belief in the hard bones and fetish dogma of an intransigent church, too much for them to bear. We cannot put ourselves in their position, though it is out of them that we have come. We cannot judge them. Their courage, their errors, their sacrifices and their faith have removed the necessity for our doing so.

Perhaps we can pity them from the vantage point of our safety. Their lives differed from ours as the old course of the Merrimack, disrupted and altered by the great glacier, differed from the powerful calm of the present sophisticated river.

Consider this note from the town records of Newbury, under date of June 1, 1638:

> Being this date assembled to treat or consult about the well ordering of the affairs of the towne, about one of the clocke in the afternoone, the sunn shining faire, it pleased God suddenly to raise a vehement earthquake, coming with a shrill clap of thunder, issuing as it supposed out of the east, which shook the earth and the foundations of the house in a very violent manner to our great amazement and wonder, wherefore, taking notice of so great and strange a hand of God's providence, we were desirous of leaving it on record to the view of after ages to the intent that all might take notice of Almighty God and feare his name.

Perhaps no man or woman in Newbury, or in all the region which felt its great shock, which was most of settled New England, could help seeing in the natural phenomena of that earthquake the voice of the Lord criticizing and warning them.

It is not easy without a more careful study of the background than most of us can make to understand the apparent paradox and the many inconsistencies of life and thought in the first New England colonies, which the Merrimack River might have led, far earlier than it did, to new life and new thought.

It should be borne in mind that there were two major forces operating in the colonization of the coast from the Connecticut River to the Penobscot. One was the political and commercial activity of certain groups of men in England, among them Mason and Gorges, many of whom never saw the New World and none of whom envisaged the idea of its being a self-governing region, men who wished to colonize and to exploit New England for their own benefit. Another and originally inconspicuous force was the religious zeal of that group of uncompromising folk who had broken with the Church of England because they almost believed that they knew all there was to know about God and the completeness of His revelation to man in the Scriptures and felt that they must set up a new church in order to preserve themselves and to save those less enlightened than they. These devout people, whom we have come to refer to rather loosely as Puritans, who came to New England under a charter and in the course of a movement which had nothing of the religious about it, ended by achieving complete domination of their part of the New World. They brought with them no true allegiance to the Crown of England, no reliance, at first at least, upon the laws of England. God was their King and God's laws, as they chose to interpret them, their laws.

They had not been in North America very long before it became apparent that absentee government, which sat in London as prescribed by their charter, was inadequate. By 1634, when they had colonized much of Massachusetts Bay from the separate colony of Plymouth to Salem and Ipswich, they had contrived to bring their government across the water with them, stretching quite out of shape the provisions of their charter in doing so, and to become a colony. Not a crown colony but an independent political entity, whose only connection with England was through ownership by Englishmen of wealth and station. It was under the political government of this colony which had become, instead of the mere remote plantation of English investors organized as "The New England Company," the Massachusetts Bay Colony, with a governor, a deputy-governor, a small group of "assistants" or magistrates and, after a period of trial, a group of deputies from the towns.

This was, in a sense, political revolution. The King of England did not rule over the colony not because it hated monarchy, but only because God was its King and any other king could only be an impostor. The colonial government of Massachusetts Bay was no democracy. It was a government by the few.

The people of the colony fell into four classes: first, the freemen, who had privileges but who also had obligations and who were in the minority in every town; second, the actual church members, not freemen, who were by no means a majority; third, those who were neither freemen nor church members but who had sworn loyalty to the purposes and aims of the colony; and fourth, those who were neither church members nor freemen and had taken no oath and were therefore, as one historian has put it, "in the colony but not of it."

The first three classes constituted the majority, although the last, the only one which could not be called wholly Puritan, cannot have been small. It was made up of miscellaneous persons such as servants and apprentices, many of whom, when not too weary to feel at all, must have felt little sympathy with the Puritans.

The colony's first governor, John Winthrop, would have shuddered at the idea, had anyone suggested it to him, that there was such a thing, or should be, as equality of opportunity among men. There were, he believed, those whom God meant to rule and those whom God meant to be ruled. In Massachusetts Bay there were few of the former and many of the latter, few of whom thought to grumble because such was the situation.

It was under such a government and its General Court, consisting of an upper house of magistrates and a lower house of deputies, that the old and new towns of Newbury were formed, though, as has already been suggested, the settlements east of the Merrimack did not for some time or for very long come under the colony's wing.

To describe this government as it is here described does not give any indication of the position of the Church in seventeenth-century New England. The church was not the government, though there was no difference of opinion between government and church. It would be misleading to state, merely as a fact, what is undoubtedly true, that the actual church members in any town of the colony were usually a minority. The elders of the church were always deferred to, by the governor as well as the General Court, as God's representatives on earth, who could give correct information about God's opinion of any contemplated enterprise.

This surprising domination of a commercial enterprise by the religious zeal of its communities was something new to English history, something regarded with great disapproval by the proprietors at home who, quite correctly, saw that such a development threatened the feudal world which they had hoped to create in America. Steps were taken to unseat the Puritans, but confusions at home and determination in the colony kept them from being successful.

In spite of the success of the Puritans in establishing a government, the very nature of their purpose kept it from being ideal as an instrument for the development of the new land. Had they had less blind confidence in their view of God, their interpretation of His word, they might have been further removed than they were from kinship with Edgar Allan Poe's people of Vondervotteimittiss, who never climbed the hills surrounding their village for the very good reason that they were perfectly certain that there was nothing on the other side of them.

DIVISION AND DESTINY

It is easy for us today to wonder why, the prospects in a new country being what they were, outsiders did not come in and disturb the balance of orthodox towns like Newbury. It should be remembered that organized towns of that day could and did keep outsiders out when they chose to by refusing to grant them or let them buy land. Thus the orthodoxy would have been self-perpetuating but for economic conditions which, as the towns grew closer together and their need of intercourse greater, operated to change the *status quo*.

We have already seen that there was a scarcity of land for crops and grazing. Farm tools and fencing were equally scarce. In 1640, troubles abroad following a political upheaval in England, an upheaval which marked with prison bars the end of Archbishop Laud's domination of the Anglican church, caused the almost complete cessation, for a time, of immigration from England. As a result of this, the somewhat inflated economy of the Massachusetts colonies suffered a severe puncture. Provisions were not at first scarce and indeed importation of them did not immediately cease when settlers ceased to cross the sea. English proprietors and merchants still hoped to profit by the colonists' need. The result was that for a time supplies piled up while cash dwindled and disappeared. Cattle declined in value by as much as 80 per cent. It was said that a man who at the time considered himself worth a thousand pounds could not, even by selling out completely, raise 250. Though men had plenty to eat, they could not pay their debts. It soon became apparent that they had neither cash nor beaver skins with which to pay for imports. The imports accordingly dwindled.

These conditions made the settlers of Newbury restless and it was at this time, after the frightful winter of 1641-1642, that they decided to divide, part going to the new location on the Merrimack. They did not realize what separation would involve.

It was unthinkable that those who were leaving to found the new town should not have a meeting house. It was their decision to take the Newbury meeting house with them. No sooner was this step planned than it was objected to. The objection, though it did not ultimately prevail, kept the town in a turmoil for several years. The meeting house was eventually moved, Old Newbury getting the short end of the stick. Perhaps those who remained in the original town were persuaded to accept defeat by the fact that in July, 1643, while the congregation was gathered within, the Almighty saw fit to produce a sudden violent storm which prophetically removed the meeting house from its foundations, miraculously without hurting anyone.

A group, including John Lowell, whose family name, through a notable relative, Francis Cabot Lowell, was later to be given to a city near Pawtucket Falls farther up the Merrimack, took up land in the new town. John Lowell was one of them, and so was William Franklin, a less worthy citizen, who before he had more than two years' use of his new property

was hanged in Boston in June, 1644, for the highly unorthodox killing of Nathaniel Sewell, a child who was apprenticed
to him. Governor Winthrop in his *History of New England*
states the case against Franklin:

> He used him (Nathaniel Sewell) with continual rigor
> and unmerciful correction, and exposed him many times
> to much cold and wet in the winter season, and used
> divers acts of rigor towards him, as hanging him in the
> chimney and so forth and the boy being very poor and
> weak he tied him upon an horse and so brought him
> (sometimes sitting and sometimes hanging down) to
> Boston, being five miles off, to a magistrates, and by the
> way the boy calling much for water, would give him
> none, though he came close by it, so as the boy was near
> dead when he came to Boston, and died in a few hours
> after.

Among those receiving a lot in the new town by the great
river was a person described as "John, Indian," though there
is no record of how he happened to be admitted among the
English as a townsman and he was not one of those who
separated themselves from Old Newbury.

The first years in the new town, which became Newburyport in 1764, were busy years of fence and housebuilding,
laying out streets and generally struggling to keep body and
soul together. Houses were built with care and skill. The
early settlers of the New England coastal towns, and Newburyport was no exception, built no log cabins, though logs
were everywhere. They built as they had seen building done
in England, hewing timbers by hand and fitting them with
remarkable exactness with mortises and pins of wood. Some
of the houses of this period are standing in Newburyport
today.

The Spencer-Pierce-Little house, one of the earliest

stone houses remaining in New England, was built about 1650, when Newbury was less than a score of years old. There is about it nothing that is primitive and much that is reminiscent of feudal England. The Noyes house, on Parker Street, dates from 1646. It would be an ornament to any dignified community today. The Tristram Coffin house on High Street, a good part of which was built in the neighborhood of 1650, is far from what one might have expected to find on a wilderness frontier three thousand miles from home. The architectural eminence of the Merrimack began in the infancy of the region, though it did not reach its peak for nearly a century.

Thus did the first ripple of the rising tide of European settlement reach the Merrimack. That it was for some time little more than a ripple was partly the result of the cessation of immigration and the diminution of trade with England in the early 1640's. The river, referred to by elders of Old Newbury in a plaintive petition to the General Court in 1646 as an "inconvenience," was ready to serve the invaders, but the invaders as yet had no use for it except as a pasture and pound for fish and as a somewhat tricky avenue leading to the sea and what commence they were beginning to develop.

4 Old England Alive in the New

The tide of settlement in the Merrimack Valley, as elsewhere in New England, lapped gently at the forest edge, only in a few places penetrating, as a beach wave may do, beyond its general line. The English settlers of Massachusetts Bay and the Piscataqua were not frontiersmen in the sense that those who developed the West in the nineteenth century earned that name. The New England colonists, whatever their economic or social position, were in a sense all in the same boat. The well-to-do had to work to keep alive as did the poor. Labor was scarce and it was a rare Puritan or Church of Englander from Connecticut to Maine who could hire his work done for him. There were, it is true, indentured men and women who served others but as soon as they had worked enough to pay off what had been advanced for their passage, they were as free as anyone. Those who had means when they landed were merely given more land than those who had not. All were given land, however, and they had either to get a living from it, go back to England or die. Not all succeeded in earning a living. Many returned to England, often by request of their fellow citizens. Incredible numbers died.

Those who succeeded in making a living and acquiring and keeping property realized that the one thing they greatly needed if they were to improve their living was capital. This could only be obtained by spending less than was earned. Thus began the too-well-known and too-little-understood New England thrift, more often called penny-pinching, the notion of which was later to be made distasteful to the naturally generous hearts of New England school children by Benjamin Franklin. Distasteful or not, the nation could not have been so easily and rapidly developed without it, inasmuch as it provided capital for eighteenth- and nineteenth-century development.

The New Englander of the first half of the seventeenth century approached the valley of the Merrimack not as a wilderness adventurer but as the builder of a New World, in a secular sense at least, as much like the old as possible, a world which for the time being had no need of territorial expansion.

Though it may be something of a digression, it must be said here that the English approach to colonization in America was entirely different from the approach of their great and bitter rivals, the Spanish and the French. The Spanish found in what we now call Latin America a rich civilization like a ripe fruit waiting to be plucked. They plucked it and sucked it dry, destroying meanwhile with ruthless lack of foresight the tree on which it grew.

The French were the great adventurers and wilderness tamers. Both cruel and shrewd, they made use of the natives of the lands they penetrated and, while the English sat in their villages along the coast, pushed up the Great River of Canada, along the Great Lakes and down the Mississippi, with dreams of empire in their heads. They built about the British a wall of outposts which might have been impregnable but was not.

The Spanish colonial empire was destroyed by the British on their own doorstep, so thoroughly, thanks to the intervention of bad weather, that it never rose again. The French Empire in America lasted until shortly after the middle of the eighteenth century, when it fell of its own weight and, be it said, of its faulty underpinning, into the slow and irresolute, sometimes almost indifferent hands of the British.

The English in America played tortoise to the French hare, not penetrating as far into the continent in two hundred years as the French had advanced in fifty. Yet in creating a real civilization, a real new world in America and a real people in the Americans, England made and had at hand the means, which no other nation could command, of receiving a continent in trust for the future.

THE FORBIDDING FRONTIER

No. The English in America were not frontiersmen in the modern sense. Once they had endured the incredible and horrible adventure of sharing with death their voyage across the Atlantic, they settled down to the process of using the English way of looking at things to create an environment more to their taste than that of the homeland in which their minds had suffered unsympathetic compulsion and their bodies denial and hunger.

It is true that a few adventurers among them traveled inland, facing "the common enemy," as the once friendly Indian had come to be considered, and the wild beasts of the dark forest. These men brought back tales of great mountains, vast areas of flooded lakes and rivers, their waters alive with fish and their valleys and hillsides startling with furred and winged game.

In 1641, the New Hampshire towns—although Exeter, founded in 1636, did not join in the alliance immediately— somewhat reluctantly accepted the invitation of Massachu-

setts to unite with that commonwealth. In 1642, the General
Court determined to locate the northern limit of the Merrimack River, which had so freely been used in charters, as a
demarcation point. Governor Endicott appointed a commission to study the problem and the commissioners, Simon
Willard and Edward Johnson, in turn hired two surveyors and
took Indian guides to learn the secret of the wilderness.

That this daring party accomplished its purpose, at least
in part, we know from actual evidence. On the beach of the
state reservation at The Weirs, nearly 250 feet higher than
the junction of the Winnipesaukee and Pemigewasset at
Franklin, under a monumental and not very graceful canopy
of granite stands a boulder, discovered in 1832 in the Winnipesaukee River at the entrance to the great lake and later
removed to its present location. Chiseled into the face of the
boulder so forcibly that even the rush of the river's water and
the abrasions of the sand and silt in which it lay for 190 years
before being discovered have not been able to obliterate them,
are the initials of the worshipful Governor Endicott and his
two commissioners:

EI   SW
WP   IOHN
ENDICUT
Gov.

Yet even this identification of one of the true sources of
the river and of the great lake from which it issued did not
draw the busy English colonists from their occupations by the
sea. The other, more northerly source of the Merrimack in
Profile Lake, was not seen by a white man until 1805.

For thirty-eight years the four Piscataqua towns, Dover,
Portsmouth, Hampton and Exeter—increased by one in 1673
when the settlement of Dunstable, out of which Nashua

grew, received its charter—remained under the government of Massachusetts. In 1679, efforts by the proprietors in England, who saw their great estates being swallowed up by the spread of popular government in the New World, took New Hampshire out of the hands of Massachusetts and set it up as the first English royal province in New England.

There followed a three-sided struggle for dominance along the Merrimack, a struggle punctuated by political stops and starts at home. The people of New Hampshire, the most important of the three contenders, were the underdogs, the Crown was in power, and the heirs of John Mason, fighting to have royal influence save their vast and vague grants to the New England territory which had been colonized by the people in possession, formed the third side of the triangle.

In 1684, Charles II canceled the agreement of 1629, which had enabled Massachusetts to operate as a practically independent commonwealth. The New England colonies were united, on paper at least, in a dominion of New England. Under James II, the dominion was apparently strengthened by the appointment of Sir Edmund Andros as governor and in 1688 was enlarged by the addition to it of New York and New Jersey.

Had this political return to the Crown remained as James intended it to, the story of the Merrimack River might have been very different. James II, however, was not the monarch he believed himself to be. After four short years of confused and confusing rule, he was driven from the throne and replaced by his daughter, Mary, and her husband.

When the New England colonists heard of this event in the spring of 1689, they put an end to Governor Andros's career in America by throwing him into prison and leaving New Hampshire excited and happy but without a government. By 1692, William and Mary, however, had given

Massachusetts a new status as a colony in its own right and finally returned New Hampshire to its position as a separate royal province.

During all this time the five towns were the only settlements in what is now New Hampshire. They sheltered less than one twentieth of the population of New England. The Merrimack Valley remained in the hands of the Indians, the same Indians who were dying out in 1623, but to whom the crass indifference and cruel exploitation of the Europeans had given a last, moribund lease on life.

As early as 1642 a party of settlers led by Darby Field, having heard of a great mountain range in the north, set out from the Piscataqua and reached the summit of Mount Washington, probably crossing the Merrimack watershed east of Lake Winnipesaukee, a feat of considerable magnitude, mountaineering not having at that time become what it has since become to the English.

RIGORS OF SPIRIT AND FLESH

The Great River remained unexplored and, except in its very lowest reaches, its valleys remained unsettled. Had the Puritans been as interested in developing the riches of the interior as they were in developing their more easily available confidence that they were the instruments of God's revelation, the Merrimack Valley might have borne its unique flower of civilization before it did.

The cutting off of men and supplies from Europe in the early 1640's forced the Massachusetts colonists to develop trade, but the only trade they knew, other than the slight commercial intercourse among the coastal towns, was that of sea-borne commerce and fishing. It is, therefore, not unnatural that the building of vessels and the provision of equipment for maritime trade dominated their commercial activities and left the rich inland forest to be another century's gold.

The seacoast towns, although they did not grow greatly in size, did broaden their culture as true frontier towns are not likely to do. The political life of the Massachusetts colony, matured early by its grave responsibilities, saw the birth, in its highly undemocratic midst, of a new principle which was destined to be the basis of the political life of a new nation, the democratic principle of majority rule and the protection of the rights of the individual, however lowly.

Yet this great development out of the overflow from feudal England did not come about without much acrimonious and petty bickering. In the Newbury which we now think of as Newburyport, while a shrewdly conducted trade was turning the depression of the 1640's into an era of comparative prosperity, a political battle within and about the church was dividing men whom the common enemy might otherwise have kept united.

It is difficult for us today to understand the fierce severity of this unhappy struggle, which reached its peak in the "new town" of Newbury in 1669 and 1670, a struggle foreshadowed by the division over the meeting house when the settlers of the new town broke away from the Parker River settlement.

The Newbury church had for some years been divided in allegiance between the Reverend Thomas Parker, their original pastor, and Mr. Edward Woodman, whom Joshua Coffin, historian of Newburyport, has described as "a man of talents, influence, firmness, and decision." The divided allegiance was not the result of any great divergence between the theological opinions of Thomas Parker and Edward Woodman but was largely a matter of what we would call today Yankee resentment at the real or imagined fact of being, so to say, "pushed around." The quarrel between Newbury church factions was described in a letter to the Council by Edward Woodman as a matter of determining "whether God hath placed the power in the elder, or in the whole church, to judge between truth and error, right and wrong, brother and brother, and all things of church concernment." It is not important historically except as it was one of the links in the evolution of New England democracy out of feudal oligarchy.

As far back as 1650, there had been a tendency on the part of the Reverend Thomas Parker to reserve the ultimate right of church discipline to himself and the assistants of his choice and to allow the congregation to participate in it only when he saw fit. A strong and not easily quieted faction in the church felt that Mr. Parker was arrogating to himself and his associates the power to say when the people could have a voice in church government. This group felt that it was the right of the people of the church to have such a voice and that exercise of it should not be limited by the elders nor made to seem a favor granted by them to the congregation.

That the temper of the Christian church on the banks of the Merrimack in the middle of the seventeenth century was keyed very high and capable of causing as much moral confusion as religious calm, is illustrated by the case of Lydia Wardwell, born Perkins, of Newbury, who was married to Eliakim Wardwell of Hampton. Eliakim had for some reason, probably friendliness with the Quakers, been censured by the elders of the Newbury church and the censure must have struck home with stupefying force. Certainly, whatever it did to Eliakim, it aroused Lydia, who remembered the treatment of three Quaker women who were stripped and lashed on their bare backs in Dover. Lydia's behavior is reported by George Bishop, whose bias was clearly not toward the church, in his *New England Judged by the Spirit of the Lord:*

His wife Lydia, being a young and tender chaste woman,
seeing the wickedness of your priests and rulers to her
husband, was not at all offended with the truth, but as
your wickedness abounded, so she withdrew and separated from your church at Newbury, of which she was
sometimes a member, and, being given up to the leading
of the Lord, after she had been often sent for to come
thither, to give a reason of such a separation, it being at
length upon her in the consideration of their miserable
condition, who were thus blinded with ignorance and
persecution, to go to them, and as a sign to them she
went in (though it was exceeding hard to her modest and
shamefaced disposition) naked amongst them, which put
them into such a rage, instead of consideration, they soon
laid hands upon her, and to the next court at Ipswich had
her, where without law they condemned her to be tyed
to the fence-post of the tavern where they sat—and then
sorely lashed her with twenty or thirty cruel stripes. And
this is the discipline of the church of Newbury in New
England, and this is their religion, and their usage of the
handmaid of the Lord, who in a great cross to her natural
temper, came thus among them, a sign indeed, significa-
tory enough to them, and suitable to their state, who
under the visor of religion, were thus blinded into cruel
persecution.

This was in 1663, a year in which the Lord's voice spoke
in the form of severe earthquakes from January to July. There
were those in town who were more constrained than ever to
feel that the men and women of the church did not have
enough to say about the falling of its hand in punishment.

In the following year the first outward sign of resentment against Reverend Thomas Parker appeared in the form
of a majority vote of the town to reduce the minister's salary
to sixty pounds per year.

Seven wolves were killed in Newbury in that year. The
canker worms came and a blight was on the wheat. Pickled

sturgeon from the Merrimack were in great demand. Men were kept busy boiling and pickling, making casks and tubs to hold them and building vessels to carry them and other fish abroad. There were some who thought that commerce had become more important than God in Newbury.

The Indians were discontented and disillusioned. The Newbury people grumbled at having to build new roads. The twenty-five-year-old Parker-Woodman war went on within the church and became almost a part of church ritual. It grew more violent and more partisan with every year. It became celebrated throughout New England. It was brought into court and apparently settled there, only to break out again. It kept Newbury from spiritual but not from material prosperity.

The colonists of Massachusetts had not since their first decade in North America been predominantly agricultural. There was the sea, already cleared and more easily plowed and tilled than the unco-operative land. Men from the Piscataqua, from the Merrimack, from Ispwich, Salem and Boston sailed north to the fishing grounds and south to the West Indies and learned not how to conquer a continental wilderness but how to manage a voyage, how to pick up a cargo in one port and sell it in another and then begin over again. The people of the Merrimack mouth prospered without growing much. The church remained small—not more than eighty souls—and still divided, but the echoes of its war were in everyone's ears, meaningless to many but vaguely suggestive of the new view of government which was struggling to be born.

THE FIRST NEW SHOOTS

New England did not stagnate but at least along the Merrimack it did not grow, held back by its own intellectual limitations, by conflicting land claims, by European politics, and by the mounting hostility of the Indians.

During the balance of the seventeenth century, the Merrimack settlements pushed only a few miles up river and along the north bank. Amesbury, Salisbury, Bradford and Haverhill, still a part of the seacoast, grew out of the settlements of Ipswich, Newbury and Rowley. Yet the population of the region was still sparse. From Boston, Cambridge and Watertown there was a slow migration a little to the west. By 1655 there were forty-four towns within the Plymouth and Massachusetts colonies. These were Boston, Salem, Ipswich, Newbury, Lynn, Gloucester, Rowley, Salisbury, Wenham, Manchester, Haverhill, Andover, Marblehead, Topsfield, Charlestown, Watertown, Medford (Mystic), Cambridge (Newtown), Concord, Sudbury, Woburn, Reading, Malden, Dorchester, Roxbury, Weymouth, Dedham, Braintree, Medfield, Plymouth, Hingham, Scituate, Duxbury, Marshfield, Hull, Taunton, Rehoboth, Barnstable, Sandwich, Yarmouth, Eastham, Lancaster, Springfield and Northampton.

Of these the only two which were more than thirty miles from the sea were Springfield and Northampton, both in the Connecticut Valley. The former was founded by William Pynchon, a discontented charter member of the Massachusetts Bay Colony, who had settled Roxbury but did not like the way it had developed. Only his extreme distaste for his surroundings in Roxbury can have sent him into the dangerous western wilderness as early as 1636. Northampton, sixteen miles up the Connecticut from Springfield, first settled in 1654, became a town in 1656, an isolated spearhead into the Indian country, more closely associated with the Connecticut towns to the south than with the settlements of Massachusetts Bay.

In 1656 a small fur-trading post called Watanic had been

established on the Nashua River close to the junction of that stream with the Merrimack, but there was only one settler there until 1660, when a number of families moved in. The locality was not organized under a town charter until 1673, when it became Dunstable.

In 1655 a group of Massachusetts men petitioned the General Court for a grant between Lancaster and the present Massachusetts border on the Nashua River. The Court set aside a tract eight miles square which was to be called Groton. No one of the grantees, however, took up residence there for several years, during which time the grant from the General Court was fortified by an actual purchase of the land involved, for some twenty-eight pounds, from the Indians who had from time to time cultivated some of the river meadows and kept fishing weirs in the river. Actual settlement probably began about 1661 but was seriously retarded in 1675 and 1676 by the incidents of King Philip's War.

Concord, on the river of the same name formed by the junction of the Sudbury and Assabet rivers, had been settled in 1635, it and Dedham being the first Massachusetts towns from at least one of whose boundaries a townsman could not have thrown a stone into sea water. From this little outpost of European civilization the Concord, or Musquetaquid River, flowed northward into the Merrimack, joining the great river below Pawtucket Falls at Weymessit, where there was a more or less permanent settlement of Indians who were at first friendly with the settlers.

It can be seen that to the northwest of Boston there was a slightly greater tendency to penetrate the wilderness than there was to the north and east, where to the uncertain temper of the natives was added the equally uncertain status of the land, clouded as it was by the confusions of the early grants by the Council for New England to Captain John

Mason, the absentee, now in death more absent than ever but also, through his heirs, more actively possessive.

Yet even on the Concord and the Nashua men dared not go about unarmed nor dwell at any very great distance from a garrison house.

5   Seeing Red

··

It is clear from what has already been said that in the Merrimack country the century and a quarter from about 1630 to the end of the French and Indian War in 1760 was dominated by the Indian, that doomed yet mobile race which, once its animosity had been aroused, knew how to make itself felt against far superior numbers.

It is almost impossible for the New Englander of today, however, to visualize, even to imagine, the conditions under which the colonists of the Massachusetts and New Hampshire border towns existed. There are still plenty of wild tracts of forest in New Hampshire and even in more thickly settled Massachusetts close to which the householder, going out to open the bars for his cows or into the wood to cut out fuel or pulpwood, may feel himself to be on the edge of primitive wilderness, mysterious, dangerous and haunting. Yet he never needs to fear the hidden presence of anything more threatening than skunk, marten, raccoon, bobcat or bear.

His ancestors, however, after the first few years of European immigration could never, even in the seacoast towns, risk going to meeting without posting an armed sentry, never go into the fields unarmed nor feel safe if living at too great a distance from what was called a garrison house to which nearby residents might retreat when alarmed by Indians in the neighborhood.

These garrison houses, of which a considerable number are standing today, were large and substantial buildings, often but not always built of brick or stone, with clapboard ends, shake roofs; heavily shuttered for defense and sometimes surrounded by a stockade of pointed logs. It is a mistaken notion that the second-story overhang found in many such structures and, indeed, in other purely peaceful dwellings, was for the purpose of shooting downward at enemies who had reached the lower-story walls. This overhang was a structural detail found in many seventeenth-century English houses, where there was no need of defense against marauders, and merely copied by the English migrants to North America.

To understand why garrison houses were needed so short a time after the English had landed in the midst of an apparently sparse population of co-operative and friendly Indians, who even went to the length of inviting the newcomers to settle among them, one thing, hitherto not suggested, should be borne in mind.

Many historians of early New England, notably Hubbard and Winthrop, who had firsthand knowledge of the conditions of which they wrote, make it plain that, however disposed toward the English the tribes of Narragansett, Massachusetts and Casco bays may have been, they were not at peace with one another or with their more distant neighbors in New York. In the first days of English settlement the members of one group of tribes when threatened by another would often mingle with the English for protection, thereby accustoming the settlers to Indians in their midst. This habit continued even after relations between the English and the Indians had passed from cordiality and mutual aid to suspicion and animosity. Its existence left the New England towns the victims of ready-made infiltration when hostilities grew from isolated cases of resentment and revenge to implacable and cruel warfare on a large scale.

The century and a quarter of life exposed to the danger of Indian attack and the often shocking violence of its execution could not fail to have a profound effect upon the mind and character of the inhabitants of the Merrimack Valley. There was between 1650 and 1750 scarcely a town in the valley which did not lose one or two men a year to the Indians, who sometimes came in groups of two or three and sometimes in companies of fifty or a hundred, in the larger and later attacks often accompanied by the French.

It was early on a March morning in 1697 that the little village of Haverhill, one of four towns along the frontier considered sufficiently vulnerable to warrant a permanent guard of Colonial troops, had its first great attack.

For ten years parties of Indians had been slipping into town, usually under cover of night, killing and capturing a man, a child or a whole family. In 1690 a large-scale attack on Salmon Falls, near Dover, New Hampshire, had sent the people of Haverhill into such a panic that they decided either to send for help or evacuate the town. Since the government of Massachusetts would not permit its citizens to abandon established frontier towns, asking for assistance was their only course. They got assistance in the form of soldiers, a few of whom were quartered in each of the town's six garrison houses after 1690.

In 1691, Abraham Whittier III, eight-year-old son of Abraham Jr. and Hannah Beane Whittier, was carried off and never heard of again. In the following year the boy's mother was killed, though it is interesting to note that another Whittier, Thomas, a Quaker ancestor of the nineteenth-century poet, who refused to take refuge in the garrison houses

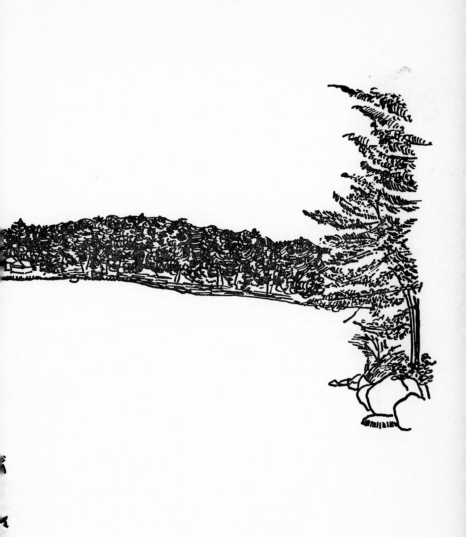

during a raid because of his pacifist beliefs, was on friendly
terms with the Indians and was never harmed.

THE WHITE CAPTIVE

March in the lower Merrimack Valley is a time of scattered snowdrifts, foggy, bone-chilling mornings, mud and
rain. On the morning of March 15, 1697, at about seven
o'clock, word got about in Haverhill that the Indians were
approaching. Whether Colonel Nathaniel Saltonstall, the
local security officer, believed it just another small surprise
raid which his troops could cope with in the open or whether
he was, as his fellow townsmen later accused him of being,
derelict in his duty, it is impossible to say. Certain it is that he
did not immediately order the populace into the garrison
houses, with the result that the fifteenth of March became a
dark day for Haverhill.

In the northwestern part of the town, where the pasture
land sloping up from the river begins to merge with the
forest, stood the house of Thomas Dustin, where he lived with
his wife, Hannah, and seven children between the ages of
two and seventeen. On the morning of March fifteenth,
Hannah was in bed recovering from the birth of an eighth
child, who lay beside her. A neighbor, Mary Corliss Neff, had
come in from next door to help Hannah and was busy tending the baby.

The house was cold, for it was unheated except by the
great fireplace in the kitchen. This, like all the fireplaces of
the time, was so spacious and attached to so large a chimney
that, unless the hearth was filled with a roaring blaze, its flue
let in more cold air than the flames could warm and send out
into the room.

Before anyone realized it, the Indians were in the house,

filling it with their stale meaty smell, the reek of half-cured deerskin and the acrid smell of pine smoke from their greasy hair. They made their way, smashing and destroying, to Hannah's room, seized her and dragged her from her bed. They overpowered the protesting Mary Neff and, taking the newborn baby by its heels, dashed out its brains against the doorjamb. The older children ran screaming and crying out of the house while Thomas Dustin, unable to save his wife, stood between his children and the Indians, holding off the yelling swarm with his gun, which he fired as rapidly as he could load it.

All over the village there were scenes of terror and panic. Arrows twanged and grew still in the clapboard walls. The choking smoke of flintlocks rose in the dark gray morning. The crash of breaking doors, shattered glass and splintered window muntins mingled with shouts of agony and fright as house after house was raided. Twenty-seven persons were killed, at least half of them children, and thirteen, among them Hannah Dustin and Mary Neff, were carried off, leaving a large part of the town wrecked and burning.

The Indians had vanished and the people of Haverhill were too stunned to follow them. Apparently the raiding party did not stick together. There were twelve or thirteen in the group which carried Hannah and her companion northward, one of them an English boy, Samuel Lenorson, who had been taken in an earlier raid on a town near what is now Worcester. The others were a squaw, six children and four warriors.

Forty-five days later, when spring had come to the Merrimack and even on the pine-clad sandy banks as far north as Penacook, some seventy-five miles by river from Haverhill, the arbutus was in bloom and trout lilies, false lily of the valley and bellwort softened the glades among the hemlocks and pines, the Indian raiders and their captives paused to rest.

What the feelings of Hannah Dustin and Mary Neff had been during their long journey we can only imagine. Hannah learned that the sannup who had captured her and whose servant she had become had once lived with an English family at Lancaster, Massachusetts, where he had been taught, and liked, the Puritan form of prayer. The French, however, had since taught him another way of praying which he thought was better. To Hannah's surprise he used the French prayer three times a day.

Whatever the feelings of the two captured women, they could not forget what had happened. Terrified at the thought of being carried all the way to Canada, there to run the gantlet, as they had been told they would be forced to do, and dreading the thought of being sold to the French, Hannah planned to put an end to the northward journey. It was not hard to persuade Mary, and the boy Samuel, though terrified, was willing to help.

The party camped on an island in the Merrimack, close to the mouth of the Contoocook, not far from where the capital city of Concord now stands. The raiders must have concluded that Hannah and Mary were docile captives, for they slept without posting a watch, and without resorting to the Indian custom of draping strips of hide over the sleeping body of a prisoner and tucking the ends under the body of an Indian sleeping on either side. Whatever their precautions, Hannah was too much for them. Early in the morning of April 29, 1697, Hannah raised herself on her elbow and listened. She heard only that infinitely various monotone of the spring tumult of the river, the overhead sound of the wind in the pine trees and the overtones of both, which make the voice of the forest.

Cautiously and silently, gathering her torn and long-unwashed clothes about her, she picked up the hatchet she had hidden beneath her and crept to where Mary Neff lay wide awake and listening beside the quivering young Samuel. With two more tomahawks taken from the sleeping Indians, the three spread out and began their work. It must have been long before dawn but their eyes had grown accustomed to the dark and they knew where each Indian lay. With incredible accuracy and desperate ferocity they split the skulls of four adults and six children and left the squaw so badly wounded that she could neither move nor utter a sound. As an added gesture of bitterness, with perhaps a touch of canniness, Hannah and her companions scalped the bloody heads they had crushed.

As soon as it was light, the three, carrying an Indian gun, a tomahawk and ten scalps, set off down the river on their long journey home, not knowing what other enemies, beast or man, they might encounter.

Hannah lived to tell the tale and her foresight in gathering the scalps of her captors enabled her, although the provincial bounty on Indians had been canceled some time before, to claim and collect a reward of twenty-five pounds. Mary Neff and the boy shared another twenty-five.

Today, on the island upon which, 260 years ago, Hannah Dustin decided that she had seen enough trouble, there stands a monument to her deed, the courage and spirit of which few who look upon that monument can imagine—as indeed few could imagine Mistress Dustin executing her fierce vengeance in the costume with which the sculptor has permanently clothed her.

LYDIA LONGLEY'S JOURNEY TO GOD

Hannah Dustin's remarkable and heroic experience was only one of hundreds of similar ones which Merrimack Valley settlers endured during the seventeenth century. Among this great number were many, however, which had different endings. One of these, which illustrates another kind of tragedy, took place on the Nashua River in Groton, Massachusetts, in 1694.

William and Deliverance Crisp Longley lived on a farm, the site of which is marked today by a small stone. Longley, in 1694, was the town clerk of Groton and a man of some property. He was the father of eight children and the owner of a considerable number of cattle.

On July 19, 1694, William Longley kept in his own handwriting the records of the town meeting of that date. He had no way of knowing that, two days before, a large body of Indians from Maine, attended and encouraged by one and possibly more French priests, had fallen upon the New Hampshire village of Oyster River (now Durham), some seventy-five miles east of Groton, killed 104 persons, captured and carried away twenty-four and burned sixty houses, which was not enough to suit all the raiders. A group of some fifty or sixty Norridgewock warriors under the sagamore, Toxus, decided to move westward in search of more skulls to split.

On the morning of July twenty-seventh, William Longley, looking from the door of his house on the little knoll in the center of his cleared land, saw that his cattle were not in the barnyard where they should have been to await the morning milking but had managed to get out and were making havoc of his shoulder-high corn. Calling to Deliverance and the children to come and help him, he rushed into the cornfield and began to drive the cattle back toward the barnyard gate. The children, with sticks and switches, spread out to keep the beasts from straying farther afield. Deliverance stood by the gate to urge them through.

Suddenly from the edges of the wood issued a series of

bloodcurdling shrieks followed by a fusillade of shots. The cattle bucked and stampeded through the corn. Longley fell and never moved again. Deliverance collapsed across the barnyard entrance under the feet of the galloping, maddened cows. Five of the eight children dropped, bleeding, among the corn rows. Three were seized by the Indians and hurried away through the woods to the river. The savages were pleased that their often-used trick of letting out the cattle for the purpose of gathering a family together to round them up had made their task so easy.

Little Betty Longley died before the raiders, hurrying down the Nashua past Dunstable and on up the Merrimack, reached Penacook. It is not recorded whether she died of wounds or the hardships of the forest journey.

John Longley was twelve years old. When his captors had gone only a little way down the Nashua, he remembered that his father's sheep were locked up in the barn and would starve if not let out. It seems strange, in view of what had already happened back at the Longley farm and of what was yet to happen to John, that thought of the sight of the bloody, mutilated bodies of his parents and five brothers and sisters lying between the cornfield and the barn should not have kept the boy from making a deal with the Indians allowing him to return and let out the sheep. Strange, too, in view of the treatment his family had received from the raiders, that he should have been willing to promise his captors that, if he were allowed to attend to the sheep, he would return and go north with them. Strange or not, John went back to the farm, apparently making no effort to communicate with neighbors or raise an alarm.

It has been said that when the neighbors finally reached the Longley farm they found Jemima Longley, one of John's sisters, tomahawked and scalped but neither dead nor dying, sitting upon a rock among the milling cattle with her family dead about her. If this is true, how could John have been content merely to let out the sheep and return to the Indians? It is certain that he did let out the sheep and hurried back into captivity without Jemima—a captivity which he endured for four years, part of the time as servant to the sagamore, Madockawando. That his life among the savages, savage enough to have destroyed seven members of his family before his eyes, appealed to him more than their ferocity dismayed him is evidenced by the fact that, when relatives at length located and came to ransom him, he was so reluctant to leave the Indians that the rescuers had to use force to separate him from them. He did return to Groton and was apparently able to divest himself of his romantic taste for the life of wigwam and forest, of sannup and squaw. He, like his murdered father, served in later years as clerk of the town. He never did, however, set down any explanation of what really happened and what passed through his mind on that dreadful July day in 1694.

That there may have been something other than fear of Indians in the life of the English pioneers in the Merrimack Valley, which made some of their children feel that there were worse things than captivity, is additionally indicated, if John Longley's story is not sufficient indication, by the mystery of Lydia Longley, John's sister, who was twenty years old at the time of her capture.

Lydia never returned to New England after being carried by the Indian raiders to Montreal, where, according to the Abenaki custom, she was offered for sale to the French. She found a purchaser, supposed to have been one Jacques LeBer, who saw to it that the taint of Protestant Puritanism was soon removed from her by baptism. In the church records appears the following statement:

On Tuesday, April 24, 1696, was baptized a young English girl named Lydie Langley, who was born at Grotten, ten or twelve leagues from Boston in New England of the marriage of William Longley and Deliverance Crisp, both Protestants, the 2nd of April, old style or 12th of the same month new style of the year 1674 taken in the month of July 1694, by the Abenakis, and living for about one month in the house of the sisters of the Congregation of Notre Dame. Her godfather was Monsieur Jacques de ber, Merchant. Her godmother, Dame Marie Madelaine Dupont, wife of Monsieur de Maricour, *Ecuyer, Capitaine d'une compagnie de la Marine*. She named this English girl Lydie Madelaine. The said ceremony was performed in the Chapel of the said Congregation and that by special permission of Messire Francois dolie *Grand Vicaire de Monseigneurs l'Illustrissione et Reverendissime* Bishop of Quebec for certain reasons.

    Signed

           Lydia Magdelaine longley

           M.Mg. Dupont

                LeBer

           M. Caille faisant les

                fonctions curiales.

What steps led from Lydia Longley's deliverance into the hands of M. LeBer and her certainly voluntary acceptance of the church of her French master to her acceptance of the vows of a nun we do not know. It must have taken a very profound stirring of heart and soul to forget that those among whom she chose to remain accepted without question the murder of her parents, who were of that company come to New England to escape priests, bishops and cardinals who they believed stood between them and the true God. Whatever it took, Lydia was, in 1733, living on the Island of Orleans, near Quebec, in the Convent of the Holy Family, of which it is supposed she was the Mother Superior. In July, 1758, exactly sixty-four years after her capture and fourteen months before the undisciplined defenders of Quebec surrendered to the English, Lydia Longley de Ste. Magdelene, Englishwoman of the Congregation of Notre Dame, died in her eighty-fifth year and was buried in the Chapel of the Infant Jesus.

No exile, and not alone among New England captives in her acceptance of a faith which most New Englanders of the seventeenth century regarded as Satan's favorite, Lydia Longley's death coincided with the end of Indian raids upon the Merrimack Valley or, in fact, upon any settlement in New England.

In 1760, French Canada surrendered to the British. France in North America, whose unscrupulous ambitions had cost the English thousands of venturesome and for the most part innocent lives, was doomed. So, too, had the world but known it, was England in America, whose rulers and would-be rulers were not made of the stuff which had gone into the making of their pioneers in America, those who sometimes in error, sometimes by default, but more often by courage and determination made North America their own.

With the signing of the Treaty of Paris between England and France in 1763, the Merrimack ceased to be a tributary-feathered arrow pointed at the hearts of New Hampshire and Massachusetts, pouring out poison and death. It became a highway to a new world.

6 Run Wild in the Mind

....

If the first 120 or 130 years of the Merrimack Valley constituted the era of the Indian, they were also years in which the New England background was becoming a part of the New England mind and character. Man can no more live on the edge of violence, fear and the undominated magnificence of nature without being affected by the contact than an axe can exist in contact with a grindstone without either becoming sharper or having the temper taken out of it.

Life in the Merrimack Valley from 1630 to 1760 did not take the temper out of its inhabitants. It sharpened them and, as in most of the remainder of New England, gave them functional form, structure and spirit which is evident and characteristic today. The New Englander's "rugged individualism" is the notice he gives that he wishes to be allowed to stand back and let things come into his mind. It produces a slow but sure resourcefulness which enables him to stand unmoved—often to the point of appearing stubborn and pigheaded—until the force applied to him has become greater than his own inertia.

He is both gullible and hard to convince, infinitely curious and exasperatingly unconcerned, quick on the trigger and hard to arouse. Yet he is what his history has made him, and what his history has made him has spread by diffusion and contagion into the life and character of the entire United

States, with the least effect upon the southeastern states.

It should not be supposed that the North American environment and the fact of being a pioneer gave to the New Englander all of that quality and spirit which brought democracy out of oligarchy and established what we today speak of with rather glib vagueness as "the American way of life." The seventeenth century saw human life in Europe and the British Isles groping for a more satisfactory world than it had yet known. England during that century was not the England which it became in the nineteenth century. The English race had, it is true, developed an almost unique respect for law and tradition, which it maintained through corruption, anarchy and revolution, but the English were by no means united in understanding of the origin, meaning and application of their law and their tradition.

What happened in North America in that fearful seventeenth century was merely an extension into an unusual and influential theater of what was going on in the mother country. Indeed the very exodus of the Pilgrims, first to Holland and then to Cape Cod and Plymouth, was merely a by-product of the same forces which cost Charles I his head, Cromwell his good sense, Charles II the respect of his people and James II his throne. England, too, was pioneering, as were her colonists in the valley of the Merrimack and the rest of the Atlantic seaboard.

What was there, then, in the physical environment of the New England colonist, other than his conflict with the aborigines, to make out of the yeoman-tradesman-artisan that he was the master of his world which he became?

The spiritual and intellectual environment of the New England immigrant of the decade which saw the settlements on the Piscataqua and at the mouth of the Merrimack was indeed limited. The Europeans who came to Massachusetts

Bay were largely, as we have seen, those who were, at home
in England, somewhat scathingly referred to as Puritans,
meaning that they did not believe that Queen Elizabeth's
church reforms had gone far enough in eliminating corrupt
practices and ceremonies from church service. They had had,
until recently, only the Bible of Tyndale or Coverdale to
read, the King James, or "authorized version," which was
completed in 1611 not yet having found its way very widely
into the hands of the common man.

When Thomas Parker and his flock settled Newbury,
John Milton was a young man of twenty-five, with neither
Lycidas nor *Paradise Lost* nor *Areopagitica* to his credit.
John Bunyan was a boy of seven who knew nothing of prison
bars; *Pilgrim's Progress* was not to appear for forty-three
years. Descartes' *Principia* had not been published, and Isaac
Newton was still seven years short of being anything which
could feel the pull of gravity. William Shakespeare, known to
hundreds of Londoners as an entertainer, had been in his grave
in Stratford for nineteen years, but his work had only reached
the reading public with the publication of the First Folio edition of his plays twelve years before.

SNAKES AND WITCHES

Those among the early comers to New England who
could read, read nothing but the Bible and a few hairsplitting
theological works now forgotten. Nature was an unknown
world, its phenomena thought of, when thought of at all,
largely as manifestations of magic or of the mood of God. Cu-
vier, Buffon and Linnaeus were decades, even generations,
away.

Small wonder that witchcraft, which began to appear in
New England in the 1640's, and other delusions took hold of

minds which had not yet learned to know better. Small wonder, too, that religious heresies should appear to the devout as attempts to unlock the gates of hell and that they should have been handled with a severity which even to us in our barbarous modern world seems sickeningly savage.

The Englishmen who waited at the frontier of the Merrimack Valley for the river to call them northward were of the same stock as the great figures to which the turmoil of the seventeenth century gave birth in England. Yet they had an added pressure of birth upon them, the pressure of new climate, new land, new necessities and requirements which were to make the eighteenth century in America unique in human history.

The inchoate mind of Cotton Mather, testy, undisciplined, overcredulous and far from serene, was the precursor of the calm serenity and disciplined judgment of Benjamin Franklin. Mather's failings were the failings of his time and place, though his state of mind might have been the suggestion for Lewis Carroll's, "I thought I saw an albatross that fluttered round the lamp. I looked again and saw it was a penny postage stamp."

A letter from a Newbury pastor, the Reverend Christopher Toppan, to Cotton Mather, in answer to an inquiry, presents an interesting view of the state of natural history at a point in time some two thirds of the way through the Indian era and nearly a century after the settling of Newbury:

> Concerning the amphisbena, as soon as I received your commands I made diligent enquiry of several persons, who saw it after it was dead, but they could give me no assurance of its having two heads, as they did not strictly examine it, not calling it the least in question because it seemed as really to have two heads as one. They directed me for further information to the person I before spoke

of, who was out of town, and to the persons, who saw it alive and killed it, which were two or three lads, about twelve or fourteen, one of which a pert sensible youngster told me yt one of his mates running towards him cryed out there was a snake with two heads running after him, upon which he run to him, and the snake getting into a puddle of water, he with a stick pulled him out, after which it came towards him, and as he went backwards or forward, soe the snake would doe likewise. After a little time, the snake upon his striking at him, gathered up his whole body into a sort of quoil, except *both heads,* which kept towards him, and he distinctly saw *two mouths* and two *stings* (as they are vulgarly called) which stings or tongues it kept putting forth after the usual manner of snakes, till he killed it. Thus far the lad. This day understanding the person mentioned before was returned, I went to him, and asked about the premises, he told me he narrowly examined the snake being brought to him by the lads after it was dead and he found two distinct heads *one at each end,* opening each with a little stick, in each of which he saw a sting or tongue, and that each head had two eyes, throwing it down and going away, upon second thoughts he began to mistrust his own eyes, as to what he had seen, and therefore returned a second time to examine it, if possible, more strictly, but still found it as before. This person is so credible that I can as much believe him as if I had seen him myself. He tells me of another man yt examined it as he did, but I cannot yet meet with him.

Postscript. Before ensealing I spoke with the other man, who examined the amphisbena (and he is also a man of credit) and he assures me yt it had really two heads, one at each end, two mouths, two stings or tongues and so forth.

Sir I have nothing more to add but that he may have a remembrance in your prayers, who is,

Sir, your most humble servant
CHRISTOPHER TOPPAN

Cotton Mather, in addition to being an eager but bad naturalist, has preserved for us a picture of the chaotic state of knowledge in New England at the close of the seventeenth century, when educated men like himself, who should have known better, let themselves be influenced by popular hysteria to believe in witchcraft. This lamentable and discreditable delusion began to trouble New England as early as 1647, when Mary Johnson was executed as a witch in Hartford, Connecticut. In the Merrimack Valley witchcraft was happily met with some skepticism, although on one occasion in 1679, thirteen years before it reached such tragic proportions in Salem, the popular pastime of witch-baiting was taken seriously enough on the shores of the Merrimack to occupy the attention of the court in Newbury, and a woman of Amesbury, on the north side of the Merrimack, was among those hanged on Gallows Hill, Salem, in the appalling July of 1692.

William Morse and his wife Elizabeth lived at the upper end of Market Street, opposite St. Paul's Church, in what is now Newburyport. William was a shoemaker, sixty-five years old, industrious, sober and godly. Elizabeth was equally well thought of by a town which scrutinized its citizens from heel to hair, eager to find some bit of getup or behavior which could be judged a breach of Christian decorum or church discipline.

The Morses, like most of the simple folk of the seventeenth century, were not very well versed in cosmology and had no knowledge of any worlds beyond their own other than that which they assumed to be presided over by His Satanic Majesty. Since they had no reason to believe that the little people in league with Satan traveled in flying saucers, they believed, instead, in witchcraft.

In December of 1679, the shoemaker began to be

troubled by the misbehavior of inanimate objects and the un-orthodox activities of such animate objects as hogs and cattle. Morse's shoemaking tools began to disappear from their proper places and rain down the chimney, accompanied by parts of chairs, baskets, bricks and other objects. At night, sticks and stones would be flung against the Morse home, although no one could be found outside. Hogs which should have been in the yard appeared in the house squealing to be let out. Cattle would not rest in their stanchions in the barn but were continually breaking loose. William was hit on the head by a shoe while he was kneeling at prayer in his downstairs room. Pots and pans fell upon Elizabeth when she went to the cellar. The harassed couple were convinced that they were receiving the attentions of witches.

At this point, Caleb Powell, the mate of a ship based at the port, who was a frequent visitor at the Morses' house, told the shoemaker that he thought he could solve the problem. With remarkably good sense Powell suggested that William let him take the Morses' young grandson with him for a day and watch to see if there was any hocus-pocus while the boy was away. Morse was willing. He later made an affidavit to the effect that, "I being persuaded to it he (Powell) Com the nex day at the brek of day, and the boy was with him until night and I had not any more truble since."

This, it would seem, should have settled the matter and resulted in a caning for the hobbledehoy. Things were unhappily ordered otherwise. Joseph Moores, boatswain on the vessel of which Caleb Powell was mate, let his opinion of Powell be known, an opinion which, though unsupported by any recorded evidence, was apparently more impressive than Powell's intelligent and perfectly understandable behavior. At least two Newbury people testified that Joseph Moores had often said, in their presence, "that if there were any wizards he was sure Powell was one."

Powell, instead of receiving the thanks of the community for exposing a fraud, was tried at Ipswich in February of 1680 for conspiracy with the forces of darkness. Fortunately for Powell, the court, having pondered the evidence, did not find that it pointed to the mate's guilt. They did, however, render a verdict which suggests the hazards of living in seventeenth-century New England. This remarkable pronouncement appears in the court records:

> Upon hearing the complaint brought to this court against Caleb Powell for suspicion of working by the devill to the molesting of the family of William Morse, of Newbury, though this court cannot find any evident ground of proceeding farther against the sayd Powell, yett we determine that he hath given such ground of suspicion of his so dealing that we cannot so acquit him but that he justly deserves to bear his own shame and the costs of prosecution of the complaint.

What Caleb Powell, so equivocally freed, thought of this curious verdict is not recorded. It is recorded that the people of Newbury were not satisfied. If the Devil was being aided by anyone in Newbury, as he must be, since it was plainly impossible that a human being could have produced without aid all of the phenomena which had tormented the Morse household, they wanted to know who his agent was. The next suspect turned out, surprisingly enough, to be hardworking and long-suffering Elizabeth Morse herself.

Elizabeth, by what train of thought we cannot guess, was brought into court at Boston, charged with being an accessory to the deed of whatever spirits were playing fast and loose with her own household.

On May 20, 1680, Elizabeth was found by a jury guilty according to the indictment which stated that she ". . . not having the fear of God before her eyes, being instigated by the Devil and had familiarity with the Devil, contrary to the peace of our sovereign lord the King, his crown and dignity, the laws of God, and of this jurisdiction . . ."

On the twenty-seventh of May, the governor, Simon Bradstreet, a man of sense, dignity and more than usual intelligence, faced Elizabeth Morse and in words it must have pained him to utter said: "Elizabeth Morse, you are to go from hence to the place from whence you came and thence to the place of execution and there to be hanged by the neck, till you be dead, and the Lord have mercy on your soul."

It was upon the soul of Simon Bradstreet that the Lord had mercy, for three days later the governor and the magistrates—the upper house of the General Court—voted to reprieve Goodwife Morse. Although the House of Deputies, in November, wanted to know why the court's sentence had not been carried out, we do not know what answer they received.

In May, 1681, however, William Morse was given a chance to answer the charges made in the testimony which had brought about his wife's conviction. He did answer them with innocent and touching naïveté. Even the Deputies were affected and Elizabeth was freed to go home and, after much wondering about her state and the public interpretation of it, to die in peace and "in Christ."

SUSANNA AND THE GIRLS

There was only one other serious case of witchcraft hysteria among the Merrimack towns. It was indeed serious, although today we are able to think that it was not without its pitiful comedy.

Although her birth date is not recorded, Susanna North Martin must have been in her late sixties in the fateful year of 1692. For six years the widow of George Martin, she lived on a little farm on Hunt's Lane, not far from the Merrimack in the western part of Amesbury.

Susanna was no old hag. In spite of the farm work which her grown sons and daughters had left her to do by herself, she was neat and trim, birdlike and bright of eye. She had a sharp tongue and a lack of charity born of the advantage taken of her by those whom she tried to get to work for her. The people of Amesbury had considered her a witch since 1669, when she had been accused of strange doings but had escaped trial, the madness not having reached its vindictive peak at that time.

On May 2, 1692, the valley of the Merrimack River shone with the silvery rose of spring. Along the river's edge and up the Powwow, the reeds and wild rice were bright with new green. The clean black water, turbulent and bubbling after the April freshets, washed high along the Amesbury shore. Red wings twanged and choughed in the cattails and in the fruit trees on the slope running up toward Hunt's Lane bluebirds warbled at their knothole nesting sites. Smoke rose from scattered chimneys among pines, oaks and elms and drifted downriver with the morning water haze.

Yet in the little settlement of Amesbury, its roofs breaking the blackness of the forest west of the Powwow, there was an atmosphere of tension.

There had been trouble, not only with the Indians, but with other settlers upriver who disputed with the Amesbury folk their right to the hay on the meadows in the flats between the Powwow and Little River. Anxiety and nervousness caused by the uncertainties of the current view of personal and public rights had made men edgy and quarrelsome.

Ill-will was everywhere. The Amesbury people and the men from Haverhill, although faced with a common and fearful danger from a common and dangerous enemy, fought each other with scythes and hayforks over the disputed grass-lands. The tension resulting from the apparent hopelessness of struggle and the meagerness of reward for labor was like a brewing storm over the heads of those working out their pre-carious existence between the river and the great forest.

The widow Martin, embittered by the town's inability to remember how great a service her dead husband—who was for nearly thirty years the official who kept track of property bounds, arbitrated disputes and helped new settlers—had rendered it, felt the general ill-will cruelly. On the morning of the second of May she may well have been so depressed by her situation that she was glad to see her good friend Orlando Bagley, the town constable, ride up to her gate, though she must have known that he could be coming to report a com-plaint from some neighbor who had taken offense at her sharp tongue.

Orlando had not come to chat, nor merely to bring a complaint. He carried with him a paper which he read to Susanna without looking at her. She did not need the words to know what had happened. This is what Orlando Bagley read, to the accompaniment of the soft twitter of bluebirds, the chatter of robins, the distant sound of sawing, the sigh of the downriver sea wind in the pines, the bleating of goats and the occasional far-off barking of dogs, those attributes of the natural world which have so little power over the unnatural:

To the Marshall of the County of Essex or his Lawful Deputies or to the Constable of Amesbury:

You are in their Majesties names hereby required forth-with or as soon as may be to apprehend and bring (be-

fore us) Susanna Martin of Amesbury in the county of
Essex Widdow at the house of Lt. Nathaniel Ingersalls
in Salem Village in order to her examination Relating
to high suspicion of sundry acts of Witchcraft donne or
committed by her upon the Bodys of Mary Walcot, Abigail Williams, Ann Putnam and Mercy Lewis of Salem
village or farmes whereby great hurt and damage to the
bodys of said persons according to complaint of Capt.
Jonathan Walcot & Sergt. Thomas putnam in behalf of
their Majesties this day exhibited before us for themselves
and also for several of theire neighbors and here you are
not to fail at your peril.

Dated Salem April 30, 1692.

John Hathorn
Jonathan Corwin assistants

If Susanna's heart sank, she did not show it. What she
said to Constable Bagley is not recorded. Whether or not
when she left with Orlando that day for their twenty-five-
mile-journey to Salem she was aware that she would never
see her farm or the Merrimack River again, we can imagine
what she must have felt as she rode downhill toward the
Newbury ferry, knowing the hostility of the Indians, the van-
dalistic venom of her own community and the uncompromising enmity of the wolves and foxes of the great forest on the
edge of which she lived.

Susanna Martin lay in Salem jail for nearly two months
before she was permitted to face her accusers and the witnesses, her own neighbors from Salisbury and Amesbury. She
was denied counsel but was brave and bitter enough to be
her own advocate. To the charge that she had practiced
witchcraft and sorcery she pleaded not guilty.

On the twenty-sixth of June the preliminary trial began.
Susanna, savagely scornful, was led into the court, past the

vengeful eyes of her neighbors, past the excited girls who were her accusers. As she took her seat Mercy Lewis fell into a fit and paid no attention to the magistrate's question. One of the other girls, Abigail Williams, answered.

"It is Goody Martin, she hath hurt me often."

The others joined Mercy in convulsions on the floor, Ann Putnam first flinging her glove at the accused woman, who burst into unpleasant laughter.

"What!" said the magistrate. "Do you laugh at it?" Susanna's reply is recorded. "Well I may at such folly."

"Is this folly?" demanded the magistrate. "The hurt of persons?"

"I never hurt man woman nor child."

At this point Mercy Lewis cried out, "She hath hurt me a great many times and pulls me down."

Susanna laughed again. The magistrate wanted to know what Susanna thought could be the matter with the girls. Susanna said that she did not know and had no desire to spend her judgment upon the matter.

"Don't you think they are bewitched?" asked the magistrate.

"No," said Susanna firmly. "I do not think they are."

The magistrate wanted to know what, in that case, she did think. Susanna shook her head. "No," she said. "My thoughts are my own when they are in, but when they are out they are another's. Their master——"

"Their master? Who do you think is their master?"

"If they deal in the black art," remarked Susanna, possibly with a toss of her head, "you may know as well as I."

The magistrate tried to make Susanna admit that the fact that her appearance sent the girls into their spells of bewitchment must have some significance. Susanna reminded the magistrate of Saul and the Witch of Endor, saying, "How do I know? He that appeared in the shape of Samuel may appear in anyone's shape."

The magistrate appears to have regarded that as the double talk of one familiar with spirits. Susanna was committed for trial and shortly faced the witnesses. She must have been baffled by what she learned of her powers and her antics, concerning which she was not permitted to question those who testified.

In a daze of rage, probably mingled with contempt, she heard John Allen of Salisbury testify that because he refused to let his ailing oxen draw a load of staves for her she bewitched the oxen. When put out to fatten on the Salisbury marshes, they suddenly went wild, infecting a dozen others with their madness, which consisted of galloping into the Merrimack and swimming to Plum Island. When their owners went to the Island to capture them, using "all imaginable gentleness," the oxen ran away with a violence which John Allen thought could be nothing but diabolical. That it was not normal seems to be indicated by the fact that the great beasts, who should have known which side their bread was buttered on, plunged once more into the Merrimack and—all but one of them—swam out to sea and were never seen alive again. The one who returned from its plunge lunged up the beach so furiously that no one could touch him, passing those who were waiting with halters and ropes to capture a creature they imagined to be exhausted. He disappeared down Plum Island, crossed the marshes, galloped through Old Newbury and, after again crossing the Merrimack, was eventually found in Amesbury, where he was presumably returning Susanna Martin to her home.

Whether Susanna lowered her eyes or raised them to heaven in agonized appeal on hearing the testimony of Bernard Peache is not recorded. Bernard swore that on a Lord's

Day night, when he was in bed, he heard a scrabbling at the window. He apparently lay still, watching Susanna Martin climb through the casement and jump to the floor. She braced herself, took hold of the deponent's feet and drew his body up into a heap. We may wonder just what kind of heap it was when we learn from Bernard's testimony that Susanna "lay upon him near two hours; in all which time he could neither speak nor stir." When he was able to move, he said, he managed to get three of the woman's fingers into his mouth and was able to bite them to the bone. This was apparently equivalent to making the sign of the cross, for it sent Susanna out of the room, down the stairs and out the front door. Other people in the house saw and heard nothing but the next day, Bernard claimed, there was a drop of blood in a bucket by the door and two upon the new snow outside. "There was likewise the print of her two feet just without the threshold; but no more sign of any footing further off."

There was much more testimony from others, but no real indication that Susanna was anything worse than an embittered termagant who enjoyed calling people names. Joseph Ring, as earnest as if he were claiming today that he had seen Susanna at many Communist meetings, claimed that he was carried about at night by demons attending any number of witch meetings, at most of which Susanna Martin was present.

John Pressey, who really did have something happen to him, blamed it impressively upon Susanna, whose house he had to pass on his way home from the ferry. He arrived home one night, bleeding and badly mauled, his clothes torn and his kerchief missing, saying that he had been attacked by wolves, which indeed he had been. His kerchief and the tracks of wolves were found in and about a thorn bush on the path which he was accustomed to use. In his testimony at

Susanna's trial he embellished his tale with a strange light which, when beaten with a stick, resisted him and threw him into a pit he knew did not exist. When he got hold of himself and resumed his exciting walk, there was Susanna, standing where the strange light had been. He was, he said, pretty much exhausted when he got home. The next day he found out that Susanna was "in a miserable condition, by pains and hurts that were upon her."

How Susanna sat through this appalling testimony we shall never know. The outcome of her trial was never in doubt and she must have known it. She never saw the old house on Hunt's Lane again.

On the nineteenth of July, five women, among them Susanna Martin, were led to Gallows Hill in Salem. Susanna was quiet but one of her companions in despair cried out to the Reverend Nicholas Noyes, who was begging the convicted women to confess, "You're a liar! I am no more a witch than you are a wizard! If you take my life away God will give you blood to drink!"

Susanna and the others were hanged by the neck until they were dead, and buried in what soil could be found on the rock of Gallows Hill. Twenty-odd miles away, on the banks of the Merrimack, Susanna Martin's goats, cattle and pigs ran wild, but there was no one to be fined for letting them do so.

7 Creatures of the Wilderness

....

There were other eyes than those of Indians and other spirits than those of witches watching from the forest and wandering through its shades. In an earlier chapter there has been given a general picture of what the Merrimack Valley forest was, and in much of its area still is, like.

The wild life of a region is not usually considered an important part of its human history. Yet it is true of New England, and particularly of the five thousand square miles of the Merrimack basin and the forest and coast to the east and north of it, that without its wild life it could not have taken nor maintained the course which its human history has taken.

The earliest settlements of the Merrimack and Piscataqua would have gone the way of Virginia's Roanoke colony without the fish which were abundant in the rivers and seas north of the forty-second degree of latitude. Without the wild life of the forest and the agricultural products of natives nourished by that wild life, the less commercial Puritans of Plymouth Plantation would have been very unlikely to have survived their first year in Cape Cod Bay.

Yet it was largely fish of river and sea, sturgeon, salmon, shad, alewives and other herring, that made the difference in Massachusetts, New Hampshire and Maine between life and death. In spite of the fact that the water was an element which man could not enter and penetrate as he could the forest, it was the water which most easily provided the seventeenth-century New Englander with nourishment.

Wild turkeys, pigeons, grouse and deer were relatively as numerous on land as fish were in the sea, but they were closer to man in their perhaps conscious desire to live and so more astute about keeping a distance between themselves and the most lethal of all predators.

There were perhaps in the first decades of the seventeenth century no more deer in the forests of the Merrimack and its tributaries than there are today and it is probable that they were seen no more often, except by deliberate hunters, than they are three hundred-odd years later. Many other wild things, more numerous then than now, were perhaps no more often seen. A few which were common in the seventeenth century are no longer found in the region, though it would not be quite proper to say that all of that few are extinct.

The wolf is no longer found along the Merrimack. The wild turkey has retreated southward and is not found in New England, though he is still fair game in Pennsylvania. The passenger pigeon, one of the most beautiful and romantic of birds, a unique example of Malthusian maladjustment aided by man's ruthless greed, is no longer found anywhere. The wolverine has indisputably gone from New England. The cougar was never common in the Merrimack basin, and today, although quite convincingly reported from New Brunswick, for a cougar not too many days' travel from the Merrimack, he seems to be seen in the region only by the uncritical.

Few other creatures known to our New England ancestors are missing from that section today, although the lynx, the moose, the black bear and the fisher are present only in greatly reduced numbers, a circumstance resulting by no means entirely from hunting pressure. Creatures of the wild are not all equally adaptable, some responding rapidly to unfavorable changes in environment and slowly to subsequent favorable changes. This is particularly true of great beasts like the moose which is in competition for subsistence with deer and has a much lower birth rate, not even bearing one offspring every year.

The cougar, which is today usually referred to in the Merrimack forests as panther, is one of the most fascinating members of the New England fauna. While it is probable that few of the early settlers in the Merrimack basin ever actually saw a panther or catamount, there is plenty of evidence of the presence of that great animal in the region. Although it is not mentioned in the account of the wild life of New Hampshire in volume three of Jeremy Belknap's great history of that state, completed in 1794, some writers, among them Captain John Smith, did mention it. There are, too, records of its presence which tell of attacks on cattle and other domestic animals and "painter stories" have been associated with the New Hampshire frontier for more than two hundred years.

THE MYSTERIOUS CAT

I recall an occasion in 1907, when I was living between Chocorua and Tamworth, New Hampshire, which left an indelible impression on my mind. On a very warm day in August I had been fishing with a companion who lived in Tamworth, the son of one of the town's selectmen, named Page. After reaching the Page house and being treated to freshly made birch beer, which Mrs. Page had been brewing in the kitchen, we went to the barn to help Mr. Page with the hay. The selectman, when we found him, was sitting on the edge of the lower mow, wiping hay dust and sweat from his fore-head. After a lapse of fifty years it is hard to remember ex-actly how the subject of panthers happened to come up, but it is my recollection that someone had reported seeing one of these great cats a short time before near Wonalancet.

However that may be, the selectman there in the shaded hay barn told a story which had been told to him as a child, a story which the boy who listened to it for the first time then believed to be unique, although I have since heard it from many mouths and in many parts of the country, each time as having happened in the vicinity of the narrator, and it ap-pears in short-story form, with the setting in Ohio, in the works of Ambrose Bierce. According to Mr. Page, his grand-father knew the man who had told the story as his own experience.

In the decade following the close of the French and In-dian War, a few years before the outbreak of the Revolution, a man and his wife—his name has not proved to have the lon-gevity of his story—traveled up the Pemigewasset to the Mad River and thence northeastward into what is now the Water-ville Valley, where no white man had been before.

The couple carried two bundles of clothing and bedding, an axe, a musket, powder and shot and a bag of seeds. Com-ing to a spot where the Mad River slowed its course as it passed through an interval of rocks and coarse grass, they set down their burdens and began to build a shelter.

Before winter set in, the man had felled and split enough trees to make boards and shakes for a cabin with a chimney of loose stone chinked with mud and moss. His wife had managed to raise, between the felled trees, a tiny crop of corn, barley and pumpkins. How they lived through the winter on corn, barley gruel, pumpkins and moosemeat is not a part of the story. What happened in the couple's first spring is.

The woman was taken sick soon after the snow had gone from the ground and, in spite of what her husband could do, fell into a coma and in a few days breathed no more. The man was crushed with grief and appalled at the prospect of burying his wife in that remote wilderness without a Christian service being said over her.

He laid the dead woman out on the floor in as decent an attitude as he could, with her arms folded on her breast and her eyes closed, took his gun and started out down the river swollen to overflowing by the melting snows. It took him all day to reach the little settlement of Plymouth on the Pemigewasset. When he reached the minister's house, he could only sit with his face in his hands and sob. After a swig of rum and a bit of food, he was able to tell his story and to persuade the preacher to return with him on the following day.

The two weary men reached the clearing on the Mad River at dusk. The pioneer stopped and pointed to the cabin. The preacher stared. Suddenly he reached out his hand and gripped his companion's arm.

From the cabin door, the hair on its back bristling, its teeth bared, its tail lashing, its shoulders hunched, came a huge panther. The beast paused a moment to snarl at the two men and then disappeared, leaping into the forest.

The astonished men hesitated and then rushed forward. The cabin was almost dark. The minister hesitated by the door while the frantic settler crept through, groping for the body of his wife. As his hand touched the homespun skirt, he gave a gasp of terrified relief.

The man rose to his feet, took a strip of birchbark from a rock near the chimney breast and knelt to pour a tiny pile of gunpowder on the hearth. Going back to the door for his gun he ignited the gunpowder with the flint of the gunlock. It burst into smoky, sulphurous flame into which he dipped the birchbark. He stood up, facing the center of the room, holding the flaming bark as he stared down at the body of his wife, whose arms were now unfolded as if frozen in a frantic clutching motion, the fingers bent like claws. The man knelt, holding the sputtering bark closer to the figure on the floor. He could see that across the throat and about her mouth were dark red stains. From between the woman's clenched teeth protruded the pad and claw of a panther's toe.

Whether this tale had its origin in an actual incident which took place in the Waterville Valley, or is merely a legend common throughout the East, establishing the awe and bitter hatred with which the panther, cougar, puma, lion, catamount or whatever you choose to call it was regarded, the dangerous beast did roam the forests of the Merrimack system until comparatively recently.

As any resident of the upper valley knows and any visitor to it will discover, the panther is far from a dead issue. You can find scarcely a town north of the Souhegan or the Suncook which does not shelter someone, man or woman, who claims to have seen, or to know someone who has seen, a specimen of *Felis concolor couguar*.

Yet the fact remains that no specimen of panther has been taken in New Hampshire since the nineteenth century. The panther never was and could not be today as abundant as current reports now seem to make him. To keep a panther going requires between fifty and sixty large deer a year. If there were today more than one panther anywhere along the Merrimack, it would be unbelievable that no trace of the beast's kills should be found. None has been found and no tracks have been positively identified, although a fairly positive track identification from Vermont was made in 1934, a specimen was killed near Moosehead Lake in Maine in 1906, and a pair of the beasts is fairly reliably reported to have roamed the woods about the Mogallaway River as recently as the early 1920's.

The probability is that most recently reported panther sightings are those of other animals, ranging from deer to fisher cat. Most of those who claim to have seen a panther turn out to have no conception of its real size or color. There are, however, a few reports which cannot be dismissed lightly. If the mysterious cat has been seen in New Hampshire recently, as it well may have been, the creature was probably not a resident but a wanderer from the less frequented forests of northern Maine and eastern New Brunswick.

THE STRANGE NURSLING

If the panther has fallen or been pushed into the category of mystery, that delightful yet untrustworthy clown, the black bear, has not. He is, as he always has been, a part of the life of the Merrimack, confined now in deference to the encroachments of industry and its suburban periphery to the river's upper reaches, where, although common, he is seldom seen. He is seldom seen, yet there is no doubt of his existence. As many as two hundred were killed in New Hampshire in 1956, during a part of which year there was a five-dollar bounty which the General Court has now had the good sense to repeal.

The Indians used bear's teeth for decoration and bearskins for warmth and bear meat was an important part of the diet of Indian and colonist alike. Although man in the Merrimack Valley as elsewhere has always regarded the bear as his enemy, his portrait in the folklore of New Hampshire is tinted with some affection, possibly because of the charm of his young, the engaging naïveté of his habits—among which is his practice of standing on his hind legs—and his somewhat incongruous vegetarian taste for nuts, fruit, berries, roots and honey.

There is a bear story from the township of Groton, New Hampshire, where a pioneer family lived in the late eighteenth or early nineteenth century, somewhere between the Cockermouth and the South Branch of the Baker River, both of which, though they run in opposite directions, are tributaries of the Merrimack.

Near the old Hood Road, between Catalochee Mountain and Kimball Hill, this pioneer family had cleared a farm and managed to get a reasonably comfortable living from the forest and the rich but shallow soil.

The man of the family had been cutting wood one day in April, over on the slope near Derby Pond. The weather was warm and sunny but the snow was deep. The falling of a large spruce which he had cut uprooted a smaller tree which grew against a rock. When the crashing of falling limbs had quieted and the disturbed snow settled, the woodcutter was startled to see a large and very emaciated she-bear emerge from the green tangle of boughs. The bear, looking very distraught and disagreeable, started for the man holding the axe, who, the story has it, stood his ground, waited until the distance was right and, taking careful aim, split the creature's skull.

When the cold sweat which had broken out all over him had turned to warmth and a glow of proud relief, the man, knowing as woodsmen do that the bear would not have been likely to attack him had she not had young nearby, searched under the fallen tree and discovered two cubs, one apparently lifeless and the other whining and crying as it climbed fumblingly about among the branches. It was scarcely larger than a good-sized rabbit.

The young of the black bear are born during late January or early February while the mother is in a dormant state and has been without food for some time. If her young were proportionately as large when born as the young of most mammals, she would not be able to nourish them for the two months before it would be possible for her to find any food for herself. The black bear's young, when born, weigh less than half a pound each although the mother may weigh three hundred or more.

When the woodcutter saw the cub of the she-bear he had killed, it was plain to him that the young one would soon join the other member of the litter which had apparently been crushed by the falling tree. As his wife, although they had five living children, was disconsolate over the loss a few days before of a three-week-old baby, he decided to take the tiny bear home with him, hoping that she might find some solace in the affection which its charm might arouse in her. He did carry the cub home with him, and, somewhat to his dismay, found his wife not only delighted with the infant creature but determined to suckle it at the breast which the death of her own child had left ready but unused.

What her other children thought of their foster brother or whether her husband regretted his decision to bring the tiny creature home we do not know. The story has it that the bear throve on his new diet and grew to be able to take care of himself and to be a playful if somewhat rough pet. When the coldest part of the winter came, he made himself a den beneath the barn where on mild days he could be heard snuffing and moving about.

In the spring he emerged in a rather surly state and before anyone knew what he was up to had, with one stroke of his paw, broken the leg of the family dog who was tormenting him. The woodcutter, who had the year before marked the cub's ear with a hog-ring, built a pen for the creature and began feeding him from a barrel of winter-spoiled apples mixed with corn.

On the first morning after the pen was built there was no bear in it. The children and their mother mourned his loss, but he was soon forgotten by the youngest. What the mother's feelings were we can only imagine.

One moonlit night in October the woodcutter heard a commotion in the pigpen, followed by a prolonged and piercing squeal. The man got out of bed, loaded his gun and flung open the door of the house. There in the moonlight stood a large black bear staring at the house door. For a moment the man hesitated, for he had never before seen a bear without young which would not run at sight of a man, and this was not the time for a bear to be with young. Yet, as there was plainly a dead pig on the ground beside the beast, he raised his gun and fired. The bear's head dropped between its forefeet which slowly collapsed. The hind legs followed and the huge creature lay still.

The man walked cautiously forward. He waited until he was sure that there was no motion in the black body and then, holding his gun, bent over it. In the moonlight he could plainly see a quill hog-ring in the dead bear's ear. As he walked slowly back to the house he saw that his wife had come to the door.

"Was it?" she said.

He nodded.

The woman gave a quick gasp and, without a word, turned and walked into the darkness of the room in which firelight flickered faintly on the hearth. The children looked silently down from the loft opening. They watched their mother cross the room in silence. One by one their faces disappeared and their tiptoe steps could be heard crossing the loft floor to their bed.

It is interesting to note that some twenty years after I first heard this story in 1913, there appeared in *The New York Times* a news item telling of a woman in New Hampshire who had been given a medal by some humane society for suckling, under identical circumstances, a bear cub the mother of which had been killed by wood choppers.

Perhaps in the Merrimack Valley, as elsewhere, folklore is the guiding spirit of reality.

8 Like No Known Habitation

....

The wild things, human and animal, and the inhuman aspects of domesticated men, women and beasts which filled the Merrimack Valley during the first century of European invasion, like the ringing of a bell which civilization was not there to hear, had little effect upon the river itself.

The rain and mists of the mountains and hills, the storms and periods of drought could only make of the river what it had been for centuries. Men, not yet in need of what it could have been to them, were powerless to change it.

It had seen changes in earth and in men and their ways, and in its silts, gravels and rocks it could record the former but not the latter. We may well wish that it could have done so, in order that we might have explanations of many things which are now inexplicable.

In an earlier chapter, I referred to the possibility that Europeans of a civilization antedating that of medieval England might have visited New England in the course of deliberate journeys which we know that they made and of accidental misadventures which, the means of travel being what they were at the time, they could hardly have escaped. The men of Scandinavia and the Celtic peoples before them were great voyagers and have left records of their travels, records which are often ambiguous if authentic. We know that the Irish were in Iceland and probably Greenland before the tenth century and, being accustomed to the sea, it is not impossible that they might have reached New England. We know that the Norsemen also colonized Greenland and it is practically certain that at some time or other they set foot in New England. There is a legend which may be more than a legend that a Scot named Sinclair reached North America in the fourteenth century. Rock markings found in Massachusetts, notably at Westford in the Merrimack basin, may possibly be associated with his visit.

From the Saga of Thorfinn Karlsefni, sometimes called the Saga of Eric the Red, we learn that Karlsefni and his men set out from Brattahlid in Greenland shortly after the year 1000 to search for Vinland, which must have been on the mainland of North America some distance to the southwest. They found a place where there was ". . . a stream that first ran down into a lake and then into the sea. There were great sandbars outside the river mouth and they could only enter the stream at high tide. Karlsefni then sailed into the river mouth and named the country Hop, because that was the Norse word for a small, land-locked bay. Here they found self-sown wheatfields in the lowlands and grapevines wherever there were hills. Every creek was full of fish."

North, or northeast, of Hop was a place which the Norsemen called Straumsfjördr, or Streamfjord. Karlsefni's party spent several winters at Streamfjord, where Karlsefni's son, Snorri, the first white child to see the light of day in America, was born.

When the Norsemen left Streamfjord to sail northeast along the coast to Markland—or Forest Land—they learned from two captive Indian boys of some strange people living in a nearby region, people who "went about in white clothes, uttered loud cries, and carried poles with banners fastened to them. It is generally believed that this must have been White Men's Land or Greater Ireland."

These words from the ancient saga, so full of romantic mystery, were to have a profound effect upon many men in America during the nineteenth and twentieth centuries.

Although the statements about time, distance and direction in the sagas are subject to many different interpretations, the descriptions of the places visited by the Norsemen have always fascinated men with a passion for the past and a tender-minded ability to overlook discrepancies, especially men eager to achieve distinction by association with some great revelation or discovery.

THE DREAMER'S GUESS

One such man was William B. Goodwin, of Hartford, Connecticut, a retired insurance man and member of a wealthy family, whose interests and enthusiasms were many. Chief among these was the pre-Columbian American past. In 1936, Mr. Goodwin was introduced by Harry A. Cheney and Malcolm Pearson to an unexplained stone ruin on the Spicket River near Cowbell Corners in North Salem, New Hampshire, six miles above the junction of the Spicket and the Merrimack at Methuen, Massachusetts.

There were local legends in and about North Salem that this curious collection of pits, walled caves, apparent rock shelters, walls of great stones and mysterious drains, had been built by a supposedly eccentric resident of the town, Jonathan Pattee. There were also published and word-of-mouth reports that the North Salem ruins were the work either of Norsemen or, better still, of tenth-century Irish monks. Since the extraordinary nature of the ruins offered convincing proof of none of these theories and seemed to have no parallel among American archeological discoveries, the romantic Goodwin felt that he had found what he was looking for.

After some negotiation he purchased the site, fenced it in with a fine and expensive six-foot fence of steel posts and mesh, hired an engineer to help him and with the added assistance of Malcolm Pearson of Sutton, Massachusetts, began the work of excavation and restoration. Goodwin was determined to find an explanation of the puzzling site, perfectly certain that it would prove to be pre-Columbian.

The history of the site which William Goodwin bought from the Dustin family—presumably descendants of the Indian-killing Hannah, whose home was not more than five miles from North Salem—has been traced back to its original granting in 1742. Every available document, every deed from the first to the last has been examined. None makes any mention of the acre or more of extraordinary structures whose baffling foundations seemed so enticing to William Goodwin.

There is no positive evidence that they ever were built at all, yet there they stand today, posing a question not seriously posed by any other New England ruin. That question, which has more than one part, is, "When and by whom were they built and for what purpose?" A look at the ruins themselves explains the existence of the last part of the question.

On a low rocky hill, some 245 feet above sea level and about eighty rods east of the Spicket River in the northernmost part of Salem township, is a complex of sturdy stone walls practically independent of the typical over-all system of stone walls of the region. In the center of these walls, on the highest part of the hill, stands what is left of an amorphous, almost deliberately irregular structure like nothing else in North America.

Vincent Fagan, Assistant Professor of Architecture at

Notre Dame University and an architect and archeologist of
note, said after his first view of North Salem:

> No amount of forewarning could prepare me for the
> amazing impact of the North Salem stone work.
>
> There was the approach from the northward which
> is, now, customarily followed and we wound upward
> through a stubble of tree-growth to the high crest of a
> vast ledge. All about stretched the grey and purple dis-
> tances of New Hampshire.
>
> From this crowning height the wild stone outcrop-
> pings cascaded southward in a tumult of forms until all
> identity was lost in the autumn jungle.
>
> Emotionally, I was aware of a terrific clash. The big
> things were too little. The little things so big. There was,
> at one and the same time, gigantic confusion and childish
> order—deep cunning and rude naïveté. There was explo-
> sive disarray held together by the fine thread of a great
> weaver. I felt flattened by the ruthless hand of Herculean
> might and restored to my feet by the beckoning finger of
> a small boy. It was as if I had been listening to the pizzi-
> catto of a solo violinist playing against a back-drop of a
> London blitz.
>
> Here was the strangest juxtaposition of antitheses I
> have ever looked at.
>
> As I made my way down the hillside nothing could
> be anticipated. The cleared areas between the structures
> were exposed basic granite but sloping at crazy angles
> such as would challenge the footing of a mountain goat.
> At hand and in unexpected places were little chambers
> and carefully constructed niches with low lintels and
> smooth, level floors of ledge stone.
>
> Things were underground where my reasoning
> would locate them on the high plateau of the acropolis I
> had just left. A huge oblong stone had a deep groove all
> around it and a spill-way at one end. It was attached to
> the side wall of a rocky gulley and stood on stone legs.
> From the native ledge—if one can hold precarious foot-
> ing—the top, guttered surface is waist high. The stone

commands no view, nor is it the focal point of any, although moving it six feet to the west would cause it to
dominate the entire architectural composition. Ten feet
to the east would have established it in an elaborate sub-
terranean edifice which was ventilated by means of stone
louvers, pivoted successfully and lying in a rebated stone
frame, well cut. Throughout this underground, or covered, building there are such details as projecting shelf-
like features expertly constructed, carefully squared cubi-
cles. Long shafts, too low and narrow for human passage,
lead off down the hillside. Their bottom is bedrock, the
sides and top are of stone. One such shaft, at eye-level
from the inside, leads straight to the space under the
table slab with the grooved top. On a stone laid hori-
zontally, and seemingly of sandy texture, is a faint line
carving. For all the lengthy premeditation evidenced in
this building, the ledge floor is uncomfortably marked by
slopes and angles. Yet the studious corbelling of the stone
walls provides easy erect passage with no sense of squeezing from the sides nor from overhead.

This is an impression, poetic and rhapsodic, but it seems
justified by the strange site. Small wonder that the impressionable enthusiasm of William Goodwin should set him plung-
ing into the past for an explanation of his fantastic relic.

Goodwin had long been interested in pre-Columbian
America and its ties to Europe, and he had read with an im-
aginativeness which ran ahead of the printed word, the Saga
of Eric the Red and its tale of Thorfinn Karlsefni's sojourn in
Vinland. He had concluded that Streamfjord—which certainly,
if the sagas are history, could be anywhere between Buzzard's
Bay and the Bay of Fundy, even at the mouth of the Merrimack—was actually the region surrounding the Piscataqua
River at Portsmouth, New Hampshire.

He concluded, too, that the place at which the men in
white clothes carrying banners were found must have been

about thirty miles from Streamfjord. In these deductions he was, like many other interpreters of the perplexing sagas, using more imagination than reason, yet it must be said that it would, from internal evidence, be as difficult to prove him wrong as it would have been for him to prove himself right. Whatever justification there may have been for his claim, he did not hesitate to make it and to announce to the world that the North Salem ruin, which is about thirty miles from Portsmouth, was a part of Irland it Mikla, or Greater Ireland, founded probably in the tenth century A.D.

North Salem being what it was and unexplained even by experts in any other terms, the press took up Goodwin's claim and carried it, with some embellishment, to a fascinated public.

Archeologists could not agree. H. O'Neill Hencken of Harvard published a long article in the *New England Quarterly* in 1939 and a shorter one in the *Scientific American* in which he made it plain that he did not believe that the North Salem structures could possibly be the work of Norsemen, Irish monks or pre-Columbian Indians; that they could not have been built before the first white settlement of the Merrimack Valley—the middle of the seventeenth century in that particular locality; and that they were probably, for the most part, the work of Jonathan Pattee, who did not occupy the site until 1826. He accounted for the amazing nature of Pattee's work by referring to his supposed eccentricity.

There was, in Hencken's remarks, much that was convincing. His description of Pattee as an eccentric, however, was merely an overready acceptance, as unscientific as Goodwin's own claims, of a confused and confusing local legend which also had it that Pattee had built the "caves" as a refuge when he was a fugitive from justice.

In any case, Hencken's pronouncements did not settle the

question of the antiquity of North Salem. Neither did Goodwin's quixotic denunciation of Hencken, which burst like a bomb in Goodwin's book, published in 1946, *The Ruins of Great Ireland in America.*

When William Goodwin died in 1950, he left the North Salem property to Malcolm Pearson, his sympathetic and faithful right-hand man, who had been impressed both by Goodwin's sincerity and by the doubts expressed by others. Pearson wanted to know the answer if it could be found.

DIGGING INTO MYSTERY

Several years after William Goodwin's death, an organization was chartered under the laws of New Hampshire for the purpose of investigating such relics of the New England past as North Salem. Malcolm Pearson became one of the directors of Early Sites Foundation, in which he was associated with a group of anthropologists, archeologists and students of architectural and human history. In 1955, Early Sites Foundation leased the North Salem site from Malcolm Pearson and under the guidance of one of its directors, archeologist Junius Bird of the American Museum of Natural History, conducted a study on the spot. Seven weeks of digging by competent field archeologists produced a vast amount of material from a sampling of test pits. None of the pits, which went down to bedrock or undisturbed earth, produced any artifacts or any other form of evidence which could be dated back farther than the end of the eighteenth century.

Meanwhile a documentary study of the history of the site owners was carried on by the Foundation. This turned up no evidence that the ruins at North Salem were those of a structure which could have been in existence earlier than the eighteenth century. The study did bring out, however, that

Jonathan Pattee, far from being an eccentric or fugitive from justice, was one of North Salem's most respected citizens, who frequently served as trustee of town funds.

The Early Sites Foundation reluctantly concluded its researches with a negative verdict, to the effect that while a pre-Columbian origin of the ruin might still be possible, the only available evidence pointed to an age of less than two centuries. There was some disposition to feel that a verdict could not properly be given while a single square foot of earth on the North Salem hilltop remained unturned. The Foundation felt, however, that the history of the Norsemen and, for that matter, of the Irish, in Iceland and Greenland pointed to the unlikelihood that artifacts and similar evidence could fail to be found by any digging wherever there had been a settlement. The Foundation came to believe, not that Norsemen or Irish had been proved to have had no connection with America or even the Merrimack Valley, but merely that further digging at North Salem would be unlikely to provide any evidence different from that supplied by the excavation already done.

The North Salem ruin still, though repeatedly attacked by vandals and heedless visitors in spite of its protection, stands as a monument of mystery. Its origin and its purpose are still uncertain. Its powerful hold upon the human imagination needs no proof, however. Even if it were nothing but the relic of a colonial agricultural age of which we know little, even if it were, as it has been said to have been, a station on the Underground Railroad along which slaves escaping from the South before the Civil War were helped on their way to Canada, it could still be an object of some awe, great interest and much wonder.

The waters of the Spicket River on their way to the Merrimack at Methuen, Massachusetts, once reflected the activities of the men who built the strange structure at Cowbell Corners. Their image has faded from the water and has left nothing to say when it was there.

Did Passaconaway and his Penacook people know of that mass of piled and corbelled stones, so different from anything ever constructed by Indians? If so, why was it never mentioned in any conversations with the Europeans who came to live in the vicinity?

Did Hannah Dustin, on her way with her captors from Haverhill to the bend of the Merrimack between Dracut and Tyngsboro, pass by that North Salem hill and see those unmortared walls and the great flat stones which roofed the caverns among them? If so, why did she not speak of them in the account she gave of her terrible journey?

Perhaps we shall never know. Yet if the ruin was not there in Passaconaway's or Hannah Dustin's day but built at a later date, why were its manifest peculiarities not recorded at the time? Whenever the acre of stone work on the hill above Cowbell Corners was built and for whatever purpose, it could not have failed to attract the attention of the community. Yet if it was put together in modern times, that is exactly what it did. It cannot be discovered that anyone ever wrote or spoke of it until the twentieth century. How that can have been is as much of a mystery as the failure of the Norsemen to leave any apprehensible trace of their undoubted visits to the North American continent.

9 The Savage Frontier

No Man's Land in the Merrimack Valley, that area between the English front stretching along the seacoast and inland across Massachusetts and the Franco-Indian front from Maine to Lake Champlain, was a vast area of potential richness inhabited by animals and mysteries but not by men. On islands and intervals along the river and its tributaries there were Indian subsistence gardens of corn and pumpkins, beans and squash, tended, between hostilities, during the short summer.

We have seen that there was a constant struggle between the heirs and assigns of John Mason, other grantees and not a few men who considered themselves bona fide purchasers from the Indians. Claiming and granting was going on all the time, but actual settling and working of the land was a different matter.

The colonists of the established towns knew from increasingly bitter experience what it meant to open up a new square mile of forest. It was, as has been said, all they could do to clear, maintain, cultivate and defend what they had. The experience of those who chose to move into that amorphous tract originally known as Dunstable in the third quarter of the seventeenth century showed what it cost in blood, sweat and anxiety to be a pioneer in the Merrimack.

Dunstable was granted in 1672 and at the time included

Litchfield, part of Londonderry, Nottingham, Tyngsboro and Dunstable, part of Pepperell and West Townsend in Massachusetts, Hollis, Brookline (New Hampshire) and those parts of Amherst (New Hampshire), Milford and Merrimack which lay to the southeast of the Souhegan River. A few intrepid folk had moved into the area between 1652 and 1672, but at the time of its official granting there were scarcely more than half a dozen families in the vast area. In 1673 the grantees, twenty-six in number, among whom was the Artillery Company of Boston (now known as the Ancient and Honorable), moved in and gave the grant its name.

Eight years later, reflecting the increased tempo of Indian enmity after open warfare broke out in 1675, there were only thirty families in the tract and in 1701, such were the hardships and dangers, there were only twenty-five. Not for more than 120 years after the date of the original grant was there any public transportation between the Dunstable settlements and Boston.

Indian depredations in the Dunstable area had reached a terrifying pitch by the first decade of the eighteenth century. Yet the men of Dunstable, like those of other towns threatened long before, were slow to act in their own defense. Although they had never known the benefits of a welfare state, the colonists of the Merrimack Valley, like their neighbors, were accustomed to be told by their government what to do and when to do it. Trees were constantly in their way, as much of a nuisance as boulders in a hayfield, yet they were only allowed to fell trees of certain kinds and under certain circumstances and were heavily fined if they disobeyed. Moreover, authority must have seemed very real to men who were told, as they were, that if a man fired a gun at anything but an Indian or a wolf he would be fined five shillings.

It is not strange that settlers should have looked to such

authority for a protection which they seldom got. Even in settlements in which there was scarcely a family which had not lost at least one member to the Indians by death or capture, men often had to be forced to take up arms against the enemy.

LOVEWELL'S FIGHTS

Captain John Lovewell of Dunstable was an exception, though his reason for being so was, possibly, more venal than patriotic. After 1722 there was in the colony of New Hampshire a bounty of one hundred pounds offered for an Indian scalp, a reward which even though reckoned in local currency instead of sterling must have seemed considerable. Perhaps with this boon in the corner of his venturesome mind, Lovewell organized a company of volunteers and after many Indian outrages in the neighborhood of Dunstable set out with his men to hunt for Indians in the vicinity of Lake Winnipesaukee, seventy miles in an air line to the northeast, across which raiding parties from the Indian headquarters at Norridgewock in Maine had been accustomed to travel on their way to the New Hampshire and Massachusetts villages east and west of the Merrimack. Lovewell's first sally across No Man's Land into the enemy trenches netted an Indian brave and a boy. The sannup was killed and scalped and the boy taken prisoner. Boy and scalp were carried in triumph to Boston where the legal bounty and a bonus were forthcoming.

This sort of crusading caught the imagination of the frontier settlements. It seemed easy and apparently not dangerous. The Indians were frightened by the recent destruction of Norridgewock in Maine by the colonists and the killing there of the remarkable French Jesuit priest, Sebastian Rasles, who controlled its many warriors and had taken pains to keep them hostile to the English. The settlers believed that they had their enemy on the run for the first time in fifty years.

Two months after his first raid Lovewell's force had increased to seventy men. Although his strength was more than doubled so was his logistical problem, a problem which he did not solve. Insufficiently equipped, he marched his seventy men again toward Winnipesaukee to the very spot where lay the rotting body of the Indian scalped on the last foray. They found no live Indians in the vicinity, and it was apparent that there was not enough food to carry seventy men farther into the Indian country and back again alive.

The men drew lots to see which of the seventy would turn back. The remaining forty went on, excited but stealthy. By this time they had passed east of Winnipesaukee and into the Piscataqua watershed. Near the present village of Sanbornville in the town of Wakefield, they came upon the tracks of the enemy plainly visible in the snow. Cautiously they followed the track through heavy woods until at dusk they saw the smoke of a campfire.

Lovewell and his men kept quiet until late at night, when they were sure that the Indians, who were careless about posting sentries, were asleep. Creeping toward the glowing embers of the fire, the hunters, silent in the snow, approached the relaxed enemy. Ten Indians, wrapped in their blankets, slept in a clearing beside a frozen pond which showed dimly white in the darkness. Lovewell disposed his men so as to cover all angles and ordered them to fire in groups of five. The Captain's first shot killed two of the enemy and another five lay dead before the remaining three knew what was happening. The second volley killed two of the survivors and the last Indian, trying to escape across the ice of the pond, was caught by a dog which had accompanied Lovewell's men and held until he, too, could be disposed of.

Lovewell was very pleased with himself, particularly as the dead Indians had left new guns and much-needed extra blankets and equipment. With the ten scalps stretched on twig hoops and mounted on poles, he and his men marched triumphantly through Dover to Boston, where they collected their thousand-pound bounty and big ideas about further Indian hunting.

In the spring of 1725, with forty-six men and the added military dignity provided by a chaplain and a surgeon, Lovewell headed for the Indian village of Pigwacket, or Pequawket, the headquarters of the group of that name who had been responsible for much trouble in the eastern settlements. The party halted on the shore of Ossippee Lake to build a stockade in which they left the surgeon, with a guard of eight, in charge of a man too sick to travel. Two of the company went home lame, leaving thirty-four to go on.

On the seventh of May, the scouts reached a pond a little over a mile from the Indian village. Here they camped for the night. Their sleep was troubled by unusual noises, which they feared were made by the enemy. In the morning, after saying prayers which for some reason seem not to have been answered, they heard a gunshot and saw a single Indian standing on the lake shore some distance away. Although they suspected that the Indian was acting as bait for a trap, they decided to approach him by way of the shore.

It was spring and the ground was moist and silent but the pines were thinly scattered. The men took off their packs and laid them unguarded among the still-small ferns. Creeping from tree to tree, they advanced toward the point on which they had seen the lone Indian who, perhaps not being a decoy at all but merely a duck hunter, left his place by the lake and started toward Pequawket. The path which the Indian took led him to the approaching raiders. Surprised, he fired at them, wounding Lovewell and another with small shot, which seemed to indicate that he had been out for ducks rather than men. He might as well have shot himself, for he was soon cut down by Lovewell's raiders. With the hunter's scalp, Lovewell and his men returned to the pine grove where they had left their packs.

Meanwhile the sagamore, Paugus, with forty-one men, returning to Pequawket from a foray along the Saco River, had come upon the company's abandoned packs and appropriated them, after noting that there were only thirty-five, seven less than their own number. The Indians hid among the trees and waited.

When Lovewell's men returned to pick up their equipment they were startled to find no trace of it.

Thus Paugus led the Pequawket tribe;
As runs the fox would Paugus run;
As howls the wild wolf would he howl:
A huge bear-skin had Paugus on.

Ah! many a wife shall rend her hair,
And many a child cry, "Woe be me!"
Other messengers the news shall bear
Of Lovewell's dear-bought victory.

While the Dunstable men were searching among the ferns and scattered pines, the Indians, with plenty of time to aim, opened fire. Nine Dunstable men, including John Lovewell, fell dead at the first volley. Three or four more were wounded. In the moment of panic which followed, the Indians, their numerical advantage increased by their successful ambush, drove the remainder of the raiding party back toward the lake, where there was a point of rocks and some large pines, offering slight shelter but no hope of escape.

All through the day the battle went on with losses on both sides. The Indians, toward evening, shrieking and yelling, demanded surrender. Fearful of what would happen to them if they yielded, the survivors of Lovewell's band kept up the fight, firing at every fair target and planting masses of lead in the lake-shore pines.

Before dark, when only nine of Lovewell's thirty-four men were left unwounded, eleven sorely hurt but able to move and three dying, the Indians stopped shooting and yelling and moved off. Those survivors who could travel made their way through the darkness to the stockade, expecting to find the surgeon, the wounded man and the eight guards. The place was deserted, but there was a small quantity of pork and bread which the others had left behind. It helped, but in the absence of the packs which the Indians had captured it was not enough.

The journey homeward through the forest must have presented a strange contrast to that of the triumphant return of the previous winter. For three more of Lovewell's men it was not to be a homeward journey. Lieutenant Farwell died of his wounds, as did the chaplain and one other man. They were left where they fell among the trout lilies and bellwort of the New Hampshire forest, never to know whether theirs was a victory or a defeat.

For the people of the Merrimack it was a victory. Not so much a victory, perhaps, as the beginning of an armistice which was to last for almost twenty years. It marked the end of an era but not the real beginning of peace between the colonists and the Indians. It was an armistice which led men to range in quest of homes farther up the Merrimack than they had yet dared to venture.

Dunstable, although its settlement was slow, retarded by Indian attacks, was a real wedge driven into the wilderness. Its early settlers made use of what they found at hand. From the pines of the forest they made turpentine; from the hardwood trees, staves for barrels in which to store and ship it. The flat lands along the river provided good ground for growing corn, pumpkins, turnips and beans. The deer and moose of the forest and the river's abundant fish provided meat which for a long time there were not enough cattle to supply. By 1695 the northern part of the town, in the vicinity of the present city of Nashua, a region which the Indians referred to as Watanic, possessed both a forge and a gristmill.

Following the Indian war, which ended after Lovewell's disastrous fight, Dunstable was ready to make use of the unmolested years to become a true farming community, a part of the cereal grain economy of northern New England, which lasted until the building of roads over the Alleghenies and the completion of the Erie Canal put an end to it by introducing low-priced Western grain to the East.

THE SCOTS FROM IRELAND

Shortly before troubles with the Indians had sent John Lovewell and his volunteers off on their campaign of profitable extermination, there appeared at the northwestern apex of the Dunstable wedge another area of settlement which was looked upon by the earlier settlers, who had done their settling in the hard way, with inimical disapproval.

During the latter half of the seventeenth century, as has been pointed out, the struggle between King and Parliament, between Cavalier and Roundhead, and the unhappy revolution of 1688, an era in which English government was struggling to find its soul, had brought interest in the American colonies, save for those who already had a stake in them, to a low ebb. The New England colonies in particular were regarded very much as Alaska was regarded by most Americans at the time of its purchase in 1867, as a cold and unhospitable land not likely to prove worth the expense and effort required to maintain it. Oliver Cromwell publicly expressed such an opinion of it.

Yet at the beginning of the eighteenth century, when the tumult and confusion of the seventeenth had begun to seem more like a bad dream than a reality, there were some who could not feel at ease in the British Isles.

A group of Scottish Presbyterians who had emigrated to northern Ireland during the reign of James I, and who, as Protestants, had had a rough time of it ever since, learned about America from one of their number who had been there and returned and had, perhaps, viewed the New World with a rosier eye than could have fed the impressions of those who had been struggling for a living in New England.

Four Presbyterian ministers and a large part of their congregations banded together in a mass migration. There were in all, it is said, about 120 families who arrived, most of them at Boston but some at Casco Bay, in the fall of 1718. The winter was coming and they had no definite place of settlement in mind, nor did they know whether or not they would be granted any land. They soon learned that the Massachusetts General Court was perfectly willing to let them take up residence in any plot up to six miles square which was not already occupied or granted to others, but could not promise them any clear title, since any acres within their reach would inevitably be subject to the as yet unjudged claims of the Masonian heirs and assigns and to the ultimate decision as to the exact boundary between Massachusetts and New Hampshire.

Sixteen of the new families decided upon a place on the Merrimack fifteen miles by land from Haverhill, north of and on the opposite side of the river from Dunstable. This region was known then and for some time after as Nutfield. The newcomers spent the winter in and about Haverhill and in the spring of 1719 the men of the group moved to their home and began preparing it for their families. The site they chose was on a brook which crossed meadows and merged with the Beaver River on its way to the Merrimack. The brook, which for another reason is celebrated in a poem by Robert Frost and has given its name to one of his volumes, was called West-Running Brook.

The settlement prospered. In 1722, Governor Shute and the Council of New Hampshire, although Massachusetts still laid claim to the territory, gave the immigrants a grant of the tract of land and a charter of incorporation. By the time of Captain Lovewell's death in 1725, six years after the settlement of the place, which had been called Londonderry since 1722, the population was four times the number of persons who had come from Haverhill with their pastor, Reverend James McGregore.

The fields, as rich as any in the state, were carefully tended and were soon highly productive. The settlement very early in its history wore an aspect of civilization uncommon in frontier towns. Because of the success of these hard-working Scottish Presbyterians, many of the descendants of earlier settlers assumed that they, who were newcomers, had been favored by the authorities over those who had been struggling for a century to clear the wilderness. There is no evidence that this was so. If the Londonderry company possessed any advantage over the older settlers, it was in their fresh point of view, unembittered by disappointment and despair, which enabled them to attack their environment as if previous attempts to do it had not been crowned with failure.

They brought with them from Ireland two things new to the New England economy—the potato, long exiled from and now returning to the continent of its origin, and the flax plant, the source of linen. They brought also a knowledge of flax-spinning and the simple but effective hand tools for making linen thread and weaving it.

In spite of enmity and misunderstanding and, to them, an infuriating tendency on the part of their fellow colonists to the south, east and west to refer to them as Irish, the settlers of Londonderry merged with the people of the Merrimack Valley and became a spearhead in the struggle to make New Hampshire a great state and the United States of America a great and free nation. It was the air of Londonderry which first filled the lungs of that extraordinary man who gave to New Hampshire its motto: "Live free or die!"

LIVE FREE OR DIE

In a meadow some three miles from the village of Derry, in the heart of old Londonderry though now separate from what is called Londonderry, is a boulder marking the site of a house built by one of the first settlers. There is now no trace of the house itself, but traces of the child who was born there in 1728 are scattered like shooting stars through the early history of the state and the nation.

John Stark was a true son of the wilderness, but he was also a true flowering of the best in that civilization which the seventeenth century brought across the Atlantic. He was a big man in both body and mind. The necessities of the wilderness taught his body and spirit toughness and ingenuity, and those qualities, in use, gave resourcefulness to his wit.

The story of his capture by the Indians in 1752, when he was twenty-four years old, illustrates the same characteristics which were apparent in him twenty-five years later during the Revolution. John and his brother William, with Amos Eastman and David Stinson, were hunting and trapping on the Baker River in Rumney, eighty-five miles north of Londonderry, in April of 1752. In the evening, when John was out on his trap line, he suddenly found himself surrounded by ten Indians who ordered him to lead them to his camp. John had no hesitation about steering his captors in exactly the opposite direction.

When he had not returned to camp the following morning, his brother and the two others, suspecting trouble, started downriver. The Indians in some way discovered Stark's trick and overtook his companions, killing Stinson and taking Eastman captive. They would have killed William Stark had not John struck up the gun of the Indian who was about to fire at his brother. William managed to escape, leaving John and Eastman to the anger of the Indians.

At St. Francis, the Indian headquarters in Quebec, to which settlement the captives were taken, Eastman and Stark had to run the gantlet between two lines of Indians armed with clubs. Eastman took the beating and suffered cruelly. Not John Stark. He seized a club from one of the Indians and went down the line knocking the others over like bowling pins. The Indians were astonished and impressed. They were still more impressed when, having been ordered by them to hoe corn, John deliberately chopped the corn to pieces and made neat rows of the weeds saying, according to legend, "It's the business not of warriors but of squaws to hoe corn." The Indians regarded Stark highly after that and treated him well.

It must have been with regret that they saw him exchanged for a horse after two months of captivity. Perhaps they solaced themselves with the knowledge that a horse was something which could be harnessed and used.

JOHN STARK AND THE FAMILY QUARREL

It was John Stark who commanded two regiments of New Hampshire troops at Bunker Hill, regiments among the best and most experienced in all the colonies, which guarded a rail fence, running from the Mystic River up the hill (actually Breed's Hill) to an earthwork behind which Prescott's Massachusetts troops were entrenched. It was in front of this fence that Stark drove a stake telling his men to withhold their fire until the British reached that point. Twice the British did reach it and twice, to their surprise and chagrin, were driven back through blinding smoke, with heavy loss from the murderous fire of the New Hampshiremen. The British did not try again in the same spot but took another route up the hill, drove out the Massachusetts men and made Stark's position untenable. The New Hampshire regiments withdrew in good order and with losses of but 107 out of some nine hundred.

Had it not been for Stark and the 1st and 3rd New Hampshire, the story of what followed Bunker Hill would have been very different.

John Stark was a proud and strong man, who knew his value. He may well be forgiven for thinking that the newly appointed Commander-in-chief of the Continental armies would see that value and use it to the best advantage. When it came to appointing a brigadier from New Hampshire to join the other seven general officers on Washington's staff,

Congress, with an ear for lobbyists even at that early day, passed over Stark and appointed the able but inexperienced John Sullivan. Washington had nothing against John Stark. It was all in the way Congress worked. It touched a sensitive spot in Stark which was again made sore after Sullivan's further promotion, when Enoch Poor, whom Stark outranked, was made a brigadier over the head of the hero of Bunker Hill. This slight—although it did not prevent John Stark from supporting Washington loyally, fighting bravely at Trenton and Princeton, and urging his men, who were ready to go home in the bad winter of 1776 as their terms ran out, to reenlist and to accept his personal guarantee that they would be paid—did cause him to resign his commission in the spring of 1777. He went back to the sawmill in Londonderry from which the news of Lexington had taken him two years before. He was a soldier, not a politician, but he could only fight when he knew where he stood. He was not left for long in any doubt on this point.

In July of 1777 the British, coming down from Quebec, forced the Continental troops to evacuate Ticonderoga and threatened to spread out eastward as they advanced toward the Hudson River. The settlers of what were then known as "the New Hampshire Grants" west of the Connecticut River, who had declared their independence in the early summer, saw themselves threatened and notified the government of New Hampshire that unless they received help they would have to abandon their lands. The New Hampshire Committee of Safety called a special session of the General Court to consider the matter. That was the end of John Stark's retirement.

Stark, who had been writing to the Continental Congress about his treatment and getting no answers, was given a New Hampshire commission as a brigadier. He was instructed to:

. . . repair to Charlestown on Connecticut river; there to consult with a committee of New-Hampshire Grants, respecting his future operations and the supply of his men with provisions; to take the command of the militia and march into the Grants to act in conjunction with the troops of that new State, or any other of the States, or of the United States, or separately, as it should appear expedient to him; for the protection of the people and the annoyance of the enemy.

Stark, with what satisfaction may be imagined and with his old fervor, followed these instructions. He moved swiftly. Receiving his commission in Exeter (then the capital of New Hampshire), he proceeded to Charlestown to organize his force and early in August was in Manchester, Vermont, conferring with General Lincoln of the Continental Army. Lincoln had been sent north to bring the state-militia units which had been covering the front south of Lake Champlain back to the safety of the west side of the Hudson River, out of General Burgoyne's way.

Stark explained to Lincoln that the suggested move, leaving the New Hampshire Grants undefended, would be as unpopular as it would be dangerous. He, he said, chose to remain on the enemy's flank by way of discovering his plans. General Lincoln, unhappy no doubt about a situation in which the authority of a sovereign state over its military forces made authority stemming from the Continental Congress powerless, reported Stark's intransigence to the Congress in Philadelphia, with the result that that anxious and confused body prepared to draw up a resolution censuring Stark. Stark knew what he was doing. Aided by volunteers from the Grants, he took up his position at Bennington and waited. He had not long to wait.

Burgoyne on the ninth of August sent Colonel Baum with one hundred Indians and fifteen hundred Germans to thrust eastward to the Connecticut River, foraging for horses, cattle and other provisions and giving the impression that he headed the vanguard of a British army on its way to Boston. Burgoyne counted on this ruse to spread panic through New England. On August thirteenth, Colonel Baum's Indian scouts were discovered some twelve miles northwest of Bennington. Stark ordered Colonel Gregg with two hundred men forward to intercept. In the evening he learned that a force of British, accompanied by artillery, was headed for Bennington. Stark marched forward with his whole force and met Gregg retreating, having found the British too strong for him.

The British, discovering that Stark's force was stronger than they had supposed, halted in a defensive position. Stark, unable to provoke them to attack, encamped about a mile to the rear and sent out skirmishers to harass the enemy. This they did so successfully in a sticky August rain that they killed two Indian chiefs and thirty others and frightened the Indians so that many of them deserted, saying that "the woods were full of Yankees."

It was not until the sixteenth of August, a hot and humid morning, that Stark took action. He had had plenty of time to learn the position of the British and to plan his attack, which he did in masterly fashion. He divided his force, sending one body to the rear of the enemy's right flank and one to the rear of his left and reserving a group of three hundred, with which he himself marched, for a frontal attack. He kept in reserve enough men to strengthen the pressure on the enemy's rear.

At three o'clock in the afternoon the attack began. By five o'clock Stark had taken the enemy's trenches, captured two cannon and a number of prisoners. Those who were not killed or taken prisoner retreated. All was not over, however. Baum had sent for help, and it was on the way.

Stark, strengthened by a New Hampshire regiment which had been left at Manchester, renewed the attack and drove the reinforced enemy back, not relaxing his pressure until it was too dark for his men to tell what they were shooting at.

The British left 226 men dead on the field, lost four cannon, all their horses, wagons and baggage. Thirty-three officers and seven hundred privates were taken prisoner and sent to Boston.

Stark reported his impressive victory to Exeter, but he took the opportunity to keep the Philadelphia Congress uneasy by not communicating with them at all. When they asked him why he had not reported to them, he wrote that his correspondence with them was closed. This was typical of Stark's tactics. His self-confidence and fearlessness worked as well with Congress as they had with the Indians a quarter of a century earlier.

Congress, instead of forwarding the resolution of censure which they had prepared a few days before, sent the Londonderry Lion a letter of thanks and a commission as Brigadier General in the Army of the United States.

Once more John Stark had presided over an action which changed the fortunes of war. This time it was a tactical as well as a strategic victory. Bennington was the prelude to Saratoga and the surrender of Burgoyne, and so the prelude to Yorktown and the surrender of Cornwallis.

No battle with an organized enemy has ever been fought on the soil of the Merrimack Valley in New Hampshire, but none of the nation's wars has been won without the help of men whose roots were and always will be in that soil. Stark was a perfect example of Merrimack Valley, which is to say New Hampshire, character. He knew which things were big and which were little and that by making the little big and the big little he could make men see and understand them better.

John Stark lived to be ninety-four. Daniel Webster, another Merrimack man of whom more will be told in a later chapter, said that he talked with him when he was an old man. Stark told him, "Well, I never knew but once what I was worth. In the war, the Indians took me and carried me to Canada and sold me to the French for forty pounds; and as they say a thing is worth what it will fetch, I suppose I was worth forty pounds."

"In the war," he said, "the Indians took me . . ."

Webster said that, to Stark, in spite of Bunker Hill, Trenton, Princeton, Bennington, Saratoga and Yorktown, "the war" was always the old French and Indian conflict. To him the Revolution was just a family quarrel, as perhaps, indeed, it was.

10 The Golden Village at the River's Mouth

It should, perhaps, be possible to see in the life of the Merrimack Valley during the four generations following the first settlement at Newbury in 1635, the genesis of the people, their institutions and their affairs, who made it what it became during the four generations following 1830. If the origins of the culture of the modern Merrimack were visible in the culture of the seventeenth and early eighteenth centuries, they must be looked for in the church, the town meeting, in the field and the forest and on the sea.

We have seen something of the bitter struggle which for three decades divided the Newbury church, yet it must be remembered that all through the conflict church members of both factions sat down side by side in faithful attendance at the services of their single church and, albeit with reservations about the preacher's church politics, listened reverently to sermon and prayer.

No matter in what variety of shapes or forms the church members of Newbury may have wished their church to abide, they had no differences over their acceptance of its dogma as a way of life. They had nothing else to which they might turn. They therefore clung to it, and their inability to agree on matters of administrative discipline indicated not a lessening of their reverence for it but a fear that, if not guided as they felt it must be guided, they might ultimately lose it and so

themselves be lost. That a small group of men, less than a hundred, could divide themselves into two hostile camps, each believing itself to be right in its dedication to the service of the church, would seem to argue that the early Merrimack colonists were not all alike. In their dissension was the seed of union.

The surprising thing is that their similarities were more noticeable than their differences. They were much more homogeneous than a single group in a modern Merrimack town could be expected to be today. The rich were not very rich, though custom and convention gave them privileges denied the less well-favored. The poor were not very poor, though they were undeniably denied participation in some of the rituals of self-government. The interests of rich and poor were at first practically identical, and the backbone of the life of both was the necessity of working for a living.

Joshua Coffin, in his *A Sketch of the History of New-*

bury, Newburyport and West Newbury from 1635 to 1845, mentions that the first settlers of that region, who were typical of all the early settlers of the Merrimack from Newbury to Dunstable, were divided into three classes: first, the rich and educated gentlemen, who "by birth or profession were entitled to the appellation of Mr."; second, the artisans or mechanics, those who came from the larger English towns, particularly of Wiltshire; and third, the yeomen, or farmers, laborers and servants. This last class probably made up much less than half of the population.

Among the ninety-one grantees of Newbury, there were two clergymen, eight were classed as "gentlemen," three were merchants, one was a maltster, one a schoolmaster, one a physician, one a sea captain, one a ship's mate. There were a dyer and a glover. There were as many as four tanners and eight shoemakers, two wheelwrights, two blacksmiths, two linen weavers and two ordinary weavers. A cooper, a saddler, a sawyer and several carpenters made up the balance of about half of the settlers. Of the rest, not individually identified, only a few were yeomen.

The ninety-one were not all church members and certainly not all "freemen," but it was the church and the town meeting which held the settlement together and gave it its character.

Although the better-off among the first Merrimack people had brought with them from England their silver, fine clothes and furniture, their homes in the New World were not very different from those of their neighbors who had little. Unity and likeness rather than discord and disparity were the cornerstones of life in the Merrimack Valley as well as elsewhere in New England.

Thus it was that a kind of involuntary democracy grew out of the essentially undemocratic organization of the first colonies. It developed in constant contact with the frontier, where differences in walk of life could not be maintained, and became first conscious, then voluntary and ultimately obligatory.

SHIPS INSTEAD OF PLOUGHSHARES

As settlements grew, like tiny buds, about the stem of the lower river, they remained as alike as the buds of a single tree and their character was the character of the English seventeenth-century village. Salisbury, Amesbury, Haverhill, Bradford, Rowley, West Newbury differed but little from one another save for minor differences in the area upon which they were planted. The ceremony and custom of their lives were identical as, for the most part, were the thoughts of their inhabitants. This unity was the result of deep dependence upon faith, molded and made firm by pressure of the wilderness which retarded the growth of the colonists, allowed their natures time to grow and gave fertility to the soil of mind and heart in which such faith is planted. It was also the result of an unwillingness, having put geographical distance between them and their old home, to burn moral and spiritual bridges behind them.

Changes took place among those who remained near the original beachhead. Although the Wiltshiremen who settled Newbury had been far from a seafaring group, the river and the sea had their way, abetted by the circumstances abroad which made it necessary for the colonists to try a trade of their own. The lower Merrimack began to develop a merchant marine and to build the vessels which such a departure required.

That there was considerable shipping out of the old Newbury settlement on the Parker River and, in spite of the difficulties presented by the bar at the river's mouth, by the new settlement on the Merrimack, is attested by a petition filed with the General Court in Boston on May 15, 1683. In February of that year, the General Court had decided that Salem should be the official loading and unloading port for shipping out of and into Marblehead, Beverly, Gloucester, Ipswich, Rowley, Newbury and Salisbury, and that vessels from those towns could not unload or load anywhere but at Salem, which is twenty miles from Newburyport as the crow flies and nearly fifty by sea.

Eleven citizens of Newbury signed a petition for relief from this uncompromising edict. The petition read as follows:

> To the honored general court now sitting in Boston, the humble petition of some of Newbury.
>
> Wee humbly crave the favour that your honors would be pleased to consider our little Zebulon and to ease us of that charge, which at present we are forced unto by our goeing to Salem to enter our vessells and thereby are forced to stay at least tow days, before we can unload, besides other charges in going and coming. That some meet person might be appointed to receive the enter of all vessells, and to act and doe according as the law directs in that case and we shall be bound forever to pray for your honors.

May fifteenth, 1683.

The petition was referred to the General Court of the following year, which apparently granted the relief desired. At least the Court appointed, on May 15, 1684, a naval officer for Newbury and Salisbury. There must have been more than a little shipping out of the Merrimack shortly thereafter— enough, at least, to attract wolves of the sea. On August 22, 1689, the brig *Merrimack* of Newbury was captured by pirates in Vineyard Sound.

By 1692, vessels were in such demand that they were occasionally built on the town common. In December of that year it was voted that anyone using the common land as a shipyard should pay the town three pence per ton for the privilege of doing so.

Lumber, fish, dried and pickled, and other provisions could be sold in the West Indies where sugar could be picked up to be sold at home and abroad. The bottoms in which to carry this trade had to be built and men who did not know how had to learn to build them.

Shipbuilding on the Merrimack began in earnest by the middle of the seventeenth century and by the early part of the eighteenth vessels up to three hundred tons or, roughly, twice as large as the *Mayflower*, were built at Newbury, Amesbury and Salisbury. The timber could be felled anywhere along the lower river, dragged to the bank by oxen and floated down to the shipyard. Fastenings were mostly of wood, in the form of "trunnels" or tree nails, but iron for the heavier fittings of a ship—cleats, bollards and anchors—was supplied by numerous forges and foundries, chief among which was the celebrated Saugus Iron Works some twenty-five miles from Newburyport, which has recently been restored by the American Iron and Steel Institute.

It was along the seacoast and the river that the lifeblood of the Merrimack region circulated. Those who farmed the narrow strip of land between the wilderness and the water could not have maintained their front without the waterborne commerce of the river towns. While the farming settler was struggling for a living, in dread of wolves and Indians, harassed by the unpredictable changes of weather and the depredations of insects, the seafaring man was not only making the inland colonist's life possible but was himself growing rich, altering to some degree the earlier democratic cohesion.

The importance of sea trade was plainly shown in 1724 —when the number of colonists who had adventured farther up the Merrimack than Londonderry cannot have exceeded a hundred—when master builders of London petitioned the Lords of Trade "not to encourage shipbuilding in New England because workmen are drawn thither."

While war with the French, which was declared in 1744, increased the emphasis on the sea and gave many a New Englander a taste for romantic and lucrative privateering, it also increased emphasis on products of the soil, which were in great demand in the West Indies and the islands and countries of the eastern Atlantic. Migration from the crowded seacoast up the Merrimack to the interior became a steady stream instead of a scattered adventure.

More than thirty towns east and west of the Merrimack, most of them on that river or its tributaries, were settled, though some of them had been granted earlier, between 1720 and 1740. Mills for the grinding of the grain which their settlers grew sprang up in many parts of the interior, as did sawmills, and, despite Indians and wild beasts, traffic in grain, cattle and lumber began to be noticeable along the wagon tracks and down the streams of the Merrimack system, which connected the coast towns with the newly opened interior.

This northward expansion kept alive the relative simplicity of the New Englander, which was the source of New England democracy and which, without constant conflict with the wilderness, might have been destroyed by the rising difference between the class of merchant-seafarers and the class of those whom they could command. Material prosperity resulting from foreign trade had, by the middle of the eighteenth century, altered beyond recognition the unity of the social and

economic life of the seacoast towns. Newburyport, by which name the settlement on the Merrimack came to be distinguished from its parent colony on the Parker River, had ceased to be a village torn merely by disputes between two factions of a single church. It had developed a character of its own, the fruit of the tree of enterprise which had its roots in shipbuilding, fishing, trading with the West Indies and Europe, and the manufacture of, among other things, rum and jewelry. Its rise to shining magnitude, which it reached in the period between the Revolution and the War of 1812, was like the brief flare of a comet, a comet with a trail of illuminated dust, brilliant and exciting. Its real brilliance disappeared as suddenly as it came in an orbit which has until now permitted no returning.

I know of no better way of presenting this startling if variable heavenly body than in the words of one of its most distinguished inhabitants. John P. Marquand is not only a brilliant satirist of the New England of his day. He is also a novelist and an essayist with a sure and genially critical sense of the past. In a paper which he read before the American section of the Newcomen Society in 1952, he has given a picture of his ancestral town which could not easily be improved upon, a picture which, as 1957 recipient of the Sarah Josepha Hale Award, he later traveled up the Merrimack and down the Sugar River to repeat at Newport, New Hampshire.

Mr. Marquand said of Newburyport:

> The most conspicuous aspects of this ancient town must have been its amazing self-sufficiency and the extraordinary self-reliance of its inhabitants, but then these attributes were an absolute necessity in that period. Federalist Newburyport was compelled to achieve a large measure of economic independence, because it was

a remote town on the seaboard of a half-explored continent, largely dependent on itself for its food, its clothing, as well as for its luxuries and entertainment. Its traditions and manner of living were derived more from Europe than from the land around it, but remoteness obliged Newburyport to create its own culture, since most of the time it was left completely alone to develop itself as best it could with the tools and graces allowed it by a very distant world. This isolation was cheerfully accepted as nothing out of the ordinary. This was all part of that distant present but it forms a social problem impossible for a modern mind to grasp. It was about a day's journey by land from the other place that mattered. Thoughts turned automatically eastward because there was not any west excepting backwoods settlements. Because of road conditions, all heavy goods had to be brought by sea and distributed from the town's warehouses to the shops, and the bluff-bowed cranky vessels of the period were utterly dependent on tide and weather.

The basic necessities of life were drawn from the hinterland farms and supplemented by foreign importations. The meat which Newburyport consumed came thither on the hoof to be processed by butchers and sold fresh in their open stalls at the foot of State Street. The clothing worn by its simpler people was local homespun. Silver, which appeared on well-to-do tables, was made by local silversmiths, and earthenware crockery was made in a pottery not far from Bartlett's Mall. Essential hardware was made by the blacksmiths, and the ships' rigging came from the old ropewalk.

The local economy and culture of Newburyport has no counterpart in the contemporary world, unless one can find a vague parallel in some walled town of central China. The truth is that a dweller in a city-state of ancient Greece, if he could have been transported through the centuries and set down at the mouth of the Merrimack River in 1800, would understand the meanings and values of Federalist Newburyport far more clearly than any modern today, because Newburyport was not far from being an Aegean city-state. It never became an Athens, but it had its own artists and artisans who developed art forms of their own and who were something more than imitators of European culture.

NEWBURYPORT'S BLAZE OF GLORY

Newburyport's rise to the glamorous and unique position which it occupied in the first years of the nineteenth century was the result of many ventures which would have whitened the hair and tightened the lips of the Newbury men of the eighteenth century and at least one of which, privateering, would not be sanctioned today as it was in Revolutionary days. The fitting out of vessels under letters of marque for the purpose of harassing the national enemy was more than merely a means of providing national defense which the government could not undertake. By conveniently ignoring the distinction between enemy and neutral, the privateer, who retained everything he captured, was able to enrich himself in a manner which made even lucrative peacetime trade seem like standing still.

By 1800, Newburyport's trade was fairly well stabilized and opportunities for investment less questionable than privateering were numerous. Wealth multiplied and with its multiplication the gap between the merchant capitalist and the folk who lacked either the gift or the opportunity for fiscal wizardry grew wider and deeper.

On one side glowed and glittered a society which believed itself and appeared to be inferior to that of no other city, although as historian Samuel Eliot Morison has pointed out most of its kingpins "were but one generation removed from the plough or the forecastle." Wine cellars containing more than a thousand gallons of fine wine were not uncommon and helped to make entertainment lavish. Along High

Street everything was done with a flourish. When the governor of Massachusetts came to town to visit a lady named Atkins, whom he had known when he was a student in Newburyport, he arrived in a four-horse coach, complete with outriders and an escort of cavalry, and the message announcing his visit was carried to the haughty hostess by a member of the town government who ascended the Atkinses' steps on his knees. On the other side of the picture, as John Marquand says: "We read of barefooted women drying cod at the river bank while their children, dirty little urchins, splashed in the shallows and sailed boats made of chips and shingles. We hear of tramps and vagrants wandering on all main roads and of witchlike women in rags riding to town on scrawny horses from a place called Dogtown, a social sore spot that was settled by unruly runaway bond servants and even a few stray Indians."

Yet in Newburyport at its peak there was probably far more abundance than poverty and the appurtenances of the abundant and glamorous life were mostly the products of the city itself. Here were made gold and silverware, jewelry, watches, wigs, fine clothes, hats and shoes, carpets and draperies; books were printed and bound—among them Bowditch's celebrated *Navigator* and Furlong's *American Coast Pilot;* dancing and the playing of the refined instruments were taught. The aspiring Newburyporter, oblivious of the back country and the agricultural pioneering going on not many miles to the north of him, could study the cultivated graces, singing, painting and even the social use of the sword.

"There were," says Mr. Marquand, "many evidences of intellectual ferment and clashes between old virtues and new luxuries. When Mr. Perkins, the inventor, offered to install in a Newburyport church a furnace of his own contriving, the congregation turned him down on the grounds of degeneracy. When a choirmaster of another church attempted to set a psalm tune by blowing a pitch pipe, the minister was constrained to shout to him from the pulpit to 'put down that papish pipe.' "

Typical of the extravagance of the place and the day was the fantastic gentleman who called himself Lord Timothy Dexter, and whose splendid house, made perhaps more dignified than it originally was by the removal of a semicircle of life-sized wooden figures which extended on either side of it like outstretched arms, still stands on High Street. Lord Timothy made money by speculation in Continental currency and by selling Bibles, warming pans and woolen mittens to that seemingly unlikely market the West Indies, the warming pans going for cooking pots and syrup ladles and the mittens being resold to vessels bound for the Baltic and North Sea ports. That he was a genuine eccentric is indicated by the fact that, as Marquand says, he "had himself driven in his own coach to the Ipswich jail, where he was confined briefly for shooting a pistol at an inquisitive visitor. He employed at various times an astrologer and a poet laureate named Jonathan Plummer, who was also an itinerant fish dealer, selling haddock and scrolls of his own works from door to door."

Along with extravagances and eccentricities of the little city went commercial and artistic virtues which were also unequaled elsewhere. Newburyport shipbuilding, aided by invention of the water-line model by Orlando B. Merrill and by the presence of such other builders as Donald McKay, John Currier and George Jackman, reached a peak of perfection which kept its yards busy as long as wooden ships were made. In the first hundred years of the American nation's existence, Merrimack River yards from Newbury to Bradford turned out at least two thousand vessels totaling four hundred thousand tons. Some of these were as large as sixteen hundred tons each.

The amazing town of Newburyport, without any such endowed restoration as has given us a revived Williamsburg, has preserved for present-day Americans perhaps the most extensive array of eighteenth- and early-nineteenth-century houses, churches and public buildings of beauty and distinction to be found anywhere in the nation. Newburyport was, as John Marquand has suggested, a kind of New England Pompeii, buried intact under the ash of an eruptive change in New England's economy, the first blast of which was the era of canal building, followed by Thomas Jefferson's Embargo of 1807-1809 and the War of 1812.

Newburyport was, however, affected no more by the Embargo and the War with the British than were Gloucester, Salem or Boston. What kept the city at the mouth of the Merrimack from the industrial development which came to the cities upriver was, ironically, a combination of the defects of the river's own mouth and the capital of some of its citizens, employed to build a canal from Boston to the Merrimack above Pawtucket Falls, thereby by-passing the old river city.

11 Harness for the Swift Waters

....

With the exception of a few adventuresome sallies into the North Country, the story of the Merrimack River has not carried the reader far above its mouth, where, as we have seen, a miniature but quite complete civilization was established before the Revolutionary War.

The upper river had to wait for history, for a revolution of a different kind. There were a number of things which might have accelerated the development of the great area between the mountain wilderness north of Lake Winnipesaukee and the low-lying region which extended from the Maine border to the Concord and Nashua Rivers. One of these was an expanding need for agricultural land, a need which, we have seen, developed very slowly. Another was a traffic in timber and furs. As there was for many years plenty of timber in the peneplain less than fifty miles from the seacoast, and as hunters and trappers did not establish permanent settlements in the deeper forest, this was not at first a very important factor in producing inland colonization. A third cause of northward settlement could have been found in the need of establishing transportation routes, a need arising out of the two factors already mentioned. Until shortly before the War of Independence transportation to and from the lake and mountain region had been largely a matter of scouting and forays by forest trails into Indian country. The French and their vassal Abenakis controlled the north until ten years before the Revolution, and there was nothing but Indian captivity and English reprisal to take New Englanders toward Canada.

Concord, New Hampshire, under the name first of Penacook and then of Rumford, was originally settled about 1727, and was an early outpost on the upper river. It became Concord in 1765 and, although it did not become the capital of New Hampshire until much later, it was a settlement of considerable importance during the Revolution and, at that time, the only settlement of any consequence on the upper Merrimack.

The need of water power could have caused an opening up of the splendid resources of the Merrimack, but until the beginning of the nineteenth century water power was of use only for sawmills and gristmills, a very small number of which could meet the needs of a large area. Until a generation after the Revolution much of the Merrimack's power might still have been classed as an inconvenience. It remained for forces of which the New England colonists of even the eighteenth century were not aware to bring about those changes in the life and society of civilized man without which the Merrimack might have remained what it was to the Indians, and given which it became in a few decades after the War of 1812 the seat of the densest population in North America, as well as the breeding ground of a culture which has influenced the entire nation.

The great sea voyages of the fifteenth and sixteenth centuries were obviously responsible for the ultimate settlement of the Americas, but their influence upon the course of events in the Merrimack Valley was more than merely geographical. They provided both a great source of wealth and a means of using it. In them was the genesis of modern capitalism, a small reflection of which has been suggested in the thrift of the Newbury men who, by spending less than they earned, made it possible to finance their infant commerce as their descendants were able to finance the railroads which opened up the West.

The expansion of commerce and the need of greater production of goods had, even in the seventeenth century, set men to considering mechanical means of increasing the output of labor, but not until the eighteenth century was there any way of replacing wind, water, hands and feet as sources of industrial power. While the people of the lower Merrimack were worrying about the ever-present danger of Indian attack, making their weapons, clothing, tools, utensils and dwellings as their fathers and grandfathers had made them before them, Thomas Newcomen and Thomas Savery were producing, in England, a relatively inefficient but startling machine. This device was known as a "fire-engine" not because it put out fires but because it used fire and water to create steam power. It was the first steam engine able to pump water, but it was far from a complete success. It had, nevertheless, provided engineers of the time with a direction. Not until 1769, however, when James Watt developed a really practical source of steam power, was the direction widely recognized.

By that time the ingenuity of devoted men, which first seems to follow and then to lead commercial and industrial development, had been manifesting itself in many ways. Diligent study of problems produced changes in many industries, chiefly in the production of textiles and iron and steel. While the steam engine was coming of age in the hands of Watt, the factory was being born in England to provide a means of applying steam power to the world-wide demand for increasing production.

Kay, Hargreaves, Arkwright, Crompton and a host of un-

named tinkerers devised mechanical means of producing textiles which had originally been produced entirely by hand.
These new developments, mutually stimulating each other,
stimulated English industry and produced spreading wealth
which, it must be said, was not unaccompanied by widespread
poverty. It was not unnatural that the possessors of the
sources of this wealth should wish to keep them in their own
hands. Had they been able to do so, the Merrimack River
would not have become what it did become.

It can almost be said, therefore, that the ingenuity of
English inventors and engineers, of which the Indian-fighting
colonists of New England were ignorant, was what filled the
wilderness of the Merrimack Valley with the cities and villages of men whose character and industry created our New
England heritage.

BIG IDEAS AND BIG MEN

To the eager men and women, no longer Europeans,
who like drops of water in a tide were reaching from the
estuary of the Merrimack up into the great country between
the sea and the mountains, the final defeat of the British at
Yorktown was like a deed to a home in which they had long
lived in jeopardy. Yet that deed did not bring with it release
from the necessity of struggle against the dominating wilderness.

Transportation, the means of linking inland settlements
of forest and interval with the seacoast centers of trade, of
which Boston had become the most important, was a problem
for which oxen, horses and human feet found a dilatory and
unsatisfactory solution. It is true that coaching and freight-
carrying by wagon reached a high point before the end of the

eighteenth century, but the more forward-looking thinkers about transportation were searching for some form of carrier with greater potential volume if not greater speed.

Coach and wagon travel was handicapped by roads that were bogs in wet weather and spring-breakers in dry and by the presence of unfordable rivers every few miles. Only one considerable river along the entire Atlantic coast—and that was the Charles, at Cambridge—had a bridge over it in 1790. The rest all had to be crossed by ferry.

It is not unnatural that water should have seemed to provide the answer. The recently improved steam engine was still so bulky that, in spite of experiments, no one had successfully mounted it on either wheels or a keel, but navigation by small vessel had reached a high point of success on waters suited to it, and the east coast from Florida to Maine was threaded with unbridged but apparently navigable rivers leading inland. Men who recalled or learned of the success of canals in Holland, Germany, France, Russia and England could not help thinking of applying the canal principle to American streams. Before 1793, eight of the original thirteen American states had incorporated a total of thirty canal companies, small and large, some of which achieved some success.

The merchants of Massachusetts were among the most active dreamers of water routes to inland producing centers. They dreamed of a waterway linking Boston to the Connecticut River, but for reasons not hard to imagine never built it. They talked of a canal through the base of Cape Cod, shortening and making safer the sea route from the northeast coast to Rhode Island, Connecticut and New York, but it was the twentieth century before they got such an improvement. They dreamed, too, of a navigable passage from Boston to the

Merrimack and, that inviting river being what it was, they did get it—the first great feat of canal engineering in North America.

Although the year 1792 was one of commercial panic, resulting from overspeculation, Boston was not as badly hit as the cities to the south of her. She was growing beyond the means of getting needed supplies from northern New England. The then flourishing city of Newburyport was getting all the benefit of the Merrimack as an avenue for the transportation to tidewater of inland produce such as granite, lumber, barrel staves, ashes for the making of soap, charcoal, butter, meat, grain and cider.

At the suggestion of James Sullivan, Attorney General of Massachusetts, a group of men in Medford, across the wide estuary of the Mystic River from Boston, planned a canal to connect the Mystic, and hence Boston harbor, with the Merrimack above Pawtucket Falls. Among these men, who received a charter as "The Proprietors of the Middlesex Canal" from Governor John Hancock in June, 1793, was one of the young nation's natural geniuses.

Loammi Baldwin, great-grandson of one of the first settlers of Woburn, Massachusetts, was born in that town in 1744. His father was a master carpenter, among other things. The family had a shop in which they sold everything from apples, hops and cider to earthenware and dry goods, domestic and imported. Loammi says in his diaries that he himself worked with his brother Cyrus at gardening, shopkeeping, bookkeeping, collecting bills, tending poultry, haying, making tool handles and doing general carpentry. Loammi was at one time or another a cabinetmaker. He went into the business of making pumps, studied drawing and mathematics on the side, and before he was twenty began experimenting with electrical apparatus.

Loammi evidently had a wide reputation as something more than an ordinary artisan. He was, in his early twenties, a friend and correspondent of the great and somewhat neglected (for a reason which will be made apparent in a subsequent chapter) Benjamin Thompson, later Count Rumford. Thompson apparently considered his friend a walking encyclopedia, as correspondence preserved in the Baker Library at Harvard indicates. One letter, from Thompson to Baldwin, dated August, 1769, asks: "Please to give the Nature, Essence, Beginning of Existence, and Rise of the Wind in General, with the whole Theory thereof, so as to be able to answer all questions thereto." The eager Loammi Baldwin was not appalled by this appalling request. His answer is interesting: "There was but few beings (for Inhabitants of this world) created before the airy Element was; so it has not been transmitted down to us how the Great Creator formed the matter thereof. So I shall leave it till I am asked only the Natural Cause, and why it blows so many ways in so short a time as it does."

Baldwin and Thompson together attended lectures at Harvard a few years after this correspondence, walking to and from Cambridge every day, a round trip of sixteen miles. The lectures were immensely important to both. It was at Cambridge in 1771 that Loammi Baldwin learned the principles of hydrostatics, hydraulics and pneumatics which gave him the background necessary for the unprecedented task of canal building which he undertook more than twenty years later.

Loammi, in contrast to his friend Thompson, fought on the American side during the Revolution and served in the Massachusetts Legislature for a term. He was given an honorary M.A. degree by Harvard in 1785. In 1793, when the Middlesex Canal became at least a paper reality, he was serving as Sheriff of Middlesex County.

Baldwin was one of the original subscribers to shares in the canal venture but, like many others, he was shaken off by repeated assessments which he did not feel that he could meet. Men of wealth in Boston, better able to hold on, took over many of the original shares. They were men of great, if blind, faith and they could not have foreseen that, although the engineering difficulties, which appeared to be more serious than the problems of operation and maintenance, could be and were overcome, the canal itself was destined to prove a white elephant.

It was easier, in 1793, to get a charter and raise money than it was to find an engineer capable of building a great canal. The only known engineers were Englishmen, and the proprietors of the new canal project were inclined to suspect that foreigners were strange, unreliable and probably immoral. Nevertheless a deal was made with great difficulty by which an English canal expert, who was in Pennsylvania supervising the construction of a canal between the Schuylkill and the Susquehanna system, came to Middlesex County to give his advice. He picked out, rather vaguely, two alternate routes covering the distance between the Mystic and the Merrimack. Loammi Baldwin, who had taken a trip to study southern canals, and another stockholder, with Loammi's sons, Benjamin Franklin Baldwin and Loammi 2nd, and brother Cyrus, helped the Englishman with his survey. They apparently had a good time doing it, dining sumptuously at taverns along the route, sometimes *al fresco,* upon roast chickens, lamb, fried fish, punch, flip, toddy and porter, at the rate of one shilling per meal per man. This pleasant fare, with its liquid fortification, does not appear to have affected the surveyors' work, which indicated that preliminary surveys had been very erratic. The old surveys had been so inaccurate that it was supposed that the junction of the canal with the Merrimack would be its highest point whereas in reality the Concord River at Billerica, one of the points on the route, was actually twenty-five feet above the Merrimack.

Baldwin's report on the southern canals—none of them, it should be said, anything like as ambitious as the Middlesex venture—added to the report of the English engineer, Weston, had a great influence on the proprietors. By 1795 they were ready to make contracts for the still largely undesigned waterway. They offered Loammi Baldwin, who had disposed of his stock and was therefore eligible, the post of superintendent. There was no one else who could have made even a start at the job, but the directors imposed so many conditions upon the eager engineer that he was many times moved to protest—at least once, in 1803, with a threat to resign, from which he was dissuaded by James Sullivan. Sullivan said that the superintendent, like a genius rather than a good executive, was trying to carry everything on his own shoulders and was blaming the directors for the resulting nervous anxiety. "It is enough," Sullivan wrote, "for you to give the carpenters the dimensions of the timber they are to use, and the position and organization of the works they are to erect. To give the spade men the level of their trenches and the direction and elevation of their banks. The stone layers the bottom and top of their walls, and the canal formers their windings and their slopes. To prepare descriptions for boats etc.—and to give directions for an effectual perfection of works on the extensive line.—To request or even to allow you to toil below this, would be degrading the rank your studies have raised you to. . . ."

The first sod turned in the construction of the Middlesex Canal was dug by Loammi Baldwin, Samuel Jaques and Judge James Winthrop on September 10, 1794, with the New England winter almost in sight. Judge Winthrop, as he turned his spadeful of earth, murmured, "May Providence give eternal prosperity to this canal." Providence, as will be seen, saw the job through but, having other matters of human development in mind, withheld the prosperity.

THE INCREDIBLE DITCH

No one in North America in the 1790's had any conception of the nature of a large-scale engineering enterprise, just as no one had any formed idea of how to develop a great continent. Mistakes were made in the construction of the canal—locks would not work properly, stone and earth construction would not stay in place; at some points at certain times there was too little water, at others too much. Some two hundred men labored from sunrise until sunset under subcontractors who often did not quite know what they were doing or how to do it. There were long and costly delays, disputes among the proprietors as to variations in route or means of avoiding unexpected obstacles. Labor shortages periodically interfered with progress. Drinking and rioting were not uncommon. Men were discharged but had to be taken on again because there were none to take their places. They were New England village men, from the towns and farm communities of the Merrimack Valley in Massachusetts and New Hampshire. They were accustomed to owning and using their own tools, something which the vast, new scale of canal work made impracticable.

It was not only a canal that was being cut across New England countryside, it was a new system, a new relationship between man and his work. The workmen who labored on the Middlesex Canal could not contribute anything but work to their employers. They did not know anything about making earth watertight, about how to carry a canal over a river, about how to make the iron fittings for locks, wagons, boats and pumps. Neither workmen nor employers knew anything about cement, being two decades ahead of the American cement industry. They had to experiment as they went along and in the course of their experimentation they suffered many disasters and delays. Yet they built America's first great canal and in doing so provided the gestation for the birth of American civil engineering, and Colonel Loammi Baldwin was the midwife.

In November of 1797 the first section of the canal, from Billerica millpond on the Concord River, which supplied the canal with most of its water, to the Merrimack River, was ready. A proud party of directors and interested citizens boarded two horse-drawn canalboats with excitement and, no doubt, some trepidation. Laborers in their best clothes, carrying spades and tamping tools over their shoulders as if they had been arms emblematic of their calling, paraded the towpath on either side of the waterway, followed by noisy throngs of men, women, children and dogs from the farms and villages along the way. The triumphant procession reached the Merrimack, where the inspection party and the soldierly company of laborers were entertained at a tavern, one of the few buildings then existing at the canal entrance, with a feast of roast beef, potatoes, bread and cider.

The passage had been made but the waterway had defects. The banks proved unstable, the locks leaked and crumbled. There was some talk of replacing Baldwin with an imported canal man, but all next summer he kept his job and by August had the six-mile section between Billerica and the Merrimack in working order for going up as well as for coming down. By the end of 1798 three more miles had been completed east and south of the Concord River. By 1800 the waterway had reached Chelmsford and by 1801, Wilmington. In the spring of 1802 a six-hundred-ton raft of timber was brought sixteen miles down the canal from the Merrimack to Loammi Baldwin's home town of Woburn and by midsummer the last link, between Medford and Woburn, was practically complete.

Yet nine years is a long time for capital to lie in a project without return—especially when unforeseen expense had run up in that period assessments amounting to over six hundred dollars per share. The directors had begun to think in terms of economizing, unwisely, as it turned out. To the great regret of Loammi Baldwin and his sons, most of the later locks on the southern section of the canal were made of wood.

On December 31, 1803, the canal was complete from the Charles River to the Merrimack, and the proprietors, who could not know what was in store for them, grew eloquent in public praise of their project, which was, as they contended, a triumph of engineering. It was a triumph for Loammi Baldwin. It created a reputation for that remarkable man, which was of greater value than the canal itself.

In 1805 Baldwin, perhaps not so much seeing the handwriting on the wall as the impossibility of continuing to work with the canal proprietors, resigned as superintendent and, after a brief return to a directorship, severed all connection with the Middlesex Canal organization. We shall see that he did not abandon his belief in Merrimack River navigation. He was well out of the Middlesex Canal, which never, even before the opening of the Boston and Lowell Railroad in 1835, paid its way and which was entirely abandoned in 1853 after years of profitless if romantic struggle.

LEVELING THE WILD WATERS

While the Middlesex Canal was under construction Judge Samuel Blodget of Derryfield (now Manchester) con-

ceived the idea of building a canal to bypass the great Amoskeag Falls, where a drop of some forty-five feet provided the
most serious obstacle to navigation between the entrance to
the proposed Middlesex Canal and Concord.

Judge Blodget spent two years and most of his fortune
on the mile of canal around the rocks and rapids of Amoskeag
Falls. After leaving the Middlesex Canal organization in 1805,
Loammi Baldwin took charge of the construction at Amoskeag. When Samuel Blodget was in his eighty-fourth year, on
the morning of May 1, 1807, the determined old gentleman
saw his vision made a reality and, with the help of the Middlesex Canal, the river made navigable from Boston to Hooksett.

Samuel Blodget's vision of a navigable river was realized,
and the Judge had sufficient awareness of the true future of
his river to suggest, in 1810, that the name of Derryfield be
changed to Manchester, after the great English textile city.
He could not have known, however, how few years would
pass before his great contribution to the navigation of the
Merrimack would seem all but worthless. To the crowds
gathered along the banks of the river above and below the
locks of the new canal, the passage of the first vessel through
it must have seemed a promise of some splendid, if not comprehended, change in their state.

Judge Blodget, on that glittering May Day, drove to the
upstream entrance to his canal in a high two-wheeled gig,
passing bareheaded through lines of men, women and children who had come from neighboring towns and farms to see
the unbelievable miracle of a leveling of the precipitous Amoskeag torrent. The Judge with the friends who had helped him
boarded a decorated raft. The upper lock gate was closed and
the water slowly released from the lock chamber, the raft
settling gently down to the level of the river below. When

the lower gates were opened and the raft emerged, the crowd broke into cheers and applause which could barely be heard above the thunder of the falls. The Judge smiled and bowed, but the river, which had no way of knowing that it was conquered, kept up its seething roar.

It was a great day for the town of Derryfield, which had been carved out of Chester and Londonderry in 1751, but the people of Derryfield did not know exactly why. The great day was made even greater during the next eight years by the addition of other canals around the falls at Hooksett and Garven's and Turkey Falls at Bow. The Merrimack was at last navigable all the way from Boston to Concord. Navigation, it is true, consisted of travel by boats from sixty to seventy-five feet in length, aided by sails when the wind was right, but actually propelled by boatmen with twenty-foot, iron-shod poles which they poked into the river bottom and clung to as they took turns walking from bow to stern.

By this means farm produce, forest products and furs could be transported to Boston from as far up as Concord in a week or ten days, depending on the condition of the river water, and a somewhat longer upstream voyage could bring to the settlers in the towns which had sprung up since the peace of 1763 those needed commodities which the Merrimack Valley land could not produce.

At the time this seemed enough of a triumph and it did, with the help of the coach roads which were being built at the same time, increase to some extent the tempo of settlement of the upper river, so much so that by 1800 the population of New Hampshire was one fourth of what it is today. It was, however, something quite apart from river navigation which made the Merrimack the greatest single factor in the economy of nineteenth century New England. This surprising change in the evident destiny of the river began, as has been suggested, with the industrial changes which were taking place in England.

12 Two Men and a Valley

••

   To select from among the many individuals whose life and work influenced the rise to importance of the Merrimack, two individuals, one of whom was neither a native American nor a resident of the valley, may seem unjustifiable. Yet without these two there is no possible doubt that the river and the textile industry which grew about it could not have reached the eminence they achieved at the time they achieved it.

   The second of these men was a sixth-generation American, descendant of the Lowells of Newbury and in that sense identified with the Merrimack from its civilized beginnings. It is from Francis Cabot Lowell that the city of Lowell, Massachusetts, took its name, and it is from the same man that the textile industry, indeed American industry in general, took its form.

   The other man whom I have chosen to illustrate the nature of the transformation which came to the great river of New Hampshire was a New Englander only by adoption, though his ideas and his career were what we like to call typically American.

   In 1783, a sensitive and well-educated English farm boy of fourteen, who had been brought up in the sturdy independence of an English yeoman's home—his father owned and farmed his own land—saw the man who understood and sympathized with him fall, one July day, from the hay wagon which he had unloaded as regularly as the bountiful English seasons let him. Slater was never to lift a hay fork or tread his acres again. It might have been the end of the world for Samuel Slater but it was, in fact, the beginning.

Samuel's father had been an enlightened man, one who took more pleasure in watching for new traits in his son than he did in thinking that here was a duplicate of himself growing up to take his place. Young Samuel had an engineering mind. His passion was mathematics, an unusual bent for a Derbyshire farm boy. In this passion the elder Slater had encouraged his son. Instead of requiring that the boy bury himself in farm work he arranged to apprentice Samuel to a neighbor, Jedediah Strutt, who had a cotton-spinning business at Crumford. Here the machinery recently devised by Hargreaves, Arkwright and Crompton was being used with considerable success in the making of yarn. Strutt was a partner of Richard Arkwright, inventor of the cotton-spinning frame and other devices. Young Samuel, after his father's death, apparently thought a great deal about his future. Strutt took a fancy to the boy and found his knowledge of mathematics very helpful.

THE MAN WITH MACHINES IN HIS HEAD

Samuel Slater studied the new machinery, fascinated by every detail, and became so proficient that at the end of his apprenticeship he stayed on with Strutt to supervise the mill and help build a new plant nearby. At this time England was doing everything she could to keep the New World dependent upon her, a tendency which was meeting with much resistance in America. The exportation of machines which might be used to build up an American industry, or of any data about them, was strictly forbidden. Although the cotton business in England was small, Peel's cylinder for printing cotton cloth not having been invented and most cloth-making still being done by hand, the secrets of the new cotton-spinning machinery were carefully guarded. Samuel's employer told the boy that he did not see much future in cotton. It would always, he thought, provide a fair living—not much more.

Samuel was not so sure. After six years he had his own ideas and they were stirred by the sight, in American papers which he read, of advertisements for men with a knowledge of textiles and textile machinery. Some state legislatures in the new nation across the water actually offered a bounty to encourage such men to leave the mother country for the New World. Samuel did not confide in anyone. He spent Sundays drawing and experimenting with machinery, and for six weeks at a time did not visit his mother and brothers and sisters although they lived but a mile away.

In 1789, the year in which George Washington took office as President of the United States, Samuel left his job and without telling anyone of his plans—he didn't even take any steps to liquidate property left him by his father—went to London and in disguise took passage for New York. Just before sailing he wrote to his mother and told her what he had in mind. Although there was close supervision of emigrants, Samuel, who looked more like a farm boy than a mechanic, aroused no suspicion. He carried no papers, no plans. Everything he had was in his head. In New York, he had no trouble getting a job, though it was not a very satisfactory one. He answered with a letter an ad which had been put in the paper by Moses Brown of Providence, who was trying in vain to get results from some badly designed wooden yarn-making machinery. Slater said he thought he could help. In April, 1790, having found the old wooden machinery hopeless, he signed a contract to reproduce Arkwright's machinery for Brown's firm. In spite of having no drawings and nothing but his memory to work by and of being unable to get tools or skilled help, he had his first yarn-making machines ready within a year. They worked. (The British have always insisted that he managed to get some actual Arkwright machines from England to America. It is certain that he did not.)

By 1793 he was a partner with the firm of Almy and Brown and married to Hannah Wilkinson, the daughter of another textile man. Slater went on, with his original partners and other partnerships, with his father-in-law for one, to develop the spinning industry. Everything he did prospered. Samuel Slater, the immigrant boy, had guessed right about the cotton-textile industry. Before he was forty-five years old he was a full-blown capitalist, using the money he had to make more.

THE BIRTH OF A GIANT

Shortly after 1800 an enterprising and resourceful Scot had brought the idea of factory manufacture of cotton yarn to the Merrimack Valley. James Sanderson built a carding mill on the Souhegan River, which empties into the Merrimack between Thornton's and Reed's Ferry near the village of Merrimack, about half way between Nashua and Manchester. Nearby, another New Ipswich man, Benjamin Prichard, a better dreamer than businessman, built a small cotton factory which lasted no more than a year.

Prichard moved up the Souhegan and on to the Amoskeag Falls, where he tried again on the Goffstown side. He had heard of the English developments in cotton machinery and he did his best to apply what he knew of them to his own plant,

but his lack of business sense kept him confused. In 1810 he sold his operation and moved away, discouraged. The mill was reorganized under the name of "Amoskeag Cotton and Woolen Manufacturing Company," and might have succeeded had it not been for the terrible blow which American industry received from the War of 1812. After the war, British imports flooded New England at a price which no native mill could meet.

The Amoskeag mill was barely able to keep alive. By 1822 it could not have remained alive without new capital. The proprietors laid their case before Samuel Slater, by that time the leading figure in cotton manufacturing, and asked him for a loan. Slater was interested but not so convinced that he felt like taking a direct risk. He refused to lend the company money, but he did offer a loan to an Attleboro friend with the suggestion that he use it to buy the Amoskeag plant and water rights. With Slater's money and a sizable mortgage, Olney Robinson stepped in. Robinson turned out to be no more of a businessman than Benjamin Prichard had been. The mortgagors foreclosed and Samuel Slater bought the unmortgaged half of the business from Robinson. In 1825 a partnership of Larned Pitcher, Ira Gay and Samuel Slater formed the "Amoskeag Manufacturing Company," putting considerable new money into an expansion of the property. In 1826, under the active management of Dr. Oliver Dean, Lyman Tiffany and Willard Sayles, the new company began operations on the west side of the Merrimack and on an island in the center of the long stretch of falls. The mill did well from the moment of reorganization. A striped cotton ticking which it turned out became extremely popular and was its mainstay for many years.

In 1831 the New Hampshire Legislature gave the Amoskeag Company a charter authorizing a capitalization of one million dollars. In 1831 a million dollars was a lot of money. Samuel Slater's belief in the future of cotton manufacturing had been justified, largely because of Samuel Slater, whose mind had brought with him from England, unaided by paper, the intricate details of complex machines. What Slater had brought with him was not, however, an industrial revolution. There was no industry in America to be overthrown and rebuilt, there were no thousands, not even hundreds, of mill workers to fear the new machines. Slater brought with him a simple and clear vision of the possibilities of machinery. He was now ready to handle the even greater complexities of a gigantic business.

The giant may be said to have emerged from its state of gestation and been truly born in 1831. For the next few years it grew gradually, as a prodigious infant should. Its parents, forseeing the necessity of satisfying a great appetite, bought up the water power at Hooksett Falls and at Concord and began gathering in parcels of land in Goffstown and on the other side of the river in what had been Derryfield but was now the village of Manchester.

When Samuel Slater died in 1835, he left at Amoskeag Falls the nucleus of a snowball with tremendous momentum and tremendous power to grow, not only to grow but to cause the entire countryside for miles along the river and east and west of the falls to grow with it.

By 1840 the Amoskeag Company had built mills on the east side for its own account—Numbers One and Two—and for others, among them the Stark Mill, the acquisition of which for its own account eighty years later marked the beginning of the end. All the mill buildings were of brick made at Hooksett. Brick homes and apartments for the rapidly growing working force appeared on the slope above the mills of the east bank. The company gave land for parks and streets to Manchester, which, though inhabited by only a few hundred villagers in 1810, became a city in 1846.

Because the corporation had more land and water power than it could use, it leased part of its water rights and continued to build mills for concerns which were virtual rivals. It could afford to be generous. To meet its own needs for machinery it built metal-working shops, machine shops and foundries. Before 1850 the great textile plant was manufacturing locomotives and by 1860 had added fire engines to its list of products. In spite of—or perhaps because of—this wide diversification, Amoskeag turned out a superior quality of cotton goods, goods of such excellence that they won, in competition with the best English materials, gold medals at the Crystal Palace Exposition of 1851.

So versatile was Amoskeag that it was able to meet the conditions imposed upon it by the Civil War, conditions which made rough going for many lesser mills. Amoskeag, in addition to its cloth, was able to and did turn out rifles for the Union Army—25,000 Springfields, 17,000 breech-loading carbines —and many cannon and other pieces of equipment, including at least a part of the turret of the famous *Monitor* which, appropriately enough, fought to a standstill the Confederate ironclad *Virginia,* built upon the hull of the captured frigate *Merrimac.*

Amoskeag attracted mechanics and artisans from many regions. Many a man who got his experience in its vast shops went out to distinguish himself elsewhere. Many remained, satisfied with the ability of the versatile giant to use their talents.

At least one young man who was employed in the office of the Amoskeag machine shops became famous in his own right. John Rogers did not feel that office work gave full scope to his talents. He, like many a New England artisan, was an instinctive artist. He began experimenting with the beige clay which the Amoskeag foundry brought down the river from Hooksett. He soon developed a characteristic modeling technique and began turning out large clay groups of figures, illustrating scenes from the domestic and agricultural life of New England. "Rogers Groups" soon were in great demand, a demand which always exceeded the supply and which anyone who tries to buy one today will know has never failed.

So celebrated was the great Amoskeag industrial prodigy at the time of the Civil War that it was visited by Abraham Lincoln. During the election campaign of 1860, when the tall Illinois politician was beginning to realize his power, he visited Manchester and made a stirring speech at Smyth's Opera House, which was filled to overflowing.

E. A. Straw, the agent, as the active manager was called, invited Lincoln to visit the mills. Lincoln, who always welcomed an opportunity to learn about the inner workings of

people and things, accepted gladly and was shown through the apparently interminable plant by a young mechanic, Edwin P. Richardson. Richardson, when sent for, did not know what was going to be asked of him, and he appeared in Straw's office in work clothes, just as he had left his machines, with his hands and face unwashed. He later said that when he told Mr. Lincoln that he did not feel that he was clean enough to shake hands, the candidate replied, "Young man, the hand of honest toil is never too grimy for Abe Lincoln to grasp."

If that is what Lincoln said, we may be fairly certain that he said it with the equivalent of a wink which Richardson either did not understand or did not see fit to record. He and the future President spent, according to his report, a congenial two hours studying the complicated organization of the huge mill which at that time was run entirely by the falling waters of the Merrimack River.

It would be interesting to know what the frontier lawyer thought of this sample of the power of industrial New England, but Lincoln never publicly referred to his visit and we have only Edwin Richardson's statement that the great man was an enjoyable companion and that he was surprised and pleased by what he learned of Amoskeag's activities, activities which were to be of inestimable value to the North during the war which filled the next four years.

It is only natural that the enraptured proprietors of the vast gold mine, developed where only a few years before had been a forest traversed by Indians and wild beasts, should have supposed it to be inexhaustible. For more than ninety years of peace and war it appeared to be not only inexhaustible but to possess the Midas touch and have the ability to turn to gold everything toward which it reached.

Perhaps no one could have foreseen its end. Yet, as we shall see, its end did come, as unbelievable as Abraham Lincoln's end. When it did come, it shook New Hampshire, indeed all of New England, to the very roots. Yet the Merrimack Valley, resourceful as when it first welcomed Samuel Slater, merely turned the page upon disaster and, unbowed, began a new chapter.

13 Dawn on the Merrimack

Although Samuel Slater's creation of the Amoskeag Manufacturing Company and the company's subsequent creation of the City of Manchester began the alteration of the river of Indians, shad, sturgeon and salmon before the idea of factory production had taken root anywhere else along its banks, the growth of textile-making in New Hampshire was soon matched by a growth below the Massachusetts line.

The first two decades of the life of the American Republic were, on the lower reaches of the Merrimack, years of frenzied canal building, some of the consequences of which I have described in telling of the beginning of manufacturing at Amoskeag Falls. Before 1800 the thirty-five-foot Pawtucket Falls were an obstacle to the driving of lumber from upriver to Newburyport and Boston. Before the canal around the falls was built, rafts of lumber floated down from the northern forests had to be hauled ashore and dragged by oxen to the pool below the falls, there to be launched again on their oceanward journey. The Pawtucket Canal, built during the construction of the Middlesex waterway under the direction of the ubiquitous Loammi Baldwin, did away with this inconvenience, increased the flow of timber down the Merrimack and greatly increased the importance of the region between the mouth of the Concord River, in what is now Lowell, and the Middlesex Canal, farther upstream, which was opened shortly after the

Pawtucket Canal. Men began to dream of a great system of navigable water channels from Boston up the Merrimack to Lake Winnipesaukee, on through the mountains to the Connecticut and across Vermont to Lake Champlain and the Hudson, connecting with projected canals across New York State to the Great Lakes and the new West.

James Watt had practically perfected the steam engine before the American Revolution and, although he regarded with distasteful horror the idea of applying his device to transportation, it was evident before his death in 1819 that his feeling in the matter could not hold the steam engine to a stationary course. The steam railroad had its period of gestation while canal building was flourishing and the application of the steam engine and related machines to manufacturing was changing the emphasis on descending water of rivers from navigation to power.

It was this emphasis on power which brought the Pawtucket Canal, bypassed and made almost unnecessary by the amazing but disappointing Middlesex waterway, back into a position of importance. Here enters the second of those two great figures of which Samuel Slater was the first.

Francis Cabot Lowell was born in Newburyport in 1775, seven years after Samuel Slater saw the light of day in England. Unlike Slater, Lowell was a fifth-generation American of the well-to-do and intelligent Lowell family, which was descended from Percival Lowell who had come to Newburyport in 1635. Francis' early days culminated at Harvard in 1793. He was always, like Slater, interested in mathematics and mechanics and, also like his contemporary, given to much thinking about the future. He went into business after leaving Harvard, but the international troubles which followed the establishment of our Republic and the young Republic's own painful spasms of teething were not good for business. Francis' health was not good, either. In 1810 an ocean voyage was recommended as a cure and he went to England, where, having time and intellectual aptitude, he became interested in the creation of machinery.

Lowell was fascinated by the idea of developing manufacturing in his own country as a stimulus to the ailing national income. When he returned home, full of enthusiasm and experimental ideas, the War of 1812 climaxed the commercial doldrums of a New England which had planted most of its eggs in the basket of sea-borne commerce. Yet when the war was over, Francis Lowell knew what he wanted to do—he wanted to work on the machine-weaving of cotton cloth. He devoted himself to the improvement of the looms already in use and, apparently independently of the English, invented a successful power loom, the first in this country.

So far, Lowell's career was, in total effect, not unlike Slater's save that Lowell concentrated, at first, on weaving and Slater on spinning. After the War of 1812, however, Lowell's ideas began to take more complex shape. He was the first to develop the idea of an integrated corporation, the first to concentrate the complete production of cotton cloth in one mill. He saw the need, in his day, for a protective tariff and went to Washington to fight for it and win, although such an idea was far from popular in England.

With his brother-in-law, Patrick Tracy Jackson, and Nathan Appleton he organized at Waltham, Massachusetts, what was really the first unit of American capitalism, a stock corporation as against a partnership or individual holding. This, even more than Lowell's extraordinary inventiveness, was his great contribution to American life. The Waltham mill was more than mere machinery. The welfare of its employees was a primary consideration. In the "Waltham Plan" it set up a social philosophy which changed the American way of looking at industrial development. Coming as it did at the beginning of the great period of national expansion, it may be said to have provided the backbone upon which every American industry has grown its nourishing flesh, although every American industry has not maintained the vision of social justice which Francis Cabot Lowell and his associates had before them and which was realized in the beginnings of the city of Lowell, Massachusetts.

WATER INTO WEALTH

Francis Lowell never saw or heard of the city which bears his name and which was largely, though not entirely, the outgrowth of his genius. His health remained bad and the demands upon it of his great energy kept it from improving. At the height of his career, in his forty-third year, only seven years after the trip to Europe which had inspired him, he died, leaving with his business associates the idea of developing still greater mills for the complete manufacture of cotton cloth.

Patrick Jackson and Nathan Appleton began, after Francis Lowell's death, to search the Merrimack Valley for a suitable water power. The Souhegan and the Nashua Rivers, though the latter possessed a fall which was later successfully developed by the Nashua Manufacturing Company, did not appear to them to offer adequate power. A friend who heard of what they were looking for suggested that they buy the Pawtucket Canal, no longer of much value as an aid to navigation. By developing this channel the entire power resulting from the

thirty- or thirty-five-foot drop of Pawtucket Falls could be made available at a single point.

Jackson, Appleton, Kirk and John Boott, Paul Moody and Warren Dutton looked over the canal in November, 1821, when the sparsely settled river banks were powdered with a light fall of snow and the river, though not in flood, ran full and strong. From the banks of the canal less than a dozen houses could be seen where now is the heart of Lowell. It did not take the inheritors of Francis Lowell's idea long to decide that they had found what they were looking for. They immediately drew up articles of organization. By the following February the Merrimack Manufacturing Company had been incorporated.

Such was the nature of the enterprise that one of the company's first acts was to authorize the building of a church, no temporary wooden structure but a substantial one of stone. The first mill wheel began turning in September 1823. In 1825 a library was built, along with several additional mill buildings. In the same year, under the presidency of Nathan Appleton, a dividend of one hundred dollars per share was paid to the stockholders, whose holdings had been increased by the issuance of stock in a canal company which controlled all of the land and water power on and about Pawtucket Falls. Power not required by the Merrimack Company was sold to others. The growth of industrial Lowell was on in full force. In 1826 the town was incorporated. The town of Lowell became a city in 1836, its rapid expansion having been speeded by the opening, in 1835, of the Boston and Lowell Railroad.

By 1840 it was a large, if utterly new city, a city of mills and boarding houses, churches, residences and schools. The Merrimack Valley was then in the process of changing from its predominantly grain economy to a sheep-raising economy. The daughters of farm and village families welcomed the op-

portunity to work in the mills of the new city, which provided
not only steady work but, astonishingly enough, unusual social
and intellectual opportunities—the outgrowth of Francis Lowell's Waltham idea carried to the banks of the Merrimack.

In 1842 a celebrated if somewhat acid-tongued traveler
from England visited New England and wrote an account of
his trip from Boston to the Lowell mills. Charles Dickens was
an eye witness, and in this case a sympathetic one, of an almost
utopian moment in American industrial history. The Lowell
of 1842 comes to life in his pages:

> I was met at the station at Lowell by a gentleman
> intimately connected with the management of the facto-
> ries there; and, gladly putting myself under his guidance,
> drove off at once to that quarter of the town in which
> the works, the object of my visit, were situated. Although
> only just of age—for, if my recollection serve me, it has
> been a manufacturing town barely one and twenty years
> —Lowell is a large, populous, thriving place. Those indi-
> cations of its youth which first attract the eye, give it a
> quaintness and oddity of character which, to a visitor
> from the old country, is amusing enough. It was a very
> dirty winter's day, and nothing in the whole town looked
> old to me, except the mud, which in some parts was al-
> most knee-deep, and might have been deposited there on
> the subsiding of the waters after the Deluge. In one
> place there was a new wooden church, which, having no
> steeple, and being yet unpainted, looked like an enor-
> mous packing-case without any direction upon it. In
> another there was a large hotel, whose walls and colon-
> nades were so crisp, and thin, and slight, that it had
> exactly the appearance of being built with cards. I was
> careful not to draw my breath as we passed, and trembled
> when I saw a workman come out upon the roof, lest
> with one thoughtless stamp of his foot he should crush
> the structure beneath him, and bring it rattling down.
> The very river that moves the machinery in the mills

(for they are all worked by water power) seems to acquire a new character from the fresh buildings of bright red brick and painted wood among which it takes its course; and to be as light-headed, thoughtless, and brisk a young river, in its murmurings and tumblings, as one would desire to see. One would swear that every 'Bakery,' 'Grocery,' and 'Bookbindery,' and other kind of store took its shutters down for the first time, and started in business yesterday. The golden pestles and mortars fixed as signs upon the sun-blind frames outside the Druggists' appear to have been just turned out of the United States Mint; and when I saw a baby of some week or ten days old in a woman's arms at a street corner, I found myself unconsciously wondering where it came from: never supposing for an instant that it could have been born in such a young town as that.

There are several factories in Lowell, each of which belongs to what we should term a Company of Proprietors, but what they call in America a Corporation. I went over several of these; such as a woollen factory, a carpet factory, and a cotton factory: examined them in every part; and saw them in their ordinary working aspect, with no preparation of any kind, or departure from their ordinary every-day proceedings. I may add that I am well acquainted with our manufacturing towns in England, and have visited many mills in Manchester and elsewhere in the same manner.

I happened to arrive at the first factory just as the dinner hour was over, and the girls were returning to their work; indeed, the stairs of the mill were thronged with them as I ascended. They were all well dressed, but not, to my thinking, above their condition: for I like to see the humbler classes of society careful of their dress and appearance, and even, if they please, decorated with such little trinkets as come within the compass of their means . . .

They had serviceable bonnets, good warm cloaks and shawls; and were not above clogs and pattens. Moreover, there were places in the mill in which they could deposit these things without injury; and there were conveniences for washing. They were healthy in appearance, many of them remarkably so, and had the manners and deportment of young women: not of degraded brutes of burden . . .

The rooms in which they worked were as well ordered as themselves. In the windows of some there were green plants, which were trained to shade the glass; in all, there was as much fresh air, cleanliness, and comfort as the nature of the occupation would possibly admit of. Out of so large a number of females, many of whom were only then just verging upon womanhood, it may be reasonably supposed that some were delicate and fragile in appearance: no doubt there were. But I solemnly declare, that from all the crowd I saw in the different factories that day, I cannot recall or separate one young face that gave me a painful impression; not one young girl whom, assuming it to be matter of necessity that she should gain her daily bread by the labor of her hands, I would have removed from those works if I had had the power.

That Dickens's view of the workings of Francis Lowell's industrial idea was not the result of a foreigner's enthusiasm for American novelty is, if Dickens's usually sharp critical comments were not sufficient evidence, indicated by the words of one of the very mill girls who had caught his eye.

Lucy Larcom was a girl of eighteen in 1842. Her widowed mother had come to Lowell seven years before and established a boardinghouse for mill employees, a task, as Dickens pointed out, which could not be undertaken by anyone whose character and credentials had not been carefully investigated by the mill management. Lucy was a girl of unusual talent, sensitive and imaginative, but she seems not to have been unique among the Lowell mill girls, even though she was a poet. The mill employees published a magazine called *The Lowell Offering,* "a repository of original articles, written exclusively by females

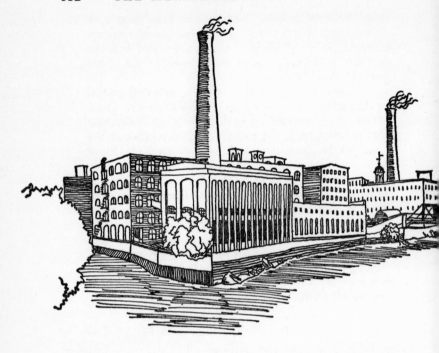

actively employed in the mills." Charles Dickens carried away with him from Lowell issues of this journal totaling four hundred pages, which he said he read from beginning to end, thus meeting Lucy Larcom, who was a contributor.

SPINDLES AND GOLDEN GIRLS

In her charming account of her early days in the Lowell cotton mills, Lucy testifies to the correctness of the Englishman's view of a mill girl's life:

> I went to my first day's work in the mill with a light heart. The novelty of it made it seem easy, and it really was not hard, just to change the bobbins on the spin-

ning-frames every three quarters of an hour or so, with half a dozen other little girls who were doing the same thing. When I came back at night, the family began to pity me for my long, tiresome day's work, but I laughed and said,—"Why, it is nothing but fun. It is just like play."

And for a little while it was only a new amusement; I liked it better than going to school and "making believe" I was learning when I was not. And there was a great deal of play mixed with it. We were not occupied more than half the time. The intervals were spent frolicking around among the spinning-frames, teasing and talking to the older girls, or entertaining ourselves with games and stories in a corner, or exploring, with the overseer's permission, the mysteries of the carding-room, the dressing-room, and the weaving-room. . . .

At this time I had learned to do a spinner's work, and I obtained permission to tend some frames that stood directly in front of the river-windows. . . . I kept myself occupied with the river, my work, and my thoughts. And the river and my thoughts flowed on together, the happiest of companions. Like a loitering pilgrim, it sparkled up to me in recognition as it glided along, and bore away my little frets and fatigues on its bosom. When the work "went well," I sat in the window-seat, and let my fancies fly whither they would,—downward to the sea, or upward to the hills that hid the mountain-cradle of the Merrimack. . . .

There was many a young girl near me whose life was like the beautiful course of the river in my ideal of her. The Merrimack has blent its music with the onward song of many a lovely soul that, clad in plain working-clothes, moved heavenward beside its waters.

This was the atmosphere of the Lowell mills in their youth, when England's distinguished novelist, who was no doubt as well thought of by them as they were by him, visited the mill girls. Lucy Larcom was, like Dickens, a reformer—

later an abolitionist—and had there been anything to reform in Lowell in the 1840's one or both of them would have seen it.

Perhaps at some point along Charles Dickens's route from the Boston and Lowell station through the streets of the young city there stood a boy, then eight years old, whose eye would have been for the gray of sky beyond the mill buildings and the more subtle tones of their newness, who saw people, their postures and motions as elements of a design and the colors of their world as a language which he might speak with his own private accent. Perhaps with him as he watched the bearded Englishman drive through the muddy streets was a woman who bore a striking resemblance to one of the best-known paintings by an American, for that boy, who was born in Lowell in 1834, was James Abbott McNeill Whistler, son of Major George Washington Whistler, who had contributed to the success of both the Middlesex Canal and the Boston and Lowell Railroad.

14 The Midas Touch

The physical nature of the Merrimack River—the obstacles and the unimpeded stretches of its course, the mountain waters which fed it through the surrounding reservoir of forest root and mold—has always been the determining factor in the human growth about it. The sandbars at its mouth kept it from being a Hudson or a Delaware or, even, a Piscataqua. The aroused Indians kept its middle reaches from becoming productive land at an early date. Its very power kept it from being navigable, and the need for navigation at first obscured man's view of its power potential. When the growth of the machine idea, America's variant of the European industrial revolution, began to demand for its roots the soil of urban centralization, the river valley could not provide a rapid enough development of transportation to supply the urban centers, though its gradually sloping banks did provide a thoroughfare first for coach travel and then for railroad tracks.

The human life of the changing valley depended always upon change—and change sometimes came in unexpected form. It was unforeseen change which in a sense isolated the self-sufficient little Athens of Newburyport; it was change which turned Amoskeag and Pawtucket and the Nashua River Falls from fishing grounds to great centers of manufacturing, and these changes were not, basically, matters of individual human initiative. Samuel Slater and Francis Cabot Lowell did not bring about the changes. They took advantage of them. They were the catalysts of alteration. They were like bees cross-fertilizing plants of opportunity already in existence. Without this fertilization the plants might have remained unproductive.

They could not, however, so intricate was the economy of the new varieties which their contributions helped to produce, control all the conditions under which those varieties must maintain their lives. In spite of the rosy picture of the early days of Lowell, in spite of the vision and planning of its founders, things had not always been as rosy as Dickens believed them. The gigantic textile industry had its growing pains, then as now being dependent upon intelligent and resourceful management, which was not always available.

Amos Lawrence was a Merrimack Valley man in a double sense. His ancestors from Suffolk, England, were among the earliest settlers of Groton, Massachusetts, on the Nashua River, where Amos was born in 1786. His father was the founder of Groton Academy (now known as Lawrence Academy and not to be confused with Groton School) which provided the peak of Amos's formal education. When the boy left the Academy in 1799 at the age of thirteen, he went to work in a local store. He was not content to remain a mere apprentice in a country town. As soon as he could he headed for Boston and by 1807 was in business there on his own account, where he was joined in the following year by his younger brother, Abbott. The partnership of Amos and Abbott Lawrence developed the commission selling of woolen and cotton cloth, domestic and imported, providing an ever-widening outlet for products of the Merrimack Valley's new industry and incidentally enriching the partners to such an extent that even the War of 1812 and the depression which followed it could not hold them back. By the time the firm of A. & A. Lawrence was a dozen years old, Amos had enough spare capital to use as a hypodermic for an ailing combination in Lowell and incidentally to set up several new mills under the control of his brother, Luther. By the early 1830's, his health not being good, Amos ceased to be the active partner. By the time that Charles Dickens visited Lowell, Amos Lawrence had decided that he was rich enough. He spent the last decade of his life giving away more than half a million dollars and reaching even beyond the gift of dollars by going about the country in his carriage or sleigh, handing out books to anyone he believed could be enriched by reading them.

Abbott Lawrence kept the Lawrence enterprises going, moving downriver from Lowell and getting control of the water power between Lowell and Haverhill. Here in 1845 the mill city of Lawrence began to take shape about a power canal built on the north side of the river by the Essex Company, of which Abbott became a director. The Lawrence bee was producing successful hybrids. The city which ripened in fields on both sides of the river at the junction of the Merrimack and the Shawsheen had, like Lowell, a phenomenal early growth, becoming a full-blown city in 1853, less than ten years from the time when it had been nothing at all.

Up the valley, where the Nashua River—after passing through Lancaster and Groton, Massachusetts, and crossing the New Hampshire line—joins the broad stream of the Merrimack, another great textile organization had its beginning. In 1822, when the farmers of the region which had begun as Indian-haunted Dunstable had commenced to recover from the War of 1812 and the equally disastrous "cold year" of 1816 in which no crops ripened and cattle and sheep died by hundreds, a group of enterprising men founded the Nashua Manufacturing Company and began the change from a fishing and farming community to an industrial center. The mill community began—as Manchester, seventeen miles above it, had already done—to attract young people from the upriver farms which were in the throes of change from produce-growing to sheep-raising and on which work for girls and boys was never-ending and never-paid.

The development of navigation on the lower river was of great benefit to the industrial enterprise of the region and in the second and third decades of the nineteenth century seemed to promise so much that efforts were made to speed upriver travel by the application of mechanical motive power. Anyone who attempted the passage of the Merrimack from the site of the entrance to the Middlesex Canal in a vessel of any size might be forgiven for wondering what made the promoters of the 1830's imagine that the river could be made navigable by self-propelled vessels.

STEAM AGAINST THE SWIFT WATER

Whatever it was, Joel Stone of Lowell and J. P. Simpson of Boston believed in it. These two enthusiastic pioneers had built for them in Amos Whitney's cooperage shop at Paw-tucket Falls a vessel ninety feet long and twenty feet wide. She was called *Herald*. With her great and uncouth steam engine mounted amidships she drew three feet of water.

On May 31, 1834, *Herald* steamed out of upper Lowell, which by that time was a community of some fourteen thousand inhabitants, and headed for the town of Nashua, carrying anyone who was willing to pay fifty cents for the ride. Her life was short and exciting if not exactly gay. It was not easy to keep her off the sandbars or to steer her considerable length around the many bends. Moreover her owners, either not believing that a steam engine on wheels could be a profitable means of transportation or being ignorant of the fact that the Boston and Lowell Railroad had almost linked those two cities, chose the worst possible time for their venture. In the year following *Herald's* first voyage the railroad reached Lowell, sounding the death knell of the Middlesex Canal, a knell which was, be it said, not immediately heard. Three years later the Nashua and Lowell Railroad put the venturesome steamboat out of business. She promptly sank in the autumn of 1838 at Wicasee Falls, near Tyng's Island, just above the entrance to the Middlesex Canal.

Her owners would not believe that she was useless. When the river ice was thick enough that winter to give a salvage crew something to work on she was raised and skidded to shore, where she was completely rebuilt. They added thirty feet to her length and launched her as a side-wheel excursion steamer with a magnificent superstructure including a "saloon" and bar. She could and did carry more than five hundred people about the wide waters between Lowell and the New Hampshire line, but evidently not at a profit. In 1839 she was laboriously taken overland around Pawtucket Falls, being too big for the canal locks, and left on the bank below. In 1840, when the spring freshets brought the river gurgling about her keel, she was floated down to Newburyport and sold. The purchasers sailed her to New York, there to end her days as a ferry, perhaps the very one on which Walt Whitman traveled so often between Manhattan and Brooklyn.

Steamboat travel, much as it has always appealed to the American imagination, was not attempted again on the Merrimack—except for barge tugs on the lower river and local pleasure boats perhaps on the upper—until 1867, when its success was no greater. In spite of early opinion, steam travel on wheels in the river valleys of New England proved to be more effective and durable than navigation by water. The railroad, which reached Lowell in 1835 and Nashua in 1838, was extended to Concord in 1842. Six years later the Northern Railroad—some of whose early locomotives were, as has already been said, produced in the shops of the Amoskeag Mills at Manchester—pushed the New Hampshire railhead to White River Junction on the Vermont side of the Connecticut River, helping to carry the industrial products of the seacoast northward and the eager young hill people southward to the great new mills which could not do without them. The Merrimack maintained its dignity, its power and its majesty, but it hired out its transportation to the steel rails which clung to its banks.

Rail development, which marked the end of the canal and river era, had a profound effect upon the Merrimack Valley. Until the last quarter of the nineteenth century railroad locomotives in New England burned almost nothing but wood. The demand for wood fuel and ties was extraordinary and had a marked effect upon the forests of the upper Merrimack. The railroad dream took the place of the canal- and river-navigation dream, both as a means of making the new industrial centers more important and as an aid in opening up new rural areas to settlement and development.

RAILS BY THE RIVER

I have brought the railroad into the portrait of the Merrimack River at this point because its introduction coincided with the beginnings of Merrimack industry which I have been describing. The railroad, however, was not immediately welcomed by everyone in the Merrimack Valley. When, after many delays caused by promoters' rivalry, shortage of equipment and disputes over right of way, the thirty-four miles of track between Nashua and Concord was opened for traffic (in the year of Dickens's already described visit to Lowell), there was definite opposition, definitely expressed, to the extension of railway traffic farther north. The northern towns were

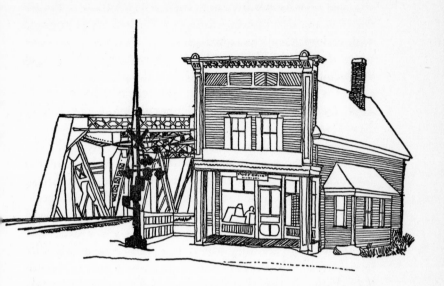

afraid of surrendering their isolation and being gobbled up by
sinister influences of the state capital and the industrial cities
in the southern part of the state. At least one of them sent a
note to the Legislature referring to the "calamity" of the possible approach of the railroad. In the same year the General
Court passed a law, making the taking possession of land for
railroad right of way almost impossible. This perhaps did not
so much represent popular feeling as it showed the political
balance between urban and rural, industrial and agricultural,
in the Merrimack Valley. That the balance was precarious
and that the trend from agriculture to industry had begun in
earnest, is shown by the fact that two years later the New
Hampshire General Court passed a new law, empowering
authorized railroad builders to take land by eminent domain.

Railroad building began again at a furious rate and the
town of Dorchester on the south branch of the Baker River,

the Merrimack's northwestern tributary, which had begged the Legislature to protect it from the fire-breathing, crop-consuming iron horse, remained protected and to this day has never been touched by a steel rail. It is worthy of note that as a consequence of this spirited isolation the population of Dorchester is today approximately 10 per cent of what it was in 1830. During the same period the population of the State of New Hampshire as a whole has more than doubled.

The two hundred years which elapsed between the settling of Newbury and the beginning of the new era of the development of textile manufacturing and of mechanical transportation are, when seen from a distance, like the breaking of a wave—a long and slowly undulating passage toward land and then, suddenly, as the depth grows less, a swift wild turbulence and seething access of speed, a wide rippling spread up the shore. The wave that broke upon the Merrimack Valley in the 1830's had been a long time finding its shore. It was destined to recede and try again. What followed the breaking of that first roller along the Merrimack was a kind of Age of Reptiles, full of great ungainly creatures who were magnificent in their mass and multitude so long as their climate and their environment did not demand of them too much adaptation. The industrial giants of Lawrence and Lowell, Nashua and Manchester could not, as it turned out, survive drastic change. Yet, as in the Age of Reptiles, there were basic elements of organic life which, when the great Saurians were no more, could gather themselves together to produce a more durable form of life, so there were in the valley of the Merrimack organic elements capable of survival. What these were can be best shown, perhaps, by pointing out some of the ramifications of the lives of a few men who were born in the Merrimack region between the Revolutionary War and the building of the first railroad.

The Lowell-Lawrence manufacturing complex is an excellent illustration of the force which the Merrimack River has exerted upon American life as a whole and of the manner in which the development of one section of the river dovetails into the development of others. The elements of which I have just spoken may be found in the history of the Lowell family and of the Lawrence brothers, who were so important to that series of communities clustered in the great bend of the lower river.

MEN OF MILL AND MANSION

Amos and Abbott Lawrence and their rather short-lived brothers were more than mere merchants, profiting by disposing of the products of the mills turned by the mountain waters of the Merrimack, into which they plowed much of their savings. Amos's health kept him from being more active than his philanthropy kept him, but Abbott, concerned with matters which affected his textile interests—the tariff and the attitude of the South—went into politics. He found time, at the height of his prosperity, to represent Massachusetts in Congress, to be a member of that difficult commission whose study of the northeastern boundary between Canada and the United States led to the Webster-Ashburton Treaty and the removal of a serious threat to Anglo-American relations. As American Minister to the Court of St. James's, after a narrow escape from becoming President of the United States in 1850, he did more than any man had done up to that time to strengthen understanding and friendship between the United States and Great Britain, a strengthening without which the relationship between the two countries during the confusions of the Civil War might have been very different. Thus did the Merrimack meet the Thames.

Speculation as to what might have happened had things been otherwise than as they were is usually profitless. It is interesting, however, to speculate upon the efforts of the Merrimack to extend its influences to the White House. Abbott Lawrence, an independent who had been a supporter of Henry Clay and was an equally strong supporter of Zachary Taylor in 1848, was much talked of as candidate for Vice-President in that year. Had he not been opposed by another Merrimack River man, the great Daniel Webster, he would undoubtedly have commanded the eight votes which he lacked to secure the nomination. Had he, instead of Millard Fillmore, secured the nomination to the Vice-Presidency, he would have become President, as Fillmore did on Zachary Taylor's death in 1850. What the accession to the Presidency of a strong and vigorous man of great political sagacity and complete honesty, a man who both loved and cherished the union and understood and sympathized with the South, might have meant to the nation in the year of the great and disputed compromise is a matter for conjecture. It is a matter of record that Fillmore's handling of the Presidency kept the riven nation in a ferment of indecision and error, which his successor, another Merrimack Valley man and a nephew by marriage of Abbott Lawrence, was unable to still.

Franklin Pierce was born on the Merrimack's largest tributary, the Contoocook River, at Hillsborough, New Hampshire. He was a man of fine character, an extremely able lawyer and a resourceful soldier, as his father Benjamin had been before him. His uncle Abbott did not support him for the Presidency because of Democrat Pierce's apparent indifference to slavery and his willingness to permit the South to extend that institution into the territories. The man from Hillsborough, New Hampshire's only President, would be better known and more honored today but for this attitude.

Because of it, his good qualities, his excellent choice of cabinet and his capable handling of foreign affairs have been all but forgotten. Anyone who travels to Hillsborough and stands in the charming white house in which Pierce was born might do worse than remember that Abbott Lawrence's talented nephew served his country well and that his failure to believe in the abolition of slavery was a matter of temperament rather than of character. Had his uncle been in Millard Fillmore's place, Franklin Pierce would probably have gone down in Merrimack River history as a brilliant New Hampshire lawyer rather than as a President who did not entirely understand what was going on about him and who was unaware that he was conniving at the approach of natural disaster. As it was, he retired after one term to Concord, New Hampshire, from which he wrote to Abraham Lincoln on March 4, 1862, after the death of Lincoln's son Willie:

Concord, N.H.
March 4, 1862

My dear Sir,

The impulse to write you, the moment I heard of your great domestic affliction was very strong, but it brought back the crushing sorrow which befell me just before I went to Washington in 1853, with such power that I felt your grief to be too sacred for intrusion.

Even in this hour, so full of danger to our Country, and of trial and anxiety to all good men, your thoughts will be of your cherished boy, who will nestle at your heart, until you meet him in the new life, when tears and toils and conflicts will be unknown.

I realize fully how vain it would be, to suggest sources of consolation.

There can be but one refuge in such an hour,—but one remedy for smitten hearts, which, is to trust in Him 'who doeth all things well', and leave the rest to—

'Time comforter & only healer
When the heart hath bled'
With Mrs. Pierce's and my own best wishes—and
truest sympathy for Mrs. Lincoln and yourself
                                    I am, very truly
                                    yr. friend
                                    Franklin Pierce

        His Excy—
        A. Lincoln
        Presdt

Franklin Pierce knew the nature of private grief and had
reason to believe that the Presidency demanded of a man a
heavier toll than he should be required to pay. In December,
1852, after his election, he and his wife and their twelve-
year-old son, Benjamin, visited Amos Lawrence in Boston,
where Benjamin, a bright and beautiful child, endeared himself to everyone, and was given a pencil by his great-uncle.
The note of thanks which he wrote from Andover on the way
home makes one wonder whether the recipient of the gift may
not, in spite of the difference in ages, have been the older of
the two.

                                    Andover
                                    Dec. 27, 1852

Dear Uncle Lawrence:
        I admire the beautiful pencil you sent me, and I
think I shall find it very useful. I shall keep it very carefully for your sake, and I hope that I may learn to write
all the better with it. It was kind in you to write such a
good little note, too; and I see that being industrious
while you were young enables you to be kind and benev-
olent now that you are old. I think that you have given
me very good advice, and I hope I shall profit by it. So,
dear uncle, with much love to aunt, I am
                                    Your affectionate nephew
                                    B. Pierce

On the sixth of January, 1853, the Pierce family left Andover by train for Concord. Benjamin and his pencil were destined never to see the White House in Washington. A few minutes out of the Andover station the train of the President-elect left the tracks and plunged down a steep embankment, the wooden cars splintering on the rocks below. Franklin Pierce and his wife were injured. Little Benjamin was the only passenger to be killed.

In 1862, when he wrote to Lincoln from his retreat on the banks of the Merrimack, Franklin Pierce remembered his lonely trip to take office and to try to fill an empty White House while his wife, unable to overcome her grief, remained at home.

15 The City at the River's Heart

The pleasant city of Concord, the focal point of New Hampshire's political activities and the hub of its transportation system, is typical of the upper Merrimack Valley in appearance as well as in culture. It has been the capital of the state for 150 years and for eighty years before that was a center of far greater importance than its population would indicate.

It was settled, after a grant from the General Court of Massachusetts, by a sturdy group of pioneers from the Merrimack towns of Massachusetts, largely Newbury and Haverhill. At the time of settlement the boundary between Massachusetts and New Hampshire had not been determined and much dispute and confusion resulted from the fact that the province of New Hampshire, not recognizing the Massachusetts grant, at about the same time granted a township called Bow in the very spot which the Massachusetts men claimed for their grant of Penacook or, as they called it, Penny Cook. The controversy over this conflict was not settled for thirty-five years, and then a royal decree affirmed the grant by Massachusetts of land over which it had lost control when the boundary line between that elastic commonwealth and the province of New Hampshire was fixed in 1742. The grantees were thus assured of their holdings, but the matter of jurisdiction between Bow and Rumford, as the present settlement was then called, was not settled until a parish was established in the town of Bow and given the name of Concord in the hope that the cessation of past discord might give the new name a reality.

The settlement founded in 1727 prospered, after a few bad winters, in spite of the topographical confusion and some degree of bigotry. There was a stipulation from the outset that no original grantee could sell or alienate his land without the permission of the entire community. This provision indicated the grantees' distaste for those hardy folk, already mentioned, who had settled Londonderry and whom descendants of earlier settlers persisted in regarding as Irish, although the Londonderry people had hardly become Irish by the process of being driven out of Scotland and persecuted in their new home because they were Protestants. The early settlers' objection to the Irish was the result of their objection to papist ritual and what they regarded as idolatry. It was so strong and became so important a part of Merrimack Valley tradition that, in spite of some efforts toward a revision, in which Franklin Pierce was prominent, the New Hampshire Constitution contained until 1877—along with its article which is still in force, sanctioning the overthrow of existing government if the people should feel that it acted abusively and that they had no redress—a provision stating that the governor and other high officials of the state must be Protestants.

Perhaps this somewhat hysterical lack of common sense and charity was no more extraordinary than the fear of the French, which helped to wreck the Federalists in the early 1800's, or the twentieth century's orgy of anti-Russian feeling. As many other hostilities have done, it eventually evaporated under personal contact.

The settlers of Penacook, which was incorporated under Massachusetts laws in 1733 as Rumford, were troubled by hostile Indians far less than their neighbors to the south, east and west. Penacook had been, at least in the warm months of the year, the home of the fabulous Passaconaway and his son Wonalancet, and in some sense headquarters of the Penacook Confederacy. Here in the intervals along the meanders of the Merrimack the Indians cultivated the land, growing the usual corn, beans, pumpkins and squash. It is said that Passaconaway's own squash patch was in the very spot now occupied by the farm of the New Hampshire State Prison, where the largest squashes in New Hampshire are grown today.

BEGIN IN BLOOD

The Penacook Indians were, when left alone, friendly with the white newcomers and in fact in the first years, before the settlers had learned how to support themselves, were instrumental in saving them from starvation. Indian hostility was more or less limited to a period between 1744 and 1760. The only serious Indian depredation took place in 1746. On August eleventh of that year a party of men from Captain Daniel Ladd's company from Exeter, with one man from a Massachusetts company, under the leadership of Lieutenant Jonathan Bradley set out from Rumford town heading for a garrison house near what was later called Millville.

Lieutenant Bradley had no kindly feelings toward the Indians. He hailed from Haverhill, where most of his relatives had had tragic experiences with the common enemy. His grandfather's house was burned by the Indians and his grandmother was twice taken prisoner, the second time when she was carrying a child to which she gave birth on her foot journey through the wilderness to Canada, a journey during which she had nothing to eat but bits of skin, beechnuts and acorns, wild onions, tree bark and lily roots. Mrs. Bradley bore

her child unaided in the midst of the forest, to the disgust of
the Indians who saw that it was sickly and would hamper
their travel. When the baby cried, they threw embers into its
mouth, a procedure which was not calculated to quiet it. Some
of the Indians wished to kill it at once, but they decided to let
it live out what maimed life was left to it if the mother would
let them baptize it in their own manner.

Mrs. Bradley, it may be imagined, had no choice in the
matter. She was compelled to watch while her captors gashed
the baby's forehead with their knives. It must have survived
this ordeal, for it was alive when later on, Mrs. Bradley not
being near, they pierced its body with a sharpened stick which
they stuck in the ground.

Jonathan Bradley had heard this tale from his mother
and knew the long list of Bradleys who had been killed in
Indian attacks, five of them, two of them children, in the raid
which had carried off Hannah Dustin and Mary Neff. On
that August day in 1746 it must have infuriated him that after
fifty years the Merrimack was not free of such a scourge. He
led his men along the path out of Rumford, ready, as he supposed, for anything.

As the party of eight soldiers marched westward along
the wooded path, one of them, Daniel Gilman, moved ahead
in search of a hawk which he had seen. When he was fifty or
sixty rods ahead of his companions, he heard shots and, thinking that the others had been lucky enough to start a deer, ran
back to a rise of ground from which he could make out what
was going on. He saw nothing but gun smoke, but he says
that he heard Lieutenant Bradley cry out to the others, "Lord
haver mercy on me:—Fight!" Then there was a confusion of
shots, yells and shrieks, during which Daniel Gilman made
tracks for home.

Abner Clough, the clerk of the company, later wrote

down what he knew of the fight. Five men, says Clough, were "killed down dead on the spot. . . . It was supposed that John Lufkin was upon the front, and Obadiah Peters on the rear: and they shot down this Lufkin and Peters the first shot, as they were in the path, about fourteen rods apart; and they shot Samuel Bradley, Jonathan's brother, as he was about twelve feet before where this Obadiah Peters lay, and wounded (him) so that the blood started every step he took. He went about five rods in the path, and they shot him right through his powder horn, as it hung by his side and so through his body—and there lay these three men, lying in the path—and Lieut. Bradley run out of the path, about two rods, right in amongst the Indians. He was shot through his wrist. It was supposed that he fought (as he stood there in the spot where he was killed,) till the Indians cut his head almost to pieces; and John Bean run about six rods out of the path on the other side of the way, and was shot right through his body;—so that there were none of these men that went one or two steps after they were shot, excepting this Samuel Bradley that was shot as above said."

The Indians stripped some of the bodies, took all their equipment, and went off with four of their own dead and a number of wounded. An oxcart was brought from Rumford and the mangled naked bodies were loaded into it and driven through lines of villagers, weeping and holding up children to see the passing horror.

A granite obelisk, close to the new Concord Hospital, marks the burial site of the victims of this bloody struggle, which kept the people of Rumford in terror for several years. Rumford men played a large part, many of them under Major Robert Rogers and the Stark brothers, in the French and Indian Wars which followed, but most of the fighting was done away from home.

By 1760 the promise of peace which had come to New England had been felt in Rumford. It was a busy farming center and a crossroads between the Connecticut River settlements and the thriving towns of the lower Merrimack.

In 1767, when the first provincial census was taken, Concord showed the following:

Unmarried men, from sixteen to sixty	62
Married men, from sixteen to sixty	125
Boys, sixteen and under	189
Men, sixty and above	18
Females, unmarried	204
Females, married	126
Male slaves	9
Female slaves	4
Widows	15
Total	752

THE EXILED COUNT

It was in 1772 that there came to Concord from Woburn, Massachusetts, as a schoolteacher, that inquiring young friend of Loammi Baldwin, Benjamin Thompson. He had shown extraordinary intellectual vigor as a child and as a fatherless boy of fourteen he was enough of a mathematician to predict a solar eclipse with an error of only four seconds. He had been apprenticed for a time to a physician in Woburn, his birthplace, during which period he spent his spare time making surgical instruments of extraordinarily fine temper and finish. While apprenticed to a storekeeper in Salem, he experimented with explosives and in the course of an attempt to create a rocket he had an accident which severely damaged not only his face and hands but his master's store. He returned to his remarried mother in Woburn after this event and it is said that he was not appreciated there, his mother believing him to be less a genius than a jack-of-all-trades destined to be master of none. It was at this time that he attended lectures at Harvard with Loammi Baldwin. The acquisition of knowledge did not immediately pay cash dividends. It was necessary for the boy to do something profitable and schoolteaching seemed a suitable employment.

Benjamin taught for a while in Bradford, Massachusetts, but soon moved up the Merrimack to Rumford, which had recently become Concord. He was, in spite of the scars of his experience with the rocket in Salem, a remarkably presentable young man who dressed with an un-Puritan flourish and rode a horse as if he were part of it. He wrote like a master of style and as a schoolteacher was often asked to compose resolutions and letters for the town government. At age nineteen, when he had been in Concord for less than a year, he attracted the attention of the widow of one of the town's leading citizens and reputedly its wealthiest man. Sarah Rolfe, then thirty-three years old, after her brief marriage to Benjamin Rolfe, an ailing man in his sixties, was perhaps predisposed toward the glamour of precocious manhood which emanated from the younger Benjamin. Thompson said that he "married, or rather I was married" to the daughter of a highly respected minister and one of the first settlers of the town. This, be it said, was an understatement, as Sarah's father, Timothy Walker, was the town's first minister, served in the pulpit until his death, a period of fifty-two years, and was always a leader in the affairs of the town. Thus Benjamin Thompson, whether he was the seeker or the sought-for, reached within a year of his arrival there the top rung of the ladder in Concord.

It is said that after his marriage he took his bride to Woburn to call on his somewhat skeptical mother. The couple arrived in a splendid carriage with Benjamin arrayed in scarlet velvet, complete with powdered wig and silken hose. What the bride wore is not recorded, but it is recorded that Ben received from his mother not a gasp of admiration but the crushing exclamation, "Why, Ben, my child! how could you spend your whole winter's wages in this way!"

Ben's style and more-than-adult dignity did, however, elicit admiration from John Wentworth, Governor of New Hampshire, who, liking the manner in which the young man sat his horse and discoursed on military matters, made him a major of militia. This was, to Benjamin, not so much a preferment as a recognition of his devotion to order and method. This devotion, which was the keynote of Benjamin Thompson's character, gave him a deep distaste for what he considered the disorder of revolutionary ideas, which were, in the Concord of the early 1770's, as thick as the leaves on her trees. The people of Concord, not as easily ravished as Sarah Rolfe by the brilliant fellow's personal splendor, came to distrust him and his link to the Governor.

The events of April, 1775, filled him with horror, a horror which even the wealth and devotion of his bride of two years could not make bearable. Leaving his wife and their year-old daughter, Sarah, in the old Rolfe mansion, Benjamin Thompson made his way to the British lines and managed to get to Providence, Rhode Island, from which place he went by boat to Boston, where General Gage gave him dispatches to carry to England to the hands of Lord George Germain.

On the Thames the young man's outstanding personality seems to have advanced him as rapidly as it had done in the simpler atmosphere of the Merrimack. By 1780 he had been made under secretary of the department for the colonies. He saw his native land once more shortly thereafter when as a lieutenant-colonel he was sent with a regiment to New York;

though the end of the war soon made it necessary for him to return to England. His ideas of personal splendor made him interested in continuing a military career, although the British Army seemed, at the moment, under something of a cloud. He decided to join the Austrian Army and find glory fighting the Turks. For this purpose he went to Strasbourg where he met Prince Maximilian, the future Elector of Bavaria, who like everyone but the Americans was fascinated by the young man from the Merrimack. The Prince invited Benjamin to join him, provided that he could get a release from British service. Thompson not only got the release but word from George III that he was now Sir Benjamin! Things were indeed going well.

Sir Benjamin Thompson spent the next eleven years at Munich as minister of war, minister of police and grand chamberlain of Bavaria. He reorganized the army and, by a clever stratagem, disorganized Munich's powerful and odious army of beggars. In one day he had twenty-six hundred of them arrested and transferred to work barracks, previously prepared, in which they were taught trades and kept working at them, the products of their industry being sold for the benefit of the state. His comment on this achievement is interesting: "To make vicious and abandoned people happy," he said, "it has generally been supposed necessary first to make them virtuous. But why not reverse this order? Why not make them first happy, and then virtuous?"

During these busy years, the exiled Woburn wizard did not neglect his scientific activities. He contributed papers to European and English scientific societies. He was instrumental, with the celebrated Sir Joseph Banks, who had been to the Pacific with Captain Cook, in founding the Royal Institution in 1779. He founded the Rumford Medal of the Royal Society and was, as a matter of fact, its first recipient.

He set up a like award, also under the name of his former home, in the American Academy of Arts and Sciences and endowed a professorship at Harvard. In 1798 he presented a paper to the Royal Society in which he successfully destroyed the then-current notion that heat was a substance. He also conducted experiments calculated to improve the efficiency of chimneys. His life should have been as happy as it was active, but it was not. The wife whom he had left in Concord died in 1792, perhaps without learning of her estranged husband's greatest honor and his most pathetic gesture in the direction of his native land. In 1791 when, having no other rewards left to bestow upon Sir Benjamin Thompson, the Elector of Bavaria made the still-young man a count of the Holy Roman Empire, Sir Benjamin chose for his title the early name of that memorable town which, when he arrived in it, was just getting used to the new name of Concord. He became Benjamin Thompson, Count Rumford, and as such he has been known ever since.

I have said that he was not happy, for all his honors. He must always have felt some poignance of regret that the banks of the Merrimack were not for him. He tried to bring the atmosphere of New England to him after his wife's death by having his daughter, then a young lady of seventeen, come to live with him abroad. Yet the Count's subsequent marriage to the widow of the great French chemist, Lavoisier, was not a happy one in spite of the lady's wealth. In 1814, separated from the former Mme. Lavoisier, he died at Auteuil, perhaps regretting that his passion for pomp and circumstance had kept him from giving his remarkable talents to the fresh and strong young country which his native land became.

His daughter, Sarah, who inherited the title of Countess of Rumford, lived abroad for twenty years but returned to

Concord to spend her last years and to distribute her considerable wealth, which her father had accumulated as a result of marriage and royal service, among several Concord institutions, chiefly the Rolfe and Rumford Asylum and the New Hampshire Asylum for the Insane.

COACHING DAYS

The Concord of the early nineteenth century was a peaceful town of slow but steady growth. Its selection as the capital of the state and its subsequent connection by boat, in 1815, with the downriver towns gave it an importance far beyond its size, as is indicated by its 1820 population of 2,838. It remained primarily a farming community, its meadows enriched by the otherwise-disturbing spring freshets of the river.

Yet it must not be supposed that river traffic was all that gave the town of Concord its push toward completeness as a community. Like other towns in the interior before the days of the factory, it produced within its own borders most of what it used or consumed, the exceptions being certain items, mostly of hardware, which were made in other regions or imported. The eighteenth century had seen an increase in the number of roads leading into and across the interior, if not exactly an improvement on their quality. Passenger and freight service by coach and wagon developed before canals had made river traffic feasible.

Concord, being a self-sufficient center of a large agricultural and lumbering region and a gateway to the north and west, became a center for coaching, freight carrying and droving. By 1818—only a few years before the canal and the railroad brought a virtual end to long-distance coaching in the East—this New Hampshire capital became the center of coach

manufacturing, and the Concord coach became celebrated throughout the world as the most perfect vehicle ever devised for road transportation behind horses.

In 1813, Lewis Downing began the manufacture of carriages in Concord and in 1828 took on as a partner a Concord man who had been experimenting with coach bodies in the Downing shop, J. Stephens Abbot. The partnership, at first under the name of Downing and Abbot, lasted for nineteen years, after which Abbot and his son set up a separate business, which they continued until Abbot and Downing came together again in 1865 as Abbot, Downing and Company. In 1873 the firm became the Abbot-Downing Company, by which name it is best known and as which it produced vehicles—at the end, motor trucks—until 1928. There is a fire engine still operating in Concord which was manufactured by Abbot-Downing.

The Concord coach is familiar to devotees of Western films as the coach of the later pioneers and Buffalo Bill's Wild

West shows. For seventy-five or eighty years the Concord coach was made and shipped from the banks of the Merrimack to the banks of the Volga, the Amazon, the Congo, in fact to every country in the world. It was a triumph of engineering and a work of art as well. A specimen built in the 1850's, found in a barn in Tamworth, New Hampshire, in the early 1900's, stood in the Boston and Maine Railroad station in Concord for many years. It was recently presented to the New Hampshire Historical Society and is on permanent exhibition at the Society's headquarters.

When coaching was at its height, there was no more coaching-conscious town than Concord. The streets in winter were always full of picturesque drivers in leather boots, fur caps and buffalo skins held about them by red silk sashes, their noses red from cold and the rum and cider provided enthusiastically by their devoted customers. Every year in Concord there was a great coaching parade, followed by a Stagemen's Ball attended by Knights of the Whip from all over New England. This glamorous and certainly boisterous festival was held in the Grecian Hall above the carriage houses attached to the Eagle Coffee-house, now the Eagle Hotel on Main Street. The ball held in January, 1840, was attended by more than 150 couples. Such happy occasions were perhaps one of the reasons for the activity in Concord during the 1830's and 1840's of a very strong temperance movement aimed at eliminating alcohol from everything but medicine.

THE VILLAGE BECOMES A CITY

Concord in the nineteenth century was a well-balanced town. As the seat of the state government it attracted families of wealth and intellectual distinction and as the center of a large productive area it attracted the most skillful mechanics and artisans. The variety of its business and other activities in 1834, at the height of the coaching era, is illustrated by the following facts taken from the directory of that year. In addition to the state buildings and institutions there were: 5 meeting houses, 3 school houses, 10 hotels and taverns, 2 banks, 1 savings bank, 11 printing offices, 10 newspapers, 26 "English and West India goods" stores, 1 hard-ware store, 1 crockery ware store, 3 apothecaries, 3 hat stores, 4 clothes and drapery stores, 6 book stores, 5 book binderies, 1 circulating library, 9 shoe stores and manufactories, 7 blacksmiths, 3 wheelwrights, 4 furniture warehouses and cabinet shops, 2 bakeries, 9 tailor and tailoress shops, 3 slaughter houses, 1 last manufactory, 1 whip maker, 1 silver plating establishment, 1 looking-glass factory, 1 carver and gilder, 4 millinery shops, 1 market house, 3 victualling cellars, 2 chair manufactories, 1 comb manufactory, 1 boat maker, 1 confectionery store, 3 watch makers and jewellers, 1 clock factory, 1 grave stone maker, 1 chemical apparatus and soap manufactory, 8 joiner shops, 5 paint shops, 1 cooperage shop, 2 livery stables and 2 barber shops.

This is a revealing picture of the activities and economy, the culture and the customs of a town of approximately forty-two hundred people in 1834, before there was a single line of railroad track in all the Merrimack Valley.

In spite of Concord's growth from a small frontier settlement to the position which it has occupied for more than a century and a quarter as capital of the state of New Hampshire, it presents to this day the aspect of a country town rather than that of a city. It is cultured yet unsophisticated, and although its physical aspect is less like what it must have been 150 years ago than is the case with Newburyport, its life and its people perhaps resemble those of the Federal era more closely than do those of the older Massachusetts city from which many Concord families came.

During the railroad age of the second half of the nineteenth century, the activities of the General Court were fantastic and picturesque, as indeed in a less frenzied manner they are to this day. Two of the novels of New Hampshire by Winston Churchill give colorful pictures of the political life of the state and capital. *Coniston* and *Mr. Crewe's Career*, both written after Churchill had served a term in the New Hampshire General Court, are full of the unique personality of New Hampshire and the little big town on the Merrimack and reflect, as the river reflects the walls and spires of the city, in a kind of genial tranquillity, the nature of the people of the valley.

MEN AND LAWS

The State House was built in 1819 of local granite with a little help from the alien marble of Vermont. Within it meets the largest—outside the Congress of the United States —and certainly the most remarkable legislative body in North America. The building has been enlarged and improved since it was first put to use, and the legislature which it houses has been enlarged also, even if its improvement is not so marked. The General Court has a personality which is characteristic of the state and the city in which it meets.

Concord and its life, thoroughly American and up-to-date, yet preserves the atmosphere of the culmination of Merrimack Valley pioneering. Just as descendants of the original settlers still walk its streets, so their character, their heartiness and their faith and courage still fill the bowl of the hill-encircled town deeper than even a spring freshet of the Merrimack ever could.

The Constitution of the State of New Hampshire, adopted after much trial and error in 1783, provided for a General Court, a legislature composed of twelve senators and one representative for each 150 rateable polls in each town, or two representatives for each 450 rateable polls. The Constitution as amended to date provides for a Senate of twenty-four members and a House of Representatives of not less than 375 nor more than four hundred members. This, in a state with a population of some 560,000 and a voting strength of at most half of that, is fairly complete representation. The result is that a session of the New Hampshire Legislature is something like a town meeting—a town meeting conducted with a high degree of decorum and dignity.

As towns which are too small for representation in every biennial session are guaranteed the privilege of sending a delegate to the General Court at least once in every ten years, there can be no complaint that the people of New Hampshire have no political opportunity to speak for themselves. It is true that they do not always wisely take advantage of the opportunity. Representatives to the General Court are often elected for reasons which have little or nothing to do with their ability to serve their fellow townsmen.

A New Hampshire senator receives the same pay as a member of the state House of Representatives—the same pay provided by the Constitution of the state when it began to operate in 1784. Two hundred dollars for a two-year tour of duty, with a mileage allowance and three dollars a day for an extra session if one is called, is not exactly attractive compensation. Since the rate of pay can only be changed by constitutional amendment and the regular constitutional conventions never come up with an amendment, it is not strange that the New Hampshire Legislature should have a very high percentage of elderly men who are either retired from business or have little or nothing else to do; nor is it strange that, such being the case, the active business of the General Court should customarily be conducted by not more than one third of its elected members. What may seem strange is that the standard of legislation is extremely high. Bad bills sometimes do become laws but few good bills are lost. When they are lost, it is usually because their sponsors failed to take the political character of the New Hampshire Legislature into consideration. Members of the General Court are, for the most part, fearful of the concentration of power, suspicious of experts and fairly certain that their individual judgment could not be improved upon. Voting is conducted more by instinctive reaction than by adherence to party lines. Lobbying is, as in other states, a factor, but in spite of the low salary of the legislators, is seldom profitable. New Hampshire lawgivers do not like to be told what to do. Some of them are not above accepting favors or entertainment, but few pay for what they get by voting as the lobbyist expects them to.

During a term which I recently served in the lower house, a bill was brought in which I and others felt endangered the liberty of the writers and publishers of books, not to mention readers. I joined those who spoke before the committee which was holding hearings on the bill, explaining my belief that it was unwise to endanger the distribution of books which contain more good than harm by attempting to establish a definition of obscenity which would be universally acceptable. I said that I believed that the laws then on the books were perfectly adequate to prevent the circulation of a book or magazine which a jury might decide was thoroughly bad. The committee seemed to agree, for the bill was unanimously reported to the House as inexpedient to legislate. The sponsor of the bill promptly rose to move that the committee's recommendation be discarded and the words "ought to pass" be substituted for "inexpedient to legislate."

After the chairman of the committee which had considered the bill had spoken in favor of the committee's recommendation, the Speaker of the House recognized me and permitted me to oppose the motion. I explained to the House what I conceived the dangers of censorship to be, explaining my belief that laws passed to correct moral abuses were all too often twisted about and made to serve quite different ends. A taste for pornography, I pointed out, is not the natural result of exposure to indecency but rather of faulty moral and spiritual education. No book, I said, could make a clean mind dirty and no law could make a dirty mind clean.

When I sat down I believed that I and the others who had joined me had carried the House along with us, in spite of the fact that one member rose and with impassioned, if irrelevant, eloquence complained that our boys in Korea were being subjected to solicitation by evil women and he wanted it stopped. With a magnificent sweep of the arm toward the portraits of Washington, Lincoln, Daniel Webster, Franklin Pierce and John P. Hale which hung from the chaste wall behind the speaker's rostrum, he shouted, "How would you like to see them up there with nothing on?" The member looked at me as he sat down, as if I had plotted to disrobe the heroes. This was a form of eloquence which I had failed to take into consideration. Combined with activity on the part of the bill's sponsor, who had explained to the committee that in the course of his crusading he had built up the finest collection of filthy postcards, pictures, books and magazines in the state, this speech won the day. The sponsor had, while the debate was in progress, gone about through the House and distributed choice specimens from his collection of pornographic

art, explaining that they had been purchased in Manchester but not explaining that the sellers could have been prosecuted under existing law. This stratagem had the effect of producing a number of very red faces in the House and enough rather emotional speeches to sway the membership in the direction of a vote to substitute "ought to pass" for "inexpedient to legislate." The Senate subsequently passed the bill, the Governor signed it, and it became a law on June 11, 1953.

I have cited this example of lawmaking in Concord as an indication of a mood, a picture of a state of mind. The House often pays little attention to the fact that a committee has studied a bill carefully and soberly before making its recommendation. The sponsor of a bill which a committee totally rejects often finds it easy to persuade the House that the members of the committee are setting themselves up as experts and authorities whose edicts should be regarded with suspicion. When the House's emotions are aroused in this manner, opposition is useless.

Yet common sense in the capitol at Concord is, happily, as it has been for 140 years, more common than emotion. The same alert obstinacy, the same refusal to budge unless convinced of the advisability of doing so, exists in the Legislature today that existed during the deliberations of that infant gathering of alarmed freemen which met in Newbury more than three hundred years ago. The New Hampshire General Court is, on the whole, as honest, sober and effective a body of legislators as is to be found in any state in the union. It often reflects, perhaps wisely, the tendency of the people of the Merrimack Valley to be slow to destroy existing things. An illustration of this tendency was provided a few years ago when several changes in the Constitution were submitted to the voters of the state. One of these was a proposal to eliminate the article 57, which had stood unchallenged since 1783, providing that the state's money should be reckoned in shillings and pence. The article was eliminated, but many people in many towns voted to retain it. New Hampshire people do not like to be pushed, either forward or, I am glad to say, backward.

The fields and forests, the towns and villages of the Merrimack Valley have changed, but the character of the people like the character of the river itself has remained basically the same. Reflected in the waters of the Merrimack from its banks and bridges is no fictional, inbred, worn-out race of diminished giants, but genial, shrewd and robust people, capable of love and faith in high degree; not perhaps entirely of one mind as to what they want and how to get it, but able to act in concert on great issues, to meet disaster and turn it into promise, to be and to create, to radiate, as always, throughout the nation that painstaking genius which is the product in flesh of three hundred years of faith, struggle and slow but sure understanding.

16 The Lion and the Lamb

It is said that a great statesman, who perhaps was not thinking of himself at the time, once accounted for the huge stone face of the Old Man of the Mountain by saying that, as merchants of the city display signs outside their doors to indicate the kind of goods to be found within, the Almighty had placed his sign on that cliff above the headwaters of the Merrimack to indicate that men were the product of the region.

This statesman was one of the greatest of the men produced in the Merrimack Valley, one of the truly massive personalities of American history whose death at the wrong time has affected posterity's estimate of him. Daniel Webster was born in 1782 in a house which is still standing between the Merrimack and the Blackwater Rivers in what was then the town of Salisbury but is now Franklin, New Hampshire, which is not far from the spot at which the Merrimack assumes its name.

It is interesting to note that another eminent man born at the other end of the river, in Haverhill, Massachusetts, although twenty-five years younger than Webster, became famous during the period of the elder man's greatness for participation in national affairs in a distinctly antithetical, but at the time more widely approved, manner. The contrasts in the expression of that great force which the Merrimack seems to have given to its sons are nowhere better illustrated than in the overlapping careers of Daniel Webster and John Greenleaf Whittier.

Daniel Webster's boyhood was spent not on the farm where he was born but in a house in the township of Franklin, nearer the Merrimack, to which Captain Ebenezer Webster, his father, and his mother, Abigail Eastman Webster, moved when Daniel was only a year old.

Daniel's father was a remarkable man, a strong patriot, a vigorous farmer, a wise and tender parent, self-educated, almost self-propelled, who never shirked a service to his country or his fellow men. He served in the General Court of New Hampshire and on the bench as a Judge of the Court of Common Pleas. Daniel and his elder brother, Ezekiel, adored the tall and handsome man who seems to have thought more of them than he did of himself. Ebenezer Webster was about as far from the literary conception of a rockbound New Englander as could well be imagined. He saw men about him going farther than he—to the Federal Congress for one thing— and he was resolved that his sons should not lack the education of which he had been unable to avail himself. The Webster family life was warm and human and sunny. Captain Webster needed help on his farm even more than he needed money, and it would have been natural with two sons at home to work them to the limit of their capacity. Yet he was aware that as a boy Daniel was frail and must not be counted on for heavy work. So the boy was taught to read early and allowed to fish and wander in the woods and fields, which to him were like a heaven about the solid earth of his home. There was so much love in the Webster household that it is small wonder that love illuminated the mind's eye through which Daniel saw the Merrimack Valley countryside. He saw the distant mountains and the nearby wildflowers and he

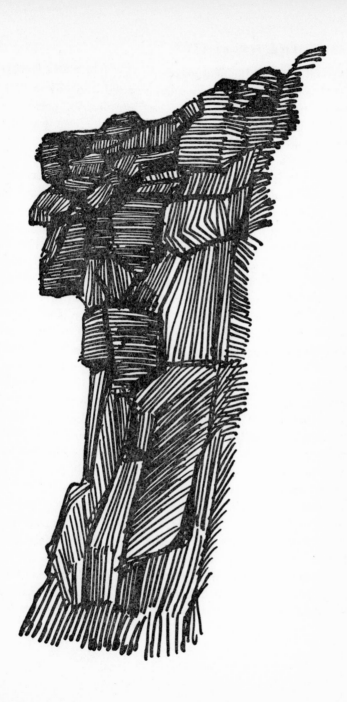

watched the wild life of woods and fields. It was he who first noted how the shad and the salmon parted company in their upriver runs, the former turning east into the Winnipesaukee and the latter clinging to the swifter, colder waters of the Pemigewasset.

Captain Webster had everything but money, but he decided that what money he had should go toward the best possible schooling for the sensitive and eager boy who, save in health, was so much like him. Daniel, while Ezekiel, two years older and far more robust, helped with the farm, was entered at the new and growing Phillips Academy at Exeter. Here his capacity and ability became known to his masters but his performance did not reach its peak. Daniel felt out of place and shy in his country-bumpkin clothes. He was not a good speller and, although his ability to read was extraordinary, he was all thumbs when it came to writing, and we have his own word for the fact that he was totally unable to stand up and recite before his class.

After nine months at Exeter, Daniel returned home and was put out to tutor, at the age of fifteen, with the Reverend Samuel Wood of Boscawen. On the way to Boscawen, Captain Webster told his son that he planned to send him to college. "I remember," said Daniel later, "the very hill which we were ascending, through deep snows, in a New England sleigh, when my father made known his purpose to me. I could not speak. How could he, I thought, with so large a family, and in such narrow circumstances, think of incurring so great an expense for me? A warm glow ran all over me, and I laid my head on my father's shoulder and wept."

Daniel made such progress under his Boscawen tutor that Dr. Wood remarked jocularly after six months that he was tired of him and was going to send him to college to get rid of him. He did. Daniel entered Dartmouth in August, 1797, at the age of fifteen.

The first year of college was to Daniel as sun is to an unopened bud. He saw for the first time what might lie ahead of an educated man, but he saw, too, that the opportunity offered him was—if it made it necessary for his brother, Ezekiel, to stick to the soil of the farm—likely to prove a widening gulf between him and the companion whom he loved. Daniel and Ezekiel talked all one night about this problem and it was Daniel's decision to tell his father that he would return to college only if Ezekiel were given an equal if belated chance to get an education.

Captain Webster, when consulted, said that, if it were up to him, he would give everything he had to educate both boys but that, as it would be hardest on their mother and two unmarried sisters, they must be consulted. Abigail Webster did not hesitate. "I will trust the boys," she said. She did not believe that she was gambling. If she was, it was on a sure thing.

Ezekiel went to school in Salisbury and Daniel went back to Dartmouth where he earned, in various ways, more than enough for his board and tuition. What he did not need could be applied to Ezekiel's expenses and a teaching job during vacation helped still more. Daniel, in Hanover, worked over his deficiencies. From a boy who could not recite before his own small class, he became a young man who could with the magic of his personality and his careful wit cast a spell over an audience of strangers. It must have amazed those who had known him at Exeter to hear that Daniel Webster, aged eighteen, had been selected by Dartmouth College and Hanover town to deliver the town's Fourth of July oration in 1800.

When Daniel graduated, he was not first in his class but,

had Dartmouth classes at that time voted for the incumbent of any such category, he would surely have been chosen "most likely to succeed." It was at the law that, with the help and advice of his father, he chose to succeed. While Ezekiel took his turn at Dartmouth, Daniel worked in the office of Thomas W. Thompson, a distinguished lawyer of Salisbury. This apprenticeship was to be a happy time for the young man, who at that time loved reading above everything. In addition to the required reading for a law clerk, he read Shakespeare and Milton and other English poets of the sixteenth and seventeenth centuries. He hunted and fished and served writs, some of which he wrote in rhyme, with gay enthusiasm.

THINKING ALONE

Reading law, pleasant and intellectually profitable as it was, produced little cash, however, and Ezekiel's expenses were increasing. True to what he believed to be his duty, Daniel took a teaching job in Fryeburg, in what is now Maine though it was then part of Massachusetts, where he earned extra money in his spare time by copying deeds for the Registrar of Oxford County. In May 1802, at the age of twenty, he rode on horseback from Fryeburg to Hanover during a week's vacation to present his first quarter's salary to Ezekiel.

Daniel Webster's ambition at this time was to see, to learn, to love and to help those whom he loved. He was gay and happy, yet he took himself seriously, rarely making a decision without considering both sides of it. At Fryeburg he considered carefully whether he should develop his sure foothold in that town and be content with a small but certain bird in the hand or risk a return to the more doubtful emoluments of the law. Even with his obligations to his family in mind, he chose the law and returned to the Salisbury office which he had left to go to Fryeburg. Here the remarkable qualities of his sure mind began to show themselves. He read and reread and, as he said, never put down a book without going over his formed opinion of it, so that the portent of his reading drawn within his mind became a part of his own thought. His amusements at this time were, as he has said, ". . . fishing, shooting and riding; and all these were without a companion. I loved this occasional solitude then, and have loved it ever since, and love it still. I like to contemplate nature, and to hold communion, unbroken by the presence of human beings, with 'this universal frame—this wondrous fair.' I like solitude also, as favorable to thoughts less lofty. I like to let the thoughts go free, and indulge excursions. And when *thinking* is to be done, one must, of course, be alone. No man knows *himself* who does not thus sometimes keep his own company."

Thus did the Merrimack country enter the mind of Daniel Webster, one of those elements of his wisdom which, like the country of literature, helped to make up for the deficiencies of the lawyer's profession.

At the close of his struggle to stay at Dartmouth, Ezekiel Webster got an offer of an excellent teaching job in Boston, which he accepted, and Daniel, his responsibility lightened, went to Boston at Ezekiel's urging and with his father's blessing to look for a job in a law office with more promise than Salisbury could offer. He found what he was looking for in the office of a brilliant and politically inclined lawyer, Christopher Gore, who later became Governor of Massachusetts and a United States Senator from that state. During his few months in Gore's office, Daniel Webster had an opportunity to visit the courts frequently and to watch the greatest lawyers in action. He was impressed but not overawed. He saw their talents, but he also saw their defects. By this time he knew

that the law was his. So much a part of his life had the law become that when he was offered the clerkship of the Court of Common Pleas of Hillsborough County, New Hampshire, a job which Ebenezer Webster had spent much effort trying to get for him, Daniel, advised by Christopher Gore, faced his father and told him that he was going on with the law and must refuse the offer.

In March, 1805, Daniel Webster was admitted to the bar and promptly returned to New Hampshire to practice, choosing Boscawen as being the place nearest his father's home, although Portsmouth was where he wished to be. In spite of the limitations of practice in Boscawen, he did not succumb to the deadly routine of the small-town lawyer. He surrounded himself with books to augment nature and never ceased to try to get within his digesting mind as much of the outside world as possible. He acquired a knowledge of European politics and their relationship to the young United States, which was of tremendous value to himself and his country at a later date. Buried, as some might have called it, in a tiny Merrimack town which offered little intellectual companionship other than that of woods and fields, he was able to see his profession as few others of his day saw it.

"Study," he said, "is the grand requisite for a lawyer. . . . Let there be a genius for whom Nature has done so much as apparently to have left nothing for application, yet, to make a lawyer, application must do as much as if nature had done nothing. The evil is that an accursed thirst for money violates everything. We cannot study because we must pettifog. We learn the law recourses of attorneyism, when we should learn the conceptions, the reasonings, and the opinions of Cicero and Murray. The love of fame is extinguished, every ardent wish for knowledge repressed; conscience put in jeopardy, and the best feelings of the heart indurated by the mean, money-catching, abominable practices which cover with disgrace a part of the modern practitioners of the law. . . . Our profession is good, if practised in the spirit of it; it is damnable fraud and iniquity when its true spirit is supplied by a spirit of mischief-making and money-catching."

In April, 1806, Ebenezer Webster died very much encumbered and Daniel voluntarily assumed the obligation of paying his debts, a task which was only completed after many years. Daniel remained in Boscawen, unrewarding as his practice there was, until his brother Ezekiel could finish a law course in Boston. When that was done, Ezekiel went to live with his mother and sisters and run the farm, taking over Daniel's practice at Boscawen. Daniel, now free to be on his own, moved to Portsmouth in September, 1807, three months before John Greenleaf Whittier, who in Stephen Bachelder (or Bacheler) had a common ancestor, was born twenty-five miles away on the banks of the Merrimack in Haverhill, Massachusetts.

TWO ROADS TAKEN

The Quaker home of the Whittiers was the center, like the Websters', of a farm. Its atmosphere was, like the Websters', one of familiar devotion. Yet there was a difference. In the Haverhill home love seems to have existed without personal pleasure, no less strong than in the homestead at the upper end of the river but less outgoing. John Greenleaf, like Daniel, not robust but inclined to make nature a companion, appears, in spite of the closeness of his family ties, to have taken less warmth from his father's parenthood than Webster did from his. Nothing human was alien to the Websters' life, but there were doors in the Whittier world which must not be opened. Whether this difference determined the directions in which the two significant lives of these two Merrimack men moved, it is not possible to be certain. It is possible that it did. It is certain that the directions were, in one sense at least, opposite.

Daniel Webster was a mature man when John Greenleaf Whittier was a hesitant boy. When in 1812 the United States, faced with two blustering enemies abroad, chose for an adversary the British instead of the French, Webster was a successful and immensely happy lawyer, making a name for himself in New Hampshire's most important city. He was making enough money to support a wife and daughter whom he adored and still to make inroads on his dead father's debts. It seemed impossible for him to make enemies or to avoid making friends without effort. Everyone was drawn to him. He had been known at Dartmouth as Black Dan, for the raven hue of his hair and eyes and the swarthiness of his complexion, yet those black eyes drew people to him and he was generally regarded as a man of great beauty. His expression was that of one whose inner self was something he could live with without pain.

Until the War of 1812, Daniel Webster had had little to do with politics. He was interested in what went on, but he did not regard political life as a path to success. He lacked that all-consuming enthusiasm for contrivance, which distinguishes the earnest young politician. He had inherited from the father whom he adored, and who gave to the concept of authority in the son's mind a benign and respect-commanding dignity, a devotion to the principles of the Federalists. Daniel was inclined to regard absolute democracy as somewhat dangerous, a belief which never entirely left him and which in his later years was to bring him his greatest disappointment. He believed—in spite of his own experience—that wealth and its opportunities produced and maintained intelligence and that the Federalist party embraced a majority of the talent, character and wealth of the nation. In his belief he was fortified by the nature of his clientele, which during his years in Portsmouth embraced more and more persons of wealth and social standing. Among them were many closely connected with the great and growing shipping interests of New England, threatened, since the coming to power of Jeffersonians, by the Embargo and the conflicts and confusions of the tariff.

Yet Webster, regarding the Federal Union as a kind and wise father, could not support those self-serving Federalists who were secretly, if ineffectually, plotting to withdraw New England from the Union. He believed that improvement in the condition of New England should come about as a result of public argument and the use of the ballot. Those who knew Webster's belief saw to it that he represented Portsmouth in a Rockingham County meeting of Federalists in 1812. At this meeting he presented a memorial against the administration's war policy, which got him nominated as a Federalist candidate for Congress, resulted in his election in November, and launched him upon a political career from which he was never afterward able to separate himself completely, a career which brought him both glory and tragedy.

After a brief but brilliant spell in the House, he gave up office-holding as a representative of the people in New Hampshire and moved to Boston, where he continued to fight publicly for free trade, sound currency and a strong Federal Union, and against the extension of slavery. His desire for free trade, however, was a result of his belief that it would benefit the harassed shipbuilders and shipowners of Massachusetts.

One of the high points of Webster's career came in 1818, when he represented Dartmouth College before the Supreme Court in an appeal against the decision of a New Hampshire court that the state had a right to alter the college's charter and make it a state institution naturally subject to political influence. Webster's argument before the Supreme Court established him at the head of his profession at the age of thirty-six. His private practice increased enormously and began to bring him an income of between fifteen and twenty thousand dollars a year, none too much for a man of his tastes, among which, in addition to a taste for meeting his long-dead-father's obligations, were a taste for the ease and richness of generous living and for often ill-considered speculation.

With his reputation as a lawyer at its peak and with confidence that at any time he wished he could make up any deficiency in his income caused by his service to his country, he was elected in 1823 to the House of Representatives from his adopted state of Massachusetts. By the time Webster returned again to Congress in 1827 as a senator from Massachusetts, he had come to believe that the future of New England lay in the growing manufacturing towns of the Merrimack and southern Massachusetts, with whose wealthy sponsors—among them Abbott Lawrence—he had become associated. This required a change in his tariff views. The mills needed protection from European manufacturers and he would see to it that they got it.

Webster never lost sight of his passionate belief in the necessity of preserving the Union. When the tariff problem caused a rift between the manufacturing North and the cotton-producing South in 1830, a rift which showed beyond it the ominous spectre of disunion, Webster made one of his greatest speeches against the doctrine of states' rights and nullification of Federal laws.

Clear-headed as he was, he began to be confused by the political confusion of the time. He had committed himself to the defense of vested interests and allied himself with the

Whig party which supported them. Although he had sided with Andrew Jackson, as he could not help doing, on the nullification question, he parted company with the President when Jackson attacked the Bank of the United States. Whether he was influenced by his own interests in this, it is difficult to say, but it is certain that the destruction of the bank which had made him loans of considerable size would have been hard on him. It is equally certain that he had always, long before he had any personal stake in the matter, supported the idea of a national bank. He fought Jackson with dignity and sound sense and believed that his fight would help him toward the Presidency, which had come to seem desirable to him. His belief was not justified. Although the Whig party in Massachusetts nominated him as their choice for President, the only electoral votes he received were those of his own state. Great figure that he was, he had overlooked the man in the street.

HOPE DEFERRED

The year 1837 was crucial in many ways. Daniel Webster, far from the calming woods and fields of the Merrimack, discouraged by his failure to be considered for the Presidency, decided to resign from Congress. His announcement of his intention raised a storm of opposition. Instead of resigning, he made a tour through the West in the interests of an idea which had an all-but-fatal fascination for him, the idea of developing with borrowed money an enormous agricultural estate in the rapidly developing Middle West. His trip was a triumphal march. He was everywhere feted and acclaimed. It must have made him feel that his hope of the Presidency was not as forlorn as the election of 1836 had made it seem. He remained in Congress to continue his fight for a sound monetary system, to predict the financial panic which swept the country in the summer of 1837 and to listen with apprehension to the ominous undercurrents of the continuing disagreement between North and South over the present and future of slavery—a disagreement intensified by the recent abolition of slavery in the British Empire, the movement to annex Texas to the Union and the rising tide of abolition sentiment in the North. Daniel Webster believed then, as always, that if the Union were not preserved, a disaster worse than slavery would overcome the country. He believed that to preserve the Union the nation's obligations under the Constitution must be fulfilled, even if they involved the continued existence of slavery in states which had come into the Union as slaveholding regions. He was opposed to the annexation of Texas because he believed that it would extend slavery, and he was unequivocally against the extension of that institution.

Webster allowed himself to be re-elected to the Senate in 1838. In the summer of 1839 he went to England with his family, hoping to get an insight into the British view of the then-serious question of the boundary between Maine and Canada and perhaps not without the idea that he might interest Englishmen in some of his recently acquired Western lands.

Meanwhile, that other dark-eyed descendant of Stephen Bachelder, at home on the Merrimack, had passed from his farm-boy existence into politics and, after serving in the Massachusetts Legislature, dreamed of big things in store for him. Greenleaf Whittier had a passion for human justice, but it was not legal justice that appealed to him. To him the Constitution and the Union it created were debased by their failure to take a firm stand against slavery. A contract which even indirectly protected something as vile as he believed slavery to be was to him no contract. He, like many other

New Englanders, regarded anyone who suggested leaving the institution of slavery alone to die a natural death as little better than a criminal. This difference of attitude between him and his remote cousin, Daniel, was more than a mere difference of temperament. It was a psychological rather than a moral or spiritual difference. How great the difference was and how far the common man was from understanding either the Webster or the Whittier point of view is illustrated by an incident which took place along the Merrimack, beginning in Haverhill and ending in the idyllic and beautiful town of Concord, New Hampshire, in August, 1835.

THE MIND AND THE HEART

John Greenleaf Whittier was serving quietly in the Massachusetts Legislature at the time, full of enthusiasm for his work with the newly formed Antislavery Society in Haverhill. An English reformer and orator, George Thompson, who had been closely concerned with the successful attempt to abolish slavery in the British Empire, came to the United States in 1834, arriving the week after Whittier had published in William Lloyd Garrison's *Liberator* a poem which contained the following stanzas:

> Shall every flap of England's flag
> Proclaim that all around are free,
> From farthest Ind to each blue crag
> That beetles o'er the Western Sea?
> And shall we scoff at Europe's kings,
> When Freedom's fire is dim with us,
> And round our country's altar clings
> The damning shade of Slavery's curse?
>
> Go, let us ask of Constantine
> To loose his grasp on Poland's throat;

And beg the lord of Mahmoud's line
To spare the struggling Suliote;
Will not the scorching answer come
From turbaned Turk, and scornful Russ:
"Go, loose your fettered slaves at home,
Then turn and ask the like of us!"

Just God! and shall we calmly rest,
The Christian's scorn, the heathen's mirth,
Content to live the lingering jest
And by-word of a mocking Earth?
Shall our own glorious land retain
That curse which Europe scorns to bear?
Shall our own brethren drag the chain
Which not even Russia's menials wear?

Up, then, in Freedom's manly part,
From graybeard eld to fiery youth,
And on the nation's naked heart
Scatter the living coals of Truth!
Up! while ye slumber, deeper yet
The shadow of our fame is growing!
Up! while ye pause, our sun may set
In blood around our altars flowing!

Oh! rouse ye, ere the storm comes forth,
The gathered wrath of God and man,
Like that which wasted Egypt's earth,
When hail and fire above it ran.
Hear ye no warnings in the air?
Feel ye no earthquake underneath?
Up, up! why will ye slumber where
The sleeper only wakes in death?

Thompson was a sincere and ardent worker for a cause
in which he believed as earnestly as did Whittier. He was
shrewd and cautious and was not, as many men believed, an
emissary from England bent upon weakening and destroying

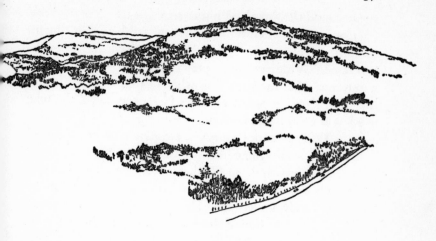

the American Union by widening the rift between North and South. He was careful not to begin his work in the larger cities.

On Sunday, August thirtieth, he left Haverhill with Whittier for Plymouth, New Hampshire, where Thompson lectured several times. On the return trip the abolitionists stopped in Concord to spend the night, their host there having made arrangements for an antislavery meeting in the Court House. Handbills had been distributed announcing that Thompson and Whittier would discuss antislavery and answer questions. Unknown to the speakers, a meeting of citizens had been held to voice a protest against the use of the Court House for such an incendiary purpose. When the time came for the meeting a large and angry crowd milled about in front of the building and became so threatening that the selectmen warned Thompson and Whittier and refused to open the doors. Thompson escaped the mob and reached his host's house in safety, but Whittier was mistaken for the Englishman and pelted with rotten eggs and stones. More eggs than stones found their mark. Whittier said that the stones, whacking against fences and walls as they missed him in his flight, made him realize how St. Stephen must have felt when he was stoned! Whittier's family preserved the egg-stained coat as a souvenir. After the Civil War when clothes were needed for the freed slaves in Southern states Greenleaf added the relic to a box of contributed clothing.

As Whittier and Thompson, escaping from the Concord mob, drove south along the Merrimack in their borrowed chaise, there was little to fill the poet's heart but bitterness against his country which he loved and its people whom he did not entirely understand. He was more than ever committed to the radicalism of the abolitionists, the more extreme among whom—of which Whittier was one—let it be known that they regarded the Union as not worth saving and the Constitution as an instrument of the Devil.

Daniel Webster, in Washington, believing as a result of deep feeling and deep thought that there was in the American Union more hope for the future of mankind than the evil of slavery could counterbalance, that the Union must be preserved and strengthened at any price and that the Constitution was the instrument of its preservation, heard with alarm the rumblings and whip-cracks of discord in his beloved New England. He, like Whittier, did not understand or trouble himself about the common man in the United States. He was perhaps inclined to feel that the safety and strength of the Union, rather than the Apollonian frenzy of the reformer, would bring life, liberty, prosperity and happiness to slave and free and that, without such safety and strength, slavery and despair would be the condition of all.

During the last decade of the first half of the nineteenth century—the decade which saw the beautiful power of the Merrimack turned to profitable, if unlovely, uses in shop and mill—two farm boys, one of the lower and one of the upper river, fought for their beliefs. Daniel Webster, with the breadth of vision which his association with broad acres, deep forests and men of scope and dignity had given him, and whose rich if sometimes tragic personal life provided a complete outlet for his emotion, gave his mind to his country, perhaps the most complete and balanced mind which has ever appeared in American public life. Whittier, whose personality, faith and intellectual limitations kept him from a fully ripened emotional life, bestowed his mind where his emotions should have been and gave his emotions to his country, which had need of something more.

COMPROMISE AND FAITH

On March 7, 1850, in his sixty-ninth year, tortured by the doom which he conceived the follies of his countrymen, North and South, to have arranged for his beloved nation, Daniel Webster arose in the Senate of the United States and spoke out as an American. He supported the efforts of Henry Clay to compromise the disagreements between North and South. Slavery, he said, was an evil, but destruction of the Union was a greater evil. Secession could not and must not take place. On the other hand, the North must live up to its obligations under the Constitution and obey laws under which Southerners had a right to claim protection. Webster believed, as few men then did, although most men do in retrospect today, that slavery must and would prove economically unsound and fall of its own weight like a diseased tree. There was no need to legislate its limitation in the far western lands, for there it could not exist.

There were many who felt, when Daniel Webster sat down on that March day, that the nation had been saved—as indeed for ten years it had—by his eloquence. There were many who felt that they, and with them Christ, had been betrayed. John Greenleaf Whittier celebrated the occasion with a poem, entitled "Ichabod," which may have made the farm boy of the upper Merrimack feel that it was he who knew what St. Stephen felt like when he was being stoned.

So fallen! so lost! the light withdrawn
Which once he wore!
The glory from his gray hairs gone
Forevermore!

Revile him not, the Tempter hath
A snare for all;
And pitying tears, not scorn and wrath,
Befit his fall!

Oh, dumb be passion's stormy rage,
When he who might
Have lighted up and led his age,
Falls back in night.

Scorn! would the angels laugh, to mark
A bright soul driven,
Fiend-goaded, down the endless dark,
From hope and heaven!

Let not the land once proud of him
Insult him now,
Nor brand with deeper shame his dim,
Dishonored brow.

But let its humbled sons, instead,
From sea to lake,
A long lament, as for the dead,
In sadness make.

Of all we loved and honored, naught
Save power remains;
A fallen angel's pride of thought,
Still strong in chains.

All else is gone; from those great eyes
The soul has fled:
When faith is lost, when honor dies,
The man is dead!

Then, pay the reverence of old days
To his dead fame;
Walk backward, with averted gaze,
And hide the shame!

Whittier's misunderstanding of the motives of his greater contemporary is illustrated by another poem, "The Lost Occasion," written years later, after Webster's death. Here the poet, while paying tribute to the great statesman's abilities, attempts to lay the blame for the Civil War upon Webster's support of the Compromise of 1850, an attempt in which it is hard to believe that Abraham Lincoln would have seconded him. On this point the words of Webster's most impartial and thorough biographer have a bearing. Written when John Greenleaf Whittier's politico-theological intransigence had ceased to be remembered, they are a direct refutation of the poet's words spoken with such bitter confidence in "The Lost Occasion":

Thou shouldst have lived to feel below
Thy feet Disunion's fierce upthrow;
The late-sprung mine that underlaid
Thy sad concessions vainly made.

The last paragraph of Claude M. Fuess's *Daniel Webster,* published in 1930, closes with the words: "When finally, after his death, Civil War did eventuate, it was Webster's doctrine, from the lips of Abraham Lincoln, which animated the North and made its victory inevitable. It is not hyperbole to say that we owe the very existence of our Union to the glowing words of Daniel Webster."

The strong waters of the mountain-fed Merrimack carry into very high places those who are fortunate enough to be washed by them, even if not by the blood of the Lamb.

17 New Men for a New World

....

There are two Concords, centers of nerve and blood, in the body of land which is the Merrimack Valley. One, of which I have already given a somewhat impressionistic sketch, gave its name to the Concord coach, and the other, at the opposite end of the feather of river quill and tributary stream, gave its name, with the help of Ephraim Bull, to the century-old Concord grape, the parent of grape culture in America.

The Merrimack not only brought about changes in the economy, the political and social life of Americans. It produced changes in the American mind and its way of dealing with the problems of life. As the number of inhabitants of the beautiful and abundantly watered valley grew beyond the number of those required merely to sustain life within it, the forces which had animated the first few generations of settlers found a fertile ground in Merrimack men who had to think. The flashes from the lives of the men already discussed, such as Webster and Whittier, illustrate to some degree what happened when the climbing vine of civilization along the river reached its blooming time and paused to let its buds unfold.

It was in the more southerly Concord, a century older than its northern opposite, that there took place one of the greatest concentrations of intellectual vitality that ever gave character to an American community. The pioneer stock of Concord, Massachusetts, bore fruit in church and school, and so full of vigor was it that not even pulpit and classroom could satisfy it. A young Unitarian minister, at a time when being a preacher seemed one of the few ways of being a scholar, began at about the time that the slightly younger Whittier was publishing his first antislavery verses to question the validity of the theology which he had inherited from his popular minister father.

Ralph Waldo Emerson, although born in Boston where his father occupied the pulpit of the First Church, was essentially a product of Concord, where for most of the town's existence his ancestors had preached. Like most intelligent men who have had an association with the Merrimack and its allied streams, he found in the open book of nature as much as he found in the books of men. What he saw of the natural world made him distrust the artificial, and it came to him early to think it strange that the Christian God should, if men did not possess some of the attributes of the Deity, let them shift for themselves while on earth and only give them His undivided attention when they had ceased to exist. This questioning attitude toward theology made Ralph Waldo Emerson a religious radical. It seemed to him that men did not regard the potentialities of man with sufficient awe and reverence. Americans had created a New World, but were they creating a New Man to inhabit it? Emerson thought not and felt that it was time they got about the task.

Before he was twenty-seven years old he had lost his father, graduated from Harvard, taught school, been threatened with tuberculosis, become a somewhat reluctant minister and traveled to Concord, New Hampshire, to marry a beautiful and talented but hopelessly frail girl who, though nearly ten years younger than he, understood him perfectly. Unfortunately Ellen Tucker Emerson lived less than two years after their marriage, her tragic death helping to resolve his doubts about the church. He resigned his ministry of the Second Church in Boston in 1831 and shortly afterwards went abroad for a year to see the art and culture of the Old World at first hand and to visit what he took to be the great figures of its literature. In most of those he was bitterly disappointed —he barely restrained himself from laughing at William Wordsworth. Thomas Carlyle was the chief exception. Largely through Carlyle, Emerson became closely associated with the somewhat vague and intellectually romantic tendencies in German idealism. He returned to America to preach for a time, without a church, and to lecture. The European heritage of his ancestors and of his recent contacts combined with that new force which was rising out of the altered lives of the Merrimack Valley pioneers to create an American thought. His lecturing and an anticipated, though not immediately realized, inheritance from his dead wife gave him time to think. He married again in 1835, without any of the passionate excitement of his devotion to Ellen Tucker, Lydia Jackson, a brilliant woman, this time his senior, who worshiped his mind and his eloquence. He was by this time returned to his ancestral home in the southerly Concord, which seemed to be a magnet for the New England genius of the day. Here Ralph Waldo Emerson developed the latent thought which his heritage and experience had imprinted upon him, creating a force which influenced the culture of New England as the minds of few men have influenced it and which, although its core of transcendentalism ultimately lost its vital pith, became a part of the heritage of American thought.

In an address delivered before the Phi Beta Kappa Society at Cambridge, Massachusetts, in 1837, Emerson fired a shot which, though perhaps not heard around the world by the same ears that heard the more real sound of guns fired at

Concord Bridge sixty-two years earlier, was none the less epoch-making. This speech which created the concept of the thinking American, the American Scholar, defined the function of the man who must be the hope of the New World:

> . . . it becomes him to feel all confidence in himself, and to defer never to the popular cry. He and he only knows the world. The world of any moment is the merest appearance. Some great decorum, some fetish of a government, some ephemeral trade, or war, or man, is cried up by half mankind and cried down by the other half, as if all depended on this particular up or down. The odds are that the whole question is not worth the poorest thought which the scholar has lost in listening to the controversy. Let him not quit his belief that a popgun is a popgun, though the ancient and honorable of the earth affirm it to be the crack of doom. In silence, in steadiness, in severe abstraction, let him hold by himself; add observation to observation, patient of neglect, patient of reproach, and bide his own time,—happy enough if he can satisfy himself alone that this day he has seen something truly. Success treads on every right step. For the instinct is sure, that prompts him to tell his brother what he thinks. He then learns that in going down into the secrets of his own mind he has descended into the secrets of all minds. He learns that he who has mastered any law in his private thoughts, is master to that extent of all men whose language he speaks, and of all into whose language his own can be translated. The poet, in utter solitude remembering his spontaneous thoughts and recording them, is found to have recorded that which men in crowded cities find true for them also. The orator distrusts at first the fitness of his frank confessions, his want of knowledge of the persons he addresses, until he finds that he is the complement of his hearers;—that they drink his words because he fulfils for them their own nature; the deeper he dives into his privatest, secretest presentiment, to his wonder he finds

this is the most acceptable, most public, and universally true. The people delight in it; the better part of every man feels, This is my music; this is myself.

In self-trust all the virtues are comprehended. Free should the scholar be,—free and brave.

AUSTERITY IN BLOOM

Among the talented young people in that Athenian village whose river feeds its waters to the Merrimack was a lad—fourteen years younger than Emerson, only twenty in 1837—just graduated from Harvard, who was as much of an individualist as Emerson's heroic "American Scholar." Henry David Thoreau, whom the talented but somewhat watery Hawthorne thought "ugly as sin," was, with his brother, John, teaching school in Concord in rather unorthodox fashion when he first attracted Emerson's attention. Emerson was fascinated by the young man, as he was also by Bronson Alcott, father of the better-known Louisa who made *Little Men* and *Little Women* out of her family, their friends and her own lively fictional sense. "I only know three persons," Emerson said, speaking of Thoreau, "who seem to me fully to see this law of reciprocity or compensation,—himself, Alcott, and myself: and 'tis odd that we should all be neighbors. . . ."

It was Thoreau who introduced Waldo Emerson to the river which the older man would have said he had known intimately from childhood. It was Emerson, excited by the sparkle of his young friend's ideas, who inspired Thoreau to keep a journal. The combination of river and journal helped to produce the Thoreau whom we know.

On the last day of August, 1839, a few months before the Whig party's nomination for the Presidency of the undistinguished and ill-fated William Henry Harrison, Henry Thoreau and his brother set out upon a voyage upon the

Merrimack system, which resulted in a picture of the river upon which the soon-to-be-perfected magic box of Daguerre could not have improved.

"I had often stood," wrote Thoreau, "on the banks of the Concord, watching the lapse of the current, an emblem of all progress, following the same law with the system, with time, and all that is made; the weeds at the bottom gently bending down the stream, shaken by the watery wind, still planted where their seeds had sunk, but erelong to die and go down likewise; the shining pebbles, not yet anxious to better their condition, the chips and weeds, and occasional logs and stems of trees that floated past, fulfilling their fate, were objects of singular interest to me, and at last I resolved to launch myself on its bosom and float whither it would bear me."

The now famous journey which resulted from this resolve is symbolic of the launching upon the stream of the human past of the American mind, which had acquired sufficient self-consciousness and self-confidence to contemplate itself, to fulfill the purpose which Emerson had outlined for it in "The American Scholar."

Thoreau, though far from the New England pioneer himself, was close enough to that hardy race to be quite conscious of its character and he was close enough to—indeed almost at the center of—the intellectual movement which was emerging from the New England struggle for life.

When Henry and John Thoreau launched their painted boat upon the quiet waters of the Concord River and headed for its junction with the Middlesex Canal at Billerica, from which point the river waters stepped downward south and north to Boston and to what Henry referred to as "New" Concord, they carried with them minds and hearts open to men and their thoughts and ways and to the book of nature which is man's chief instructor.

A Week on the Concord and Merrimack Rivers is full of a great many side journeys down endless channels of the mind, along which the happy boatmen saw visions of the past, the Greek philosophers and poets, the enticing spiritual glories of the Bhagavad-Gita, the early giants of English letters, and the historic and traditional relationships among men. The core of the narrative is, however, the simple journey, by sail and oar, through quiet and strong stretches of canal and river, through locks and rocky passages; camping on islands and at the mouths of tributaries, talking with unkempt and uncouth but intelligent and dignified inhabitants, and understanding the relationship of changing men to their changing land.

From the river, along which the railroad then ran as far as Manchester, the habitations and works of man were not always visible. It was a wild and unspoiled stream, which for the most part spoke more of the life of kingfishers, herons, frogs, woodchucks and muskrats than of the life of man.

Here and there the boatmen from Old Concord came upon the sand-buried campfires of the Indians, reminding them of the days of Hannah Dustin and her endangered contemporaries. Here and there there were sheep, suggesting the imagined El Dorado of the day. The Thoreaus lived as much as they could off the land, eating fresh bread, milk and melons as they went, fish when they could and game when they were lucky.

They passed Nashua and Manchester without being more than vaguely conscious of the mills which had begun to turn the river into something more than an idyllic avenue lined with basswood, chestnut, oak, maple, spruce and pine. The tenders of the locks, the canal boatmen, the farm families interested them more than cotton cloth and its potentialities. Perhaps the perceptive Henry realized that in the course of time men would change less than their industrial fortunes and would always be the chief product of the river.

Henry and his brother got as far as Hooksett, New Hampshire, by boat but, since they feared that farther penetration northward by water would involve much laborious portaging, they left the skiff in the mouth of a small stream on the east bank just below the Hooksett pinnacle. Hanging up their tent and stowing the bulkiest of their equipment, such as their buffalo robes, in the barn of a hospitable farmer, they continued on foot along the riverbank to Concord, and thence up the Merrimack and the Pemigewasset through the notch at its head and on to the summit of Mt. Washington.

FEAR NOT THAT THE RACE WILL WAVER

Thoreau returned, enriched by what he had seen, to become a part of that impressive but curious philosophical burgeoning which took place in his native town of old Concord. He lived for two years shortly after his return as a kind of spiritual as well as physical handyman in the home of the more staid Emerson, whose theological radicalism beside the revolutionary intransigence of his young friend seemed tame indeed. Thoreau's philosophy was in one sense a practical application of the self-reliant individualism of Emerson's, but in application Waldo was a little frightened by it. He was also troubled by Thoreau's desire to know the details of the lives and nature of plants and animals. This seemed to him likely to turn the mind, which should be an altar for the worship of things in their entirety, into a confused and confusing lumber-room and attic of facts.

Henry Thoreau brought home with him from his week on the Merrimack a sense of the vitality of its people, a sense which simply did not exist in Emerson and, for a different reason, was foreign to Daniel Webster. Neither of these two great products of the Merrimack could have brought himself to say, as Thoreau did, "I love to see the herd of men feeding heartily on coarse and succulent pleasures, as cattle on the husks and stalks of vegetables. Though there are many crooked and crabbed specimens of humanity among them, run all to thorn and rind, and crowded out of shape by adverse circumstances, like the third chestnut in the burr, so that you wonder to see some heads wear a whole hat, yet fear not that the race will waver or fail in them. . . ."

Emerson's radical interposition in the course of American thought, like the interposition of the canal builders in the course of New England economy, blazed for a while and, because there was so much it did not take into account, subsided and all but died. Yet unlike the canals and the vessels with their sails and crews of pole-men which Thoreau met on the river, it did not vanish without leaving a trace. No future American philosopher or poet could ignore it, as the railroad builders could ignore the principle of the canal. Thoreau's variety of Concord radicalism was more enduring, perhaps because his love, his imagination and his pen were closer to reality than Emerson's. Yet Thoreau, like Webster, missed something of the achievement to which his gigantic stature should have led him. As Emerson said of him:

> His virtues, of course, sometimes ran into extremes. It was easy to trace to the inexorable demand on all for exact truth that austerity which made this willing hermit more solitary even than he wished. Himself of a perfect probity, he required not less of others. He had a disgust at crime, and no worldly success could cover it. He detected paltering as readily in dignified and prosperous persons as in beggars, and with equal scorn. Such dangerous frankness was in his dealing that his admirers called him "that terrible Thoreau," as if he spoke when

silent, and was still present when he had departed. I think the severity of his ideal interfered to deprive him of a healthy sufficiency of human society. The habit of a realist to find things the reverse of their appearance inclined him to put every statement in a paradox. A certain habit of antagonism defaced his earlier writings,—a trick of rhetoric not quite outgrown in his later, of substituting for the obvious word and thought its diametrical opposite. He praised wild mountains and winter forests for their domestic air, in snow and ice he would find sultriness, and commended the wilderness for resembling Rome and Paris. "It was so dry, that you might call it wet."

The tendency to magnify the moment, to read all the laws of Nature in the one object or one combination under your eye, is of course comic to those who do not share the philosopher's perception of identity. To him there was no such thing as size. The pond was a small ocean; the Atlantic, a large Walden Pond. He referred every minute fact to cosmical laws. Though he meant to be just, he seemed haunted by a certain chronic assumption that the science of the day pretended completeness, and he had just found out that the *savans* had neglected to discriminate a particular botanical variety, had failed to describe the seeds or count the sepals. "That is to say," we replied, "the blockheads were not born in Concord; but who said they were? It was their unspeakable misfortune to be born in London, or Paris, or Rome; but, poor fellows, they did what they could, considering that they never saw Bateman's Pond, or Nine-Acre Corner, or Becky-Stow's Swamp. Besides, what were you sent into the world for, but to add this observation?"

Had this genius been only contemplative, he had been fitted to his life, but with his energy and practical ability he seemed born for great enterprise and for command; and I so much regret the loss of his rare powers of action, that I cannot help counting it a fault in him that he had no ambition. Wanting this, instead of engineering for all America, he was the captain of a huckleberry party. Pounding beans is good to the end of pounding empires one of these days; but if, at the end of years, it is still only beans!

This comment on Thoreau's lack of ambition says as much of Emerson as of Thoreau.

THE ICE ON THE STOVE LID

Something of both of these men of the Merrimack is to be found in another poet, whose relationship to the river is not unlike Emerson's, a philosopher whose contribution to the spirit of man and to American letters will possibly outlast that of any of those who flourished in and about old Concord in the days when Ephraim Bull's Concord grape was something new.

Although he was not born until more than a decade after Thoreau's too-early death and only eight years before the not untimely death of Emerson, Robert Frost belongs beside them here. Not only was his birth far removed in time from those of his two great predecessors, he was born miles away from the Merrimack in San Francisco, California. Yet he was a true creature of the Merrimack. His father, to whom politics was as a taste for drink is in some men, had been born in Kingston, New Hampshire, from whose southwesterly corner the Spicket River flows past the ruins of North Salem into the Merrimack; and at the time of Robert's birth in far-away California, his grandfather was living in Lawrence, Massachusetts, partaking of the fruits of the best days of the cotton-textile industry.

Had William Prescott Frost not died in San Francisco when Robert was a boy of ten, the career of New England's and America's greatest poet might have been very different and the human life of the valley of the Merrimack might have been less well recorded. After the death of his father, Robert and his Scottish mother traveled east to Lawrence to live with Grandfather Frost in an atmosphere of weir and water power, spindle and loom. Robert took schooling in his stride and soon made it apparent that he had always been a New Englander. The virus of enthusiasm for the apparently boundless possibilities of the textile industry found little in the boy's blood to sustain it. He was, like Thoreau, a rebel, a lover of nature and a shrewd listener to and observer of men. He attended Lawrence High School, worked briefly in the mills of that mill-ridden city and, long before he was certain what he did want to do, understood what he did not. In San Francisco, his own mind and personality undeveloped, he felt the force of his father, who had him much with him in torchlight parades. William Frost gave his son at the same time a sense of power and mystery, each of which filled the boy with a kind of fascinating suspicion made up, it may be, of half love and half distaste.

Back in New England, with no father, the boy looked about him for a vessel for his purpose, that utensil which some people call God. Like Emerson and Thoreau he found much of it not so much in himself, a self which like a scientist's is full of doubt and questioning, as in the awful and unlimited scope of his own understanding.

During one season Robert Frost tended the fish weir at the Lawrence dam, and perhaps, like the lock-keeper whom Thoreau met near Amoskeag Falls, had time and inclination to think of other things than those pertaining to his occupation. Frost was perhaps nearer to Thoreau than to Emerson in his ability to resist all social currents which might turn him from his course, but he was nearer to Emerson than Thoreau in his belief that it is the function of a poet and philosopher to be a poet and philosopher and that he must resist passion and the focus-destroying speed of emotional judgment. Frost has been more successful, publicly at least, in sticking to his last than have those earlier workers at the fashioning of New England's philosophic shoe.

Robert Frost in his youth seems to have been guided by an intuition surer than that which animated Thoreau and Emerson. More often than they did, he ran away from what was not meant for him. Among the things which were not meant for him were the cotton mills, the harness and livery of a completed formal education, the necessity of subordinating his mind and its creative genius to the task of showing the world that he was the pattern of a good provider; the role of farmer, of schoolteacher, of settled man of substance. As a young man he was constantly at war with himself and so with any who assumed that they knew what he was.

Without his knowing it, the Merrimack drew him and worked over him. His journey along its length began as a kind of boiling over of the tasteless broth of Lawrence and continued as a kind of sizzling on the stove lid, riding like a piece of ice on his own melting, which has been going on ever since and is perhaps recognized in his "The Figure a Poem Makes," the preface to the 1939 edition of his *Collected Poems*. The first important stop in Frost's Merrimack journey —which he did not at the time think of as a journey and does not now regard as a close association with the river—was at Derry, that small center of education, farming and shoemaking which was, in 1827, split from the Londonderry settled by the Scotch-Irish in 1719. Here he farmed with love and curiosity rather than enthusiasm, and began his family life. When farming seemed more likely to become his uncharitable master than his profitable slave, he turned to teaching at one of those typical New England endowed academies whose establishment showed that the New World pioneer never, even in the wilderness, forgot where lay the sources of human hope. Pinkerton Academy marked for Frost the building of a canal about the first rapid in his path, and it led to a journey farther up the river to the normal school at Plymouth, which in turn led, as Emerson's far less exacting rejection of a settled church led him, to the Old World.

Robert Frost, as he journeyed up the Merrimack, was seeking not political, not theological, not social nor economic liberty. He was seeking himself, the explanation of the inexplicable ferment in him which made him always feel that he was too near a thing to see it and so kept him moving on. This ferment had, ever since his school days, when the poetry of Edgar Allan Poe had stirred him with its alchemy of sense, expressed itself in the form of verse. He had sold an occasional piece to the *Independent* and been pleased with the editor's kind words, but there did not seem to be much of a market for him. When, just short of the river's source and a discovery of his own, he took himself and his family to Europe, he was, without being quite sure what he was doing, looking for that place to stand which Archimedes said was all a man needed in order to be able to move the world.

In England, where he made friends and what to another man would have been enemies, as stones are enemies of a brook that is trying to reach the sea, he found this place to stand. Here, far from his native California and his ancestors' New England, his work was first published in book form. Like the sound of a voice which precedes a memorable man into a room, his printed words reached home before he did. England, not entirely satisfactory as a home and made difficult by the approach of war, had become impossible; and Robert Frost returned to New England, to the very town in which the Old Man of the Mountain, advertising, as Webster said, the fact that New Hampshire's chief product is men, watches over the birth of the Merrimack in the mountain-shadowed waters of Profile Lake. It was here, in a little white house at the foot of a high hill in Franconia, that his own country found him. It was during his five years in Franconia that he became inseparably identified with New Hampshire if not with the Merrimack. It was here that for the first time he felt relative freedom from the pressures which even an extraordinary man with a family but without money is bound to feel. Yet even here he felt things impinging upon him and was again seized by an urge to move, to look at the sun of his thought from another point in his orbit around it.

In 1920 he moved away, and in moving seemed to have reached a more settled point than he had theretofore found. He has said:

> It's restful to arrive at a decision,
> And restful just to think about New Hampshire.
> At present I am living in Vermont.

This establishment of a kind of permanent retrospect is characteristic of Frost and of the true poet. Never, he seems to say, get so involved with nearness that you lose that perspective sense which gives the world more than two dimensions. This is the secret of his understanding of his fellow men. He travels through them as he travels through lands and books, but he is aloof from them and so sees them as they are, not as his presence among them makes them, when he writes about them. This aloofness, this detachment, leaves him open to the suggestion that, since he takes no side, he is cautious rather than sincere. Yet his very refusal to let his listeners on one side or the other claim that he is arguing for them ends not in teaching, nor in preaching, but in showing them, as he has said that the poet must, things which they did not know they knew.

Can it be of no significance that the waters which make up the body of the Merrimack have played an accompaniment to the lives of such men as Frost, Webster, Emerson, Thoreau? It was of a tributary to the Merrimack that Robert Frost wrote in "West-Running Brook":

> "Speaking of contraries, see how the brook
> In that white wave runs counter to itself.
> It is from that in water we were from
> Long, long before we were from any creature.
> Here we, in our impatience of the steps,
> Get back to the beginning of beginnings,
> The stream of everything that runs away.
> Some say existence like a Pirouot
> And Pirouette, forever in one place,
> Stands still and dances, but it runs away,
> It seriously, sadly, runs away
> To fill the abyss' void with emptiness.
> It flows beside us in this water brook,
> But it flows over us. It flows between us
> To separate us for a panic moment.
> It flows between us, over us, and *with* us.
> And it is time, strength, tone, light, life, and love—
> And even substance lapsing unsubstantial;
> The universal cataract of death
> That spends to nothingness—and unresisted,
> Save by some strange resistance in itself,
> Not just a swerving, but a throwing back,
> As if regret were in it and were sacred.
> It has this throwing backward on itself
> So that the fall of most of it is always
> Raising a little, sending up a little.
> Our life runs down in sending up the clock.
> The brook runs down in sending up our life.
> The sun runs down in sending up the brook.
> And there is something sending up the sun.

It is this backward motion toward the source,
Against the stream, that most we see ourselves in,
The tribute of the current to the source.
It is from this in nature we are from.
It is most us."

18 Eddies in the Flow of Faith

In the flood of human life which worked its way slowly but surely upstream along the Merrimack there were many currents, and not the least of them was that turbulent flow of faith which the first settlers imagined to be the cause of the tide on which they rode. The history of the settlement at Newbury, which was the seed from which grew the stout tree of civilization whose branches match the other branchings of the river, shows plainly that settlement in a land where men might make their own rules of worship did not solve all the problems whose existence had induced them to leave their English homes.

It might have been supposed that, once the confidently devout Reverend Thomas Parker had settled his flock by the river which later bore his name, where its members were to spread out and on up the Merrimack, it would not have been necessary for any outsider to come to Newbury to bring the good tidings of the Gospel. Yet the dissent of the Puritan immigrants did not put an end to dissension, from within the church or from without. I have mentioned in an earlier chapter the thirty-year-war of the Newbury people within their congregation. The early New England church did not differ from its parent church in England by being free from schism. In fact it was constantly tending to reproduce itself by fission like any basic cell. Sometimes it was evangelistic pressure from the outside which caused division, evangelistic pressure not of hitherto-unknown good tidings but of personality.

The summer of 1740 in Newbury, Massachusetts, was wet and cold. The corn would not ripen. The Merrimack rose and carried seaward houses, cordwood, hay and shipbuilding timber and scattered them along the Plum Island beaches. There was something unusual in the air. Men were querulous and irritable and cattle restless and alarmed. On September tenth, a remarkable personage stood on the High Street and with Bible in hand spoke to the people of the parish for the first time. Being not within the walls of a meeting house, he could speak to people whom the church, though it influenced their government, their behavior, their thought, did not reach emotionally. The New England church had been so much concerned with its theology and its politics that it did not appeal very strongly to the average man, whom it took no pains to interest. In the 1730's this had become so apparent that a movement to bring religion to more people had begun. Jonathan Edwards of Northampton, a brilliant and forceful preacher, who was a person as well as a theological mouthpiece, had begun to attract the attention of those who had never learned to believe that there was a living church. His efforts had shown that the man in the street could be interested in religion and that there was a field for the evangelist.

George Whitefield was not a native New Englander and he had not come to settle on the Merrimack. He was born in Gloucester, England, in a tavern kept by his father and when he had quit school at fifteen, he worked at the bar. He was a good scholar and was passionately fond of plays. After a year of so of bartending he prepared for Oxford and entered there in 1733. Here he came under the influence of John Wesley's Methodism and grew so devout that his career was plainly the ministry. He was ordained as a deacon at the age of twenty-two and immediately set out to bring the Gospel to the western cities of England. Wesley sent him to Georgia, where he thought he saw something of the need of settlers in a new land for the compensations of uninquiring belief. He returned to England to become a full priest and to gain confidence and stimulation from preaching in the open to huge crowds of British miners near Bristol, simple men whose grimy faces were streaked with tears before he finished speaking. Whitefield was better at presenting than at composing his sermons. None of his works is impressive reading, neither being well written nor making very good sense, yet his manner of presentation made his listeners feel that the heart of God himself was being opened to them. In August, 1739, by which time his forensic success had alienated the clergy, he sailed for America to carry his message to the colonists of the northeast.

In Newburyport he at first found a tempered enthusiasm. On at least one occasion, as he stood before the meeting house on High Street, his great voice thundering at the throng before him, someone pelted him with stones, all but knocking the Bible from his hand. This sign of hostility troubled him not at all. He held the Bible high. "I have a warrant from God to preach. His seal is in my hand and I stand in the King's highway." There were no more stones thrown. The crowd heard him through and, perhaps believing that poor crops, floods and bitterly unseasonable cold were punishment for the sins of which Whitefield made them feel that they were guilty, came back for more. The great religious awakening took deep hold upon the Merrimack. Newburyport was torn again. Some supported Whitefield and some reviled him, but religion had become an issue with many who had heretofore been content to leave it to others. The established church was never again so arrogantly secure as it had been.

Yet Whitefield, for all that he was stoned, received no such treatment as had been offered the Quakers in Massachusetts Bay during the seventeenth century, when they were under such a cloud that men were threatened, exiled and even hanged for sheltering Friends. In the eighteenth century some semblance of religious freedom began to exist in America. The way was open for religious experiment and many took the way.

THE HERITAGE OF ANN LEE

In August, 1774, four years after George Whitefield had been buried in the Presbyterian Church which he helped to found at Newburyport, a remarkable woman arrived with her family in New York City. Ann Lee was the daughter of a blacksmith in Manchester, England. She had early shown that she had unconventional and quite spirited ideas based upon those of a variant sect of Quakers, known as the Shaking Quakers, which had sprung up in Manchester. Like other supporters of the religious awakening of the 1730's, the Shaking Quakers believed that there were a great many forms of sin and that they should all be attacked with outspoken fury. Among the sins, Ann Lee believed, was the lust of generation, a belief which caused her husband Abraham Stanley some anguish. Although she believed in celibacy, Ann bore him four children, all of whom died in infancy if not actually at birth. Ann was frequently seized with paroxysms of inspiration, under the influence of which she indulged in dancing and shouting in the streets. For such behavior she was as frequently imprisoned. It was while she was in jail in Manchester that she had a vision which bade her work against the "lusts of generation" and to urge everyone that the only hope of salvation was to confess everything done under their influence. This vision marked Ann Lee as a special person and caused the Shakers to designate her their mother. She had other revelations, among which was that which bade her take her husband, her brother William, and her niece Nancy and several other followers to America.

On her arrival Ann was promptly and perhaps understandably deserted by her husband. The band of Shakers moved up the Hudson to Watervliet, New York, where the organization of the Shaker sect, the official name of which was "The United Society of Believers in Christ's Second Appearing," was begun. From the banks of the Hudson the Shaker colonies spread into Massachusetts, Connecticut, New Hampshire and Maine. In 1792 a Shaker settlement was established at East Canterbury, New Hampshire, not far from the farm above the Merrimack, on the opposite side of the river, where ten-year-old Daniel Webster was reading *Don Quixote* and strengthening his unshaking faith in nature and man's freedom from sin.

Ann Lee, the true visionary, believed things of herself which may or may not have been true. She believed that Jesus represented the male principle of God on earth and that she was destined to represent the female. She claimed that under a spell of vision she had been able to address her questioners in seventy-two different languages. She died in 1784, but the Shakers were firmly established in their union against sin; and their colonies, separated from the world, prospered as communal units in which the sexes were separated even in ritual, property was held as a consecrated whole, and marriage, though not expressly forbidden, was considered unchristian.

The colony at Canterbury is one of very few still in existence where the kind of life lived by the Shakers may be seen. It is scarcely a colony today, as might be expected of a sect which proscribes procreation, but rather a museum in which still exists evidence of the powerful and long-lasting effect in simple purity of an emotional idea which was born in somewhat disorderly, if inspired, hysteria. There have been no recent converts and when the present handful are gone, Shakerism will be extinct. Yet it is not long since, through the towns and among the summer hotels of the Merrimack Valley and the White Mountains, the quiet and gentle Shakers used to go by horse and carriage, carrying for sale trunks full of Shaker capes, sweaters, straw boxes, wooden ware, candied orange peel and even small pieces of beautifully made and exquisitely proportioned furniture. At their height the Shaker colonies developed, as self-contained communities often do, skilled workers at many trades, artisans of perfection, artists where art was the natural expression of the narrowed gap between the spirit and the flesh.

MARY OF BOW

The idea of a new form of Christian belief is not likely to visit many Americans of today, though religious revivals come and go and there are always evangelists. It is perhaps not strange, considering the transcendental movement of the nineteenth century, which in America grew out of the southerly Concord, that the only successful new Christian sect of recent times should have taken its inspiration from a native of the upper Merrimack. Mary Ann Morse Baker was born in the little settlement of Bow, New Hampshire. In 1821, Bow was not so much a village as a small collection of farms about a meeting house and a school. Mary Ann was the youngest of six children of Mark and Abigail Baker, a typical farm family of the region and the period. Mark Baker was a deeply religious, hot-tempered man, who seems to have believed that others, no doubt including his own family, should live and think as he did.

Little is known of the early years of Mary Ann's childhood save that she was delicate and subject to temper, backaches and hysteria, some of which may have resulted from the difficulty a youngest child might have in getting her own way in a strong-willed family. When Mary Ann was fifteen, the family moved up the Merrimack to Tilton, where, though her opportunity for companionship with more than her kin was increased, her unexplained spells of illness and her moods of introspection were also intensified.

Tilton is not far from Canterbury, and it is certain from some of Mary Baker's early letters that she visited the Shaker Colony there. It is probable that the Shaker background was known to her and that what she knew of it had an effect upon ideas which she later developed. Mary Ann Baker and Ann Lee, separated by a century in time, had much in common.

Mary reached a frail physical maturity in Tilton. Her emotional life at that time is something of which we know little. We do know that in December, 1843, she was married at the Baker farm to George Washington Glover, an apparently robust and jolly fellow, son of neighbors of the Bakers at Bow. "Wash" Glover had gone south and built up a small contracting business at Charleston, South Carolina, whither he carried his bride. Mrs. Glover has said that her husband was well-to-do and owned several slaves, a circumstance which did not keep her from going about Charleston talking abolition. Glover, when he was called to Wilmington, North Carolina, did not dare leave his bride to get into trouble with their Southern neighbors. He took her with him even though she was pregnant, inadvertently exposing her to a worse danger than any with which angry Southerners could have threatened her. It turned out that Wilmington was in the grip of an epidemic of yellow fever.

It was George Washington, not Mary, who failed to escape the danger. The fever took hold of him and in nine days he was dead, leaving Mary and her unborn child alone in a strange city, without means of support. As soon as she could, she went back home to her parents' farm, where she bore her son. She was unable either to nurse the child or to keep herself on an even keel. Her old spells of illness returned in aggravated form. She was so tensely hysterical that she could not bear the sound of horses' hoofs on the road outside, nor could she sit still. The road was covered with tanbark to deaden the sharp sound of horseshoes on road metal and her sister devised a cradle in which she could be rocked like a child.

In her moments of freedom from illness she tried unsuccessfully to earn a living by teaching school and, with equal lack of success, to ward off the results of emotional tension by writing poetry. Her son was, as he remained, little trouble to her. He was farmed out in the family of a neighboring blacksmith whose daughter had sometimes cared for Mary Glover in her illness. When little George Glover was four years old, Mahala Sanborn married and was allowed to keep the boy with her at her husband's home in Groton, New Hampshire, near Newfound Lake.

In 1853, Mary Glover married a second time, proving that she was not in all respects a spiritual sister of Ann Lee. Daniel Patterson, the groom, was a Franklin dentist with a taste for flashy clothes and a likable personality, but the marriage failed to serve as a lightning rod for the threatening bolt of the bride's nervousness. Dr. Patterson traveled about a good deal, apparently enjoying himself but not making enough money to suit his tastes. The couple's existence became more and more unhappy. The mortgage on their house was foreclosed, Patterson began to wander more and more, and Mrs. Patterson declined into a chronic illness, experimenting occasionally with spiritualism and animal magnetism and thinking her own curiously disordered thoughts. When the Civil War broke upon the nation, Daniel Patterson somehow got himself into the medical department of the Union Army and was taken prisoner by the Confederates at Bull Run. He remained a prisoner throughout the war. Although Mary wrote a poem lamenting the Doctor's fate, there is little evidence that his absence made much of a change in her life. As one of her biographers says, "At forty she found herself alone, unloved even by her relations and her own son, poverty-stricken, pain-racked, purposeless. Regarding her son old Mark Baker once declared, 'Mary acts like an old ewe that won't own its lamb.'"

THE HEALER AND THE SICK

It was at this time that Mary Baker Glover Patterson became interested in the work of a Portland, Maine, faith healer, Phineas Parkhurst Quimby, an honest, primitive fellow who did not have quite the intellectual equipment to understand all of what he was doing but who, since it appeared to effect cures, did it anyway. Quimby had begun by being a hypnotist and a healer who used drugs as a side line. He gradually evolved a system of healing, however, which discarded both hypnosis and pills. For them he substituted faith, thereby approaching the type of healing practiced by Jesus and his disciples, although Quimby made no claim to being a religious man and did not believe his cures were brought about by supernatural means. He believed that he had made a great discovery, which he shared with his patients to the extent of asking each of them to teach his method to at least two others. He referred to his system of healing as "The Science of Health" or "The Science of Christ" and is said sometimes to have used the term "Christian Science."

Mary Patterson and Quimby were sympathetic to each other from the first. She took a course of treatment from him and was immensely benefited by it. He in turn, having heard that she was an authoress, showed her his manuscript notes of his theories and practices and began to count on her help in getting a wider circulation for his ideas. How wide a circulation his ideas were to receive at the hands of his astonishing patient and the form which they eventually took would have startled and perhaps confused and saddened Phineas Quimby had he lived longer than he did. He died in 1866, leaving Mary Patterson possessed of his secret but not yet sure what to do with it.

That she was groping for the answer to the question of how best to use what she knew is indicated by her recovery from a severe fall shortly after Quimby's death. Mrs. Patterson, although treated by a physician who seems not to have shared her own grave view of her condition, was confident that it was not medicine but God that had cured her through the agency of her own will to deny sickness. This was, perhaps, the starting point of her public career, though it was many years before she emerged from the wilderness of confusion.

Shortly after his wife's miraculous cure, Daniel Patterson, back from his sojourn in a Southern prison to resume his unsuccessful career as a dentist, decided that he had had enough of Mary and returned to his native town of Saco, Maine, there to go from bad to worse, ending in Potter's Field, via the poorhouse, thirty years later. Shortly after her husband's departure Mary Patterson, who had been asked to leave her boarding place but felt unable to do so, was formally evicted for nonpayment of rent of $1.50 per week. This was a low ebb indeed in the tide of Mary Baker Glover Patterson's fortunes. For some time she went from place to place alternately making friends and quarreling with them, trying her hand at healing, teaching Quimby's methods and constantly writing at what she called her "Bible." In her book she sought and found release from her frustrations, her fears and her suffering.

In 1870, Mary formed a partnership with Richard Kennedy, a young man from Amesbury who had been her pupil. The two set up an office in the shoemaking town of Lynn. Mrs. Patterson, who had returned to the use of her first husband's name of Glover, let Kennedy do the healing, at which he was enormously successful, and set herself up as a teacher of "Moral Science." Kennedy shared with her the profits of his healing and she charged students at first $100 and later $300 for twelve lessons, sometimes demanding a percentage of what the students might make after they set up teaching on their own. The Kennedy-Glover partnership was a highly profitable one, but Mary Glover was unable to maintain it. She quarreled with her young and gifted partner, accusing him, of all things, of cheating at cards. He burned his contract with her, dissolved the partnership, dividing its assets fairly, and set up in business for himself, leaving Mrs. Glover with $6000 and a lucrative teaching practice.

In 1873, annoyed by the unavoidable legal necessity of using Patterson's name, Mrs. Glover successfully brought suit for divorce on the grounds of desertion. Two years later she bought a house in Lynn where she continued her highly profitable teaching, using Quimby's "Questions and Answers" as the basis of what she taught. But Mary Glover was no passive paraphraser. Her own personality, so complex and at first confused, had in it an ingredient of determined fire which affected her students strangely. It was almost as if she taught more than she knew. Her success, combined with her new freedom from want, gave her a sense of power which was like a wind blown upon the coals of her fire. Quimby began to disappear from her consciousness and his teachings to become so much a part of her that she no longer regarded them as his.

It was in the little house on Broad Street in Lynn that Mary Baker Glover Patterson finished the book on which she had been working for years. She was not successful in finding a publisher until two of her students put up the money to finance it—a total of more than $2000. Though the author later stated that the title of the work was suggested to her in a dream by God himself, it is noteworthy that Phineas Quimby had used the words of the title in his writings.

THE TRIUMPH OF THE WILL

Science and Health did not immediately become the best seller which it later, after much editing and amending, turned out to be. Yet in it was, from the first, the germ of the idea which made its author a very compelling religious leader. This was, to generalize, the application of religious ecstasy to the task of healing by suggestion. It was this combination which was extremely appealing to many who could find in formal religion alone little inspiration and in the practice of unin-spired healing by suggestion without the fervor of religion little that was attractive.

Mrs. Glover's career after the publication of her book had hatched it was one which did not immediately use its wings. She turned to many assistants for support. Devoted helpers served her until they could no longer serve, sometimes because of their own limitations and sometimes because of hers, one of which was a morbid conviction that people who turned against her in any way could ruin her health by merely thinking evil about her.

One of Mary Glover's students, coming to her after a disappointing experience with another, was Gilbert Eddy, younger than Mary and not impressive to anyone but his teacher. Mary's followers were indeed surprised when on New Year's Day, 1877, Mary Glover became Mary Baker Eddy, the name by which she has since been known to the world. It gave the astonishing woman a sense of security from evil to have so intimately loyal a protector, but it did not keep her safe, in her own view, from the mental ravages of those who did not wish her well.

The Christian Science Church had been formed and its members were increasing in number. Revenue from licensed teachers and practitioners kept pouring in, but there were at the outset troubles over the founder's extremely personal domination of her organization. In 1881 eight of her students rebelled and withdrew, to Mrs. Eddy's amazement and alarm. It seemed best for her to leave Lynn and move to Boston. Here she founded the Massachusetts Metaphysical College, with herself as president, for teaching the application of her principles to the treatment of disease.

Shortly after the college was opened, Asa Gilbert Eddy came down with an illness which Mrs. Eddy diagnosed as arsenical poisoning resulting from malicious animal magnetism applied against him by one of her enemies. It must have been malicious indeed and very powerful, for Mary was unable to save him. He died in June, 1882, and his body, which in Mary's view did not exist, was taken up the busy Merrimack to bustling Tilton where it was allowed to continue its nonexistence under the elms of the cemetery by the river, his grave marked by a still visible marble shaft.

Gilbert Eddy's removal from her household left Mrs. Eddy in a difficult position and subject to all her former ailments. She had to have someone else and, though she never married again, she found her best helper in Calvin A. Frye, who with a devotion which was almost fanatical served her for the remainder of her life, becoming so much a part of her existence that neither could have existed without the other.

The Christian Science Church grew and prospered, its work spreading throughout the nation. Mrs. Eddy never for one moment relinquished the slightest element of control over it. It was and it remained until her death in 1910 her personal property, a reality which in her eyes could have had no more existence than a dream but which at her death was real enough to be recognized by the law as an estate of some $3,000,000.

Mary Baker Eddy spent most of her last years, from 1892 to 1908, almost a recluse, in the region of her birth. When her presence in Boston, where she was accessible to the leaders of her church, became an annoyance to her, she returned to the banks of the Merrimack, in Concord, New Hampshire, where she built up an estate in which she could live privately with her proven retainers about her. Her removal from Boston intensified, if anything, the strange miracle of her leadership. In spite of opposition, in spite of actual attack, she remained in the eyes of many what Ann Lee before her had claimed to be and Mary Patterson had determined to be —the embodiment on earth of the female principle of God. She was the product of those influences of the Merrimack country which made Daniel Webster a gigantic figure of a different sort, a different but no more likely to be forgotten feature of the portrait of the river.

19 The Phoenix and the Turtle

....

It is apparent that the Merrimack and its people have been a great combined force in American life, thought and history, helping to shape political, intellectual, religious and social ideas, to win wars, to develop new ways of producing wealth and of taking sustenance from the earth. It is apparent, too, that the civilization of the valley has been something like a growing vine, sending out strong shoots which sometimes have found the ground too shallow for rooting and withered back to the main stem to begin groping outward all over again. The idea of canal and river traffic failed. Coaching and droving, once the stronger stem of the railroad asserted itself, could find no sustenance. The economy of grain and vegetables gave place to sheep, which in turn, as the West opened up, could not be produced in quantity at a profit and disappeared, leaving the river hills bare, the wild life and the forest driven northward and the river channels free to flood. The railroad and the fabulously productive giant units of the textile industry lasted for a century, but they, too, failed and had to change.

The recovery of the nation from the terrible disasters of the Civil War and the need of developing the West made the second half of the nineteenth century a deceptively prosperous period. The devising of means of production of inexpensive steel in enormous quantities helped to make the growth of transportation, manufacturing and construction so easy that it was not always possible to see where the growth might end or what it might carry along with it. The Merrimack Valley seemed to be a gold mine, and no one could believe that its wealth was not inexhaustible. Perhaps it still is inexhaustible, but its exploiters had and still have much to learn.

What happened in the city of Manchester, New Hampshire, happened to most of the other industrial cities of the valley. It is an excellent illustration of the dangers to which commercial success exposes men when they no longer face life as if it might at any moment be necessary to begin all over again at the bottom. It was the textile industry, sent off to a flying start by Francis Cabot Lowell and his associates at Waltham and Lowell, which gave to North America the conception of industrial capitalism. It was the textile industry, which, after a century of triumph, demonstrated that the potentialities of capital without freshness of vision and scrupulous control may be as destructive as they might, under other circumstances, be creative.

The Amoskeag Manufacturing Company, of whose beginnings and rise to greatness I have given a picture in Chapter 12, had, after the First World War, reached what appeared to be a peak of success. The policy of the company's early days, which had been one of aiding competitors, was reversed. The large profits and mounting surplus were used to buy up and incorporate into the gigantic enterprise all those firms in the neighborhood of Manchester, many of whose plants had been built with Amoskeag money, which were engaged in the production of similar products. The last of these to be purchased, in 1922, was the huge Stark Mills, whose buildings were almost a part of the Amoskeag plant. Shortly before this purchase, the Amoskeag Corporation had shown a year's profit of some $8,000,000 and in 1920 the stockholders re-

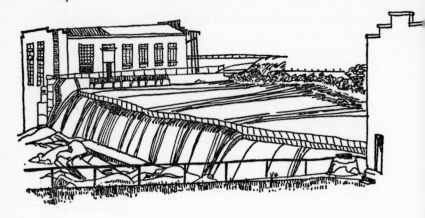

ceived a dividend of 100 per cent. The corporation's surplus had reached something like $30,000,000.

This state of affairs looked to the general public like success, as well it might. Yet within the giant's system there were signs of malignancy. Some of these were the result of a threatening postwar depression, felt by most industries, which came to a head in the commodity panic of 1921. Others were the result of internal conditions peculiar to such a gigantic structure and to the appearance in the company's management of elements which regarded acquisitive control of the company's finances as more important than imaginative control of its production and markets.

As early as 1920, in spite of excellent profits, Amoskeag curtailed its production, reducing both the amount of work it offered its employees and the rate of pay for what was left for them to do. Wages were cut 22½ per cent. There was no way out for the employees, who trusted the company not to do any more wage-cutting since practically the entire city of Manchester depended upon what they had to spend. Unhappy as they were, the workers were made still more unhappy a little more than a year later when the management announced a further 20-per-cent wage cut and a six-hour increase in the length of the work week. This was not too easy for the employees to take or for the management to explain. The United Textile Workers sent an officer to Manchester to take a poll of Amoskeag employees. More than twelve thousand said that they were unwilling to take the cut; 118 voted to accept it.

In February, 1922, a strike was declared, whereupon the company closed all its mills in Manchester and implied that they would stay closed. Neither the company nor the workers, however, had any idea that the strike would last as long as it did. It was nine months before the strikers went back to work, accepting some rather humiliating conditions in exchange for the privilege of doing so—a work week of fifty-four hours and the proviso that strike leaders were to be barred from returning to their jobs.

By 1923, Manchester was back to something like normal, but the New England textile business was not. The threat of Southern competition which grew after the First World War became still more noticeable and fabrics of synthetic fibres, replacing the old-fashioned cotton ginghams which had been an Amoskeag stand-by for years, were capturing the market. In spite of the artificial prosperity which prevailed in the nation until 1929-30, the cotton-textile business was shaky. At first few suspected that Amoskeag, that industrial Gibraltar, had really reached a crisis and that its intransigence in the 1922 strike had weakened it dangerously.

In the first years of the depression the company lost money and another serious strike in 1933 hurt the corporation even more than it hurt the now desperate workers, by this time much reduced in number by frequent layoffs. Although the holding company which controlled the Amoskeag Manufacturing Company still had many millions of cash, the corporation's policy had been to let its plant become obsolete and incapable of keeping its top place in the world market.

When in 1935 the great plant, stretching as far as the eye could reach along the Merrimack and its tributary canals, almost hiding from sight the great Amoskeag Falls, closed its doors, few could believe that they would never open again. The Amoskeag mills had made and sustained the city. What was to become of it if there was no Amoskeag, which at its height had employed nearly one third of the total population of the city? The company owned the houses in which most of its employees lived. It simply could not be. Yet it was.

On December 24, 1935, 104 years after its incorporation, the Amoskeag Manufacturing Corporation filed in the United States District Court a petition in bankruptcy accompanied by a plea that it be allowed to reorganize. The city was stunned. The court ordered the company to submit its plan for reorganization, which it did on March 9, 1936. As if to emphasize a distaste for the burden which its once hale and hearty offspring had imposed upon it, the Merrimack River staged, in the same month, a protest of such violence that it shook the entire state. The most disastrous flood in the history of New Hampshire, resulting from a combination in the highlands of the upper river of heavy snow, ice and torrential rain, roared down the river destroying everything in its path. While the referee in bankruptcy was studying the Amoskeag Manufacturing Company's petition, the river which had given the great corporation its life and wealth was savagely trying to tear its physical property to pieces.

On July ninth, when the ravages of the river along its banks in Manchester were still unrepaired, Arthur Black, Special Master in Bankruptcy, solemnly denied the company's plea for reorganization and ordered its liquidation. It was planned to hold an auction for the sale of the corporation's real estate and machinery, a procedure which if carried out might well have meant doom for the city.

UP FROM THE ASHES

The cities of the Merrimack are not easily doomed. A group of Manchester citizens looked into the matter and learned that the property of the bankrupt giant had been appraised at $5,000,000. The court, in the person of the Master in Bankruptcy, agreed to allow the property to be sold for that amount. The citizens' committee, well aware of what would happen if the machinery of the plant were sold at auction and moved out of the city, sat down to try to figure out where to get $5,000,000. They canvassed the city and received pledges totalling $560,000. The New Hampshire Public Service Company offered to buy the water power and steam plant for $2,250,000. Savings banks in Manchester agreed to put up the remaining $2,190,000 in the form of mortgages on the plant and equipment. A new corporation, called Amoskeag Industries, Inc., was formed to take over the property and those who pledged the $560,000 became its stockholders. It is probable that not one of those foresighted citizens realized that he was doing much more than helping to postpone disaster. It is certain that not one subscriber to the stock of Amoskeag Industries had the slightest hope of getting his money back. In any case, by October, 1936, the threatened city of Manchester had in its hands the means of saving itself.

The directors of Amoskeag Industries knew that they could not hope to find or to create a single manufacturing concern capable of operating the gigantic plant as a producing unit. They knew, too, that there was much equipment not likely to be needed by any new occupants of the plant and which, if wisely sold, could produce the working capital needed to keep the property going. How the directors worked and with what success has been told by Colonel William Parker Straw, one of the prime movers in the struggle to save Amoskeag. Speaking in 1946, Mr. Straw said:

> A machinery salesman of the highest reputation was engaged who began to sell pickers, cards, spinning frames, and looms, not only in accordance with the plan of orderly liquidation, but also to furnish the much needed working capital, for it was costing almost a thousand dollars a day to operate the business—taxes, interest charges, coal for heating, insurance, repairs, and a host of incidental expenses were mounting rapidly.
>
> Mills were sold for whatever the purchaser would give, in many cases with a small down payment and a comparatively large mortgage: floor space was rented at ridiculously low figures: every inducement, every encouragement was offered to anyone, who showed any promise, to buy or rent property for manufacturing purposes—to give employment and develop a pay roll for the city.
>
> As soon as a portion of the mortgage was paid, more money was borrowed to start in operation one of the old mills, the Jefferson Mill, to demonstrate to the public that Manchester was, as claimed, a good place in which to live and manufacture. This concern, Amoskeag Fabrics, Inc. was soon sold to a New York Company which still is carrying on the business upon a profitable basis. The money from this sale was invested in a *second* company which soon was sold, and then a *third, fourth,* and *fifth* were organized in rapid succession, each started on its way and then turned over to new owners, the Industries, in every case, retaining for a time a portion of its original investment.
>
> One venture was a failure and four, as it happened, were reasonably successful, but they caused much anxiety

at times because many thousands of dollars were invested in them.

Amoskeag Industries started business in the Fall of 1936 and now, ten years later, is finishing the job it undertook. All the machinery in all the mills, all the unimproved land within the yard, all the houses and tenements, and much of the land owned throughout the city have been sold. Every building and every mill have been disposed of and, happily, the floor space is practically all occupied. In fact, there are now 113 concerns operating in the old Amoskeag property, employing more than 11,000 people, with weekly payrolls which must in the aggregate far exceed the roll which the Amoskeag had at the height of its glory.

Amoskeag Industries has almost finished the work which it had to do. It never sought to make money merely for money's sake; it never rejected any reasonable proposition which would bring industry to Manchester; it has spent thousands of dollars in advertising, and through industrial agents has sought to induce corporations outside the state to come to this city. It has had many disappointments; it has met with failures; it has made mistakes, but it has had a comforting measure of success.

Since 1946 that success has become complete. Manchester is itself again, although the force which first made it what it is is now only a name. The city is no longer dependent upon a single huge venture by whose success or failure it must stand or fall. It has been proved that the Merrimack can hold those who depend upon it if only they are wise enough and willing enough to change when conditions change. Manchester was not alone in proving that this is so. Nashua, where the great Nashua Manufacturing Company had a similar experience, found a like way out. Lowell, Lawrence and Haverhill in differing degrees have had the same problem. Even Newburyport, whose rise was interrupted before any of the upriver cities had thought of industrialization, is alive, alert and busy, safe like the others not in concentration but in diversity.

PIONEER TO PLAYGROUND

One very important change in the life of the Merrimack Valley, as in the life of most of New England, which would have made the seventeenth-century settlers at the Merrimack mouth acutely uncomfortable, is the emergence of the idea of making an industry out of the task of giving to men, women and children in search of pleasure and relaxation exactly what they want and, if possible, more than they might ordinarily hope to get. It is true that for a century or more people have been coming to the Merrimack Valley and the mountains about it and beyond it for summer rest and recreation. Only since the rise of the motorcar and motorboat, however, has the beauty and wonder and invigorating excitement of New England become something susceptible of being marketed in every corner of the United States. Incredibly beautiful and almost unspoiled Lake Winnipesaukee, New Hampshire's largest body of water, has been for years one of the East's great playgrounds, providing boating, swimming, fishing and almost unlimited facilities for recreation in an incomparable setting. Only since the rise in popularity of the ski has it been possible to get large numbers of people to turn the discomforts of snow and cold into pleasures by visiting the slopes of New Hampshire mountains in winter.

The profits from these enticements of summer and winter have become not pin money but an important part of the economy of the region. Although the original cost is far higher, a flock of motel cells will bring in, in a season, a far greater revenue than a flock of sheep and the always adaptable people of the Merrimack, from the sea to mountains,

have not been slow to discover the fact. What effect the enormous vacation business of summer and winter is having upon the permanent residents of the Merrimack Valley it is difficult to say. It is difficult, too, to say what might have been the effect upon Daniel Webster, the Merrimack's greatest son, had Ebenezer Webster run a motel instead of a farm and had the woods and fields through which Daniel loved to roam and hunt and fish been full not merely of rabbits, grouse, wild pigeons, foxes, bears and deer, but also of out-of-state hunters, skiers and hikers. It is difficult to say, and, fortunately, unnecessary. As Daniel Websters are needed, the Merrimack Valley, so resourceful is its gentle power as a maker of men, will undoubtedly produce them.

Here, by this alternately turbulent and tranquil river, nothing it seems is entirely a wasted effort, nothing is entirely lost. The canal is lost, but its spirit of enterprise remains in the railroad. The steam railroad is lost, but its spirit of enterprise remains in the internal-combustion engine of track and highway. The discords and intolerances arising out of the early settlers' fear of letting go of the moral and physical controls of their ancestors were lost in the struggle for union and understanding, which has created not a jealous collection of colonies but a great nation with a real but not always recognized unity of faith and feeling, hope and purpose, where a new race of men has found a home in the New World.

TODAY AND TOMORROW

Strong and compelling as have been the Merrimack Valley's influences upon men, those influences cannot continue to operate automatically. I have pointed out some of the mistakes of judgment, the blind alleys of hope and enthusiasm which its people have made and wandered into. In seventeenth-century Newbury there were some who saw dangers in too much concern for commercial success, the danger of becoming blind to the spiritual side of life, the danger of killing the goose that seemed in the habit of laying golden eggs. Those dangers are in the offing today, ready to sweep in and harm us if the guarding pressure of intelligent vision is relaxed. Two dangers which threaten the valley will ever call for vigilance on the part of its people. The first is the danger of flood. Most residents of the valley are fully aware of what Merrimack floods can do, but many, exercising the Yankee taste for distrusting experts, have been reluctant to make the sacrifices necessary to control them. Flood-control measures, which often involve the turning of good farm land into beds for emergency reservoirs, have met with opposition from those who do not see why they should be inconvenienced to save from drowning downriver men, women and children whom they never see, who, living in another state perhaps, are practically foreigners.

There are signs, since the Massachusetts and Connecticut floods of 1955, that the people of the upper valleys are beginning to understand and accept their obligation. Massachusetts and New Hampshire have jointly assumed responsibility for flood control on the Merrimack and several essential control dams opposed a few years ago have now been approved. Perhaps it will not take another disaster to broaden the base, in the Merrimack Valley, of the feeling that one man cannot have either perfect peace or complete liberty at the expense of another's safety.

The other current danger is less obvious than danger from rampaging and ravaging water. Yet this danger is inherent in the very flow of the river. Although it has been recognized by law, little has been done to combat it, and its existence threatens the prosperity of that growing industry of recreational hospitality of which I have just been speaking.

Before the growth of industry and the spread of the congested population which it carries with it, salmon, shad, sturgeon and other valuable and tasty fish were plentiful at all points in the Merrimack. Mills and the dwellers in cities regarded brooks and rivers as convenient sewers, and used them as such. Long stretches of the river and its tributaries are now torpid, discolored and stinking instead of quicksilver bright or white as cold milk where rapids wash between granite boulders. Fish will not breed there and only a few will travel in the fouled water. Vacationers will not, indeed should not, swim in it, or even trail their hands in it from their pleasure boats.

Between the mill towns tumble glaciers of cans and rubbish, old automobile tires, old automobiles themselves, rusted and greasy, bedsprings, bottles and cartons, punctured mattresses, crockery and broken chairs. Who will come from far away to look at such as this? Who will spend his savings to build a house by a stream which is only an open sewer?

The Merrimack and its tributaries are a proud part and possession of American life and those who live it. Can it be that the men who have taken from it all that they have and are will not find ways of keeping its waters pure and as sweet as the mountain lakes? The ingenuity which its people have always exhibited can surely find ways of doing this. It is to their interest to want to.

This valley was made by a glacier for life which could not co-exist with ice. The life which followed the ice could not exist half savage and half civilized. The valley changed. Its people changed and will change, for the better, we believe. We have climbed the stream as the salmon and shad once did and may again. There are reminders of the past everywhere and promises of the future. Men may remember and still keep the promises. A river always flows from past to present and on into the sea of the future, and while there are men, they will be found in its valley and with them will be found their heights and depths, their triumphs and their defeats. A river and its people are inseparable. They ultimately grow to resemble each other.

Acknowledgment

....

To acknowledge indebtedness in the preparation over a period of years of a book such as this is to run the risk of expressing gratitude to some and slighting others. Assistance in such a project must sometimes be intangible.

I must, however, gratefully acknowledge the co-operation of John P. Marquand of Newburyport, Massachusetts, Robert Frost of Ripton, Vermont, Henry Christman of New York City and of Carl Carmer and Jean Crawford, editors of the Rivers of America Series.

I could not have gone far without the generous help of Mildred McKay, State Librarian, and the staff of the New Hampshire State Library in Concord, nor without the use of the extraordinarily well arranged facilities of the Baker Library of Dartmouth College. Jean Claggett, Librarian of the Richards Library, Newport, New Hampshire, has also been a great help.

To Barbara Perkins of New York I am indebted for material provided, and to my wife for labors on the manuscript which I could not possibly have performed myself, and without which this book would not exist. I have also to thank Sherwood C. and Marjorie Badmington for generous help in copy reading.

Bibliography

ALBREE, JOHN, ed., *Whittier Correspondence from the Oak Knoll Collections, 1830–1892*. Salem, 1911.

ANDREWS, CHARLES M., *The Colonial Period in American History*. 3 vols. New Haven, 1935.

BATCHELDER, SAMUEL, *Introduction and Early Progress of the Cotton Manufacture in the United States*. Boston, 1863.

BELKNAP, JEREMY, *American Biography*, Vol. 2, John Winthrop. 1789.

BELKNAP, JEREMY, *The History of New Hampshire*. Comprehending the Events of One Complete Century from the Discovery of the River Piscataqua. 3 vols. 1812.

BENNETT, WHITMAN, *Whittier, Bard of Freedom*. Chapel Hill, 1941.

BISHOP, J. L., *History of American Manufactures from 1608 to 1860*. Philadelphia, 1861–68.

BLOOD, GRACE E. *Manchester on the Merrimack*. Manchester, 1948.

BOUTON, NATHANIEL, *The History of Concord*. Concord, 1856.

BRADFORD, GAMALIEL, *As God Made Them*. Boston and New York, 1929.

BROWN, JOHN MARSHALL, *Coasting Voyages in the Gulf of Maine, Made in the Years 1604, 5 and 6 by Samuel Champlain*. Bath, 1875.

BROWNE, GEORGE WALDO, *The Amoskeag Manufacturing Company of Manchester, New Hampshire. A History*. Manchester, 1915.

BROWNE, GEORGE WALDO, *Indian Nights*. New York, 1927.

BROWNE, GEORGE WALDO, *The River of Broken Waters*. Manchester, 1918.

BUTLER, CALEB, *History of the Town of Groton, Including Pepperell and Shirley*. Boston, 1848.

CAMPBELL, DOUGLAS, *The Puritan in Holland, England and America*. An Introduction to American History. 2 vols. New York, 1892.

CAREY, ROBERT LINCOLN, *Daniel Webster As an Economist*. New York, 1929.

CAVERLY, ROBERT B., *Heroism of Hannah Dustin*. Boston, 1874.

CAVERLY, ROBERT B., *The Merrimack and Its Incidents*. Boston, 1886.

CHAMPLAIN, SAMUEL DE, *The Voyages of Samuel de Champlain*. 3 vols. Boston, 1878–82.

CHANDLER, WILLIAM EATON, *Reminiscences and Events in Concord's History*. Concord, 1904.

CHURCHILL, WINSTON S., *A History of the English-Speaking Peoples*. 4 vols. New York, 1956–1958.

CLAFLIN, MARY B., *Personal Recollections of John Greenleaf Whittier*. New York, 1893.

CLARKE, THOMAS C., AND OTHERS, *The American Railway*. Its Construction, Development, Management, and Appliances. New York, 1889.

COBURN, F. W., *History of Lowell and Its People*. New York, 1920.

COFFIN, JOSHUA, *A Sketch of the History of Newbury, Newburyport and West Newbury from 1635 to 1845*. Boston, 1845.

COLEMAN, EMMA LEWIS, *New England Captives Carried to Canada Between 1677 and 1760 During the French and Indian Wars*. 2 vols. Portland, 1925.

Collections of the New Hampshire Historical Society.

COOK, HOWARD M., *Wayside Jottings*. Concord, 1909.

COOLIDGE, A. J., AND MANSFIELD, J. B., *History and Description of New England. New Hampshire*. Boston, 1860.

CURRIER, JOHN J., *Historical Sketch of Shipbuilding on the Merrimack*. Newburyport, 1877.

CURTIS, GEORGE T., *Daniel Webster*. 2 vols. New York, 1870.

DAKIN, EDWIN FRANDEN, *Mrs. Eddy*. New York, 1930.

DAVIS, REBECCA I., *Gleanings from the Merrimack Valley*. Portland, 1881. Sheaf No. 2, Haverhill, 1887.

DICKENS, CHARLES, *American Notes*. Boston, 1890.

Dictionary of American Biography. New York, 1953.

DRAKE, SAMUEL G., *Annals of Witchcraft in New England*. Boston, 1869.

DRAKE, SAMUEL G., *Biography and History of the Indians of North America*. Boston, 1834.

DRAKE, SAMUEL G., *The Witchcraft Delusion in New England*. Roxbury, 1866.

EARLE, ALICE MORSE, *Stagecoach and Tavern Days*. New York, 1900.

ELLIS, G. E., *Memoir of Sir Benjamin Thompson, Count Rumford, with Notices of His Daughter*. Boston, 1871.

EMERSON, RALPH WALDO, *Nature, Addresses, and Lectures*. Boston, 1897.

Encyclopedia Britannica. Eleventh Edition. Cambridge, 1910–11.

FARMER, JOHN, AND MOORE, JACOB B., *Gazeteer of the State of New Hampshire*. Concord, 1823.

FROST, ROBERT, *Collected Poems*. New York, 1939.

FUESS, CLAUDE MOORE, *Daniel Webster*. 2 vols. Boston, 1930.

GILBERT, A. B., *History of Salem, New Hampshire*. Concord, 1907.

GILMAN, ALFRED, *The Merrimack River, Its Sources, Affluents Etc.* (Old Residents' Historical Association Contributions). Vol. 2. 1883.

GOLDTHWAIT, LAWRENCE, *The Geology of New Hampshire*. 3 vols. Concord, 1951–56.

GOODWIN, WILLIAM B., *The Ruins of Great Ireland in New England*. Boston, 1946.

GOODWIN, WILLIAM B., *The Truth About Leif Ericsson and the Greenland Voyages to New England*.

HAKLUYT, RICHARD. *The Principal Navigations, Voyages and Discoveries of the English Nation, etc.* London, 1589.

HAPGOOD, NORMAN, Daniel Webster. Boston, 1899.

HAUGEN, EINAR, Voyages to Vinland. The First American Saga Newly Translated and Interpreted. New York, 1942.

HILL, HAMILTON A., Memoir of Abbott Lawrence. Boston, 1884.

HILL, HOWARD F., The Merrimack: Sources, Navigation and Related Matters. n.p. n.d.

HITCHCOCK, C. H., AND HUNTINGTON, J. H., The Geology of New Hampshire. A Report Comprising the Results of Explorations Ordered by the Legislature. Concord, 1874.

HOWELLS, JOHN MEAD, The Architectural Heritage of the Merrimack. New York, 1941.

HURD, DUANE HAMILTON, History of Essex County, Massachusetts. Philadelphia, 1888.

HURD, DUANE HAMILTON, History of Merrimack and Belknap Counties, New Hampshire. Philadelphia, 1885.

JOHNSON, GERALD W., America's Silver Age; the Statecraft of Clay-Webster-Calhoun. New York, 1939.

Journal of the New Hampshire House of Representatives, January Session. 1953.

LARCOM, LUCY, A New England Girlhood. Boston, 1889.

LAWRENCE, WILLIAM, Life of Amos A. Lawrence, with Extracts from His Diary and Correspondence. Boston, 1887.

LAWRENCE, WILLIAM R., ed., Extracts from the Diary and Correspondence of the Late Amos Lawrence with a Brief Account of Some Incidents in His Life. Boston, 1856.

LYFORD, JAMES O., ed., History of Concord, New Hampshire. Concord, New Hampshire, City History Commission, 1903.

MARQUAND, JOHN P., Thirty Years. Boston, 1954.

MATHER, COTTON, Magnalia Christi Americana. 2 vols. Hartford, 1853.

MATHER, COTTON, The Wonders of the Invisible World. London, 1693.

MEADER, J. W., The Merrimack River: Its Source and Its Tributaries. Boston, 1869.

MERRILL, ELIPHALET, Gazeteer of the State of New Hampshire. Exeter, 1817.

MERRILL, JOSEPH, *History of Amesbury.* Haverhill, 1880.

MERRIMACK RIVER VALLEY SEWAGE BOARD, MASSACHUSETTS, *Joint Board To Investigate . . . Disposal of Sewage in the Merrimack River.* Boston, 1947.

MILLER, PERRY, *The New England Mind. The 17th Century.* New York, 1939.

MILLER, PERRY, *The New England Mind. From Colony to Province.* Cambridge, 1953.

MIRICK, BENJAMIN L., *The History of Haverhill, Massachusetts.* Haverhill, 1832.

MOORE, JACOB BAILEY, *Annals of the Town of Concord in the County of Merrimack and State of New Hampshire, from Its First Settlement in the Year 1726 to the Year 1823.* Concord, 1824.

MOOREHEAD, WARREN R., *The Merrimack Archaeological Survey.* Salem, 1931.

MORGAN, LEWIS H., *Houses and Houselife of the American Aborigines.* n.p. 1881.

MORISON, SAMUEL ELIOT, *The Maritime History of Massachusetts.* Boston, 1921.

MORISON, SAMUEL ELIOT, AND COMMAGER, HENRY STEELE, *The Growth of the American Republic.* 2 vols. New York, 1937.

NEW HAMPSHIRE FISH AND GAME DEPARTMENT, *Biological Survey of the Merrimack Watershed.* Report of Earl E. Hoover, Biologist in Charge of Survey to the New Hampshire Fish and Game Commission and Director . . . New Hampshire Fish and Game Department. Rochester, 1938.

New Hampshire: Public Acts and Joint Resolutions of the Legislature of 1953. Published by the Secretary of State.

PARKMAN, FRANCIS, *Pioneers of France in the New World.* Boston, 1886.

PENHALLOW, SAMUEL, *History of the Wars of New England with the Eastern Indians.* New Hampshire Historical Society Collection, Vol. 1. 1824.

PICKARD, SAMUEL THOMAS, *Life and Letters of John Greenleaf Whittier.* Boston and New York, 1894.

POHL, FREDERICK J., *The Sinclair Expedition to Nova Scotia in 1398.* Princeton, 1950.

POOR, ALFRED, *Historical and Genealogical Researches and Recorder of Passing Events of the Merrimack Valley.* Haverhill, 1857–58.

PRESCOTT, WILLIAM, *Report on the Alterations in the Channel of Merrimack River.* New Hampshire Historical Society Collections, Vol. 7. 1863.

RAFN, CARL CHRISTIAN, *Antiquitates Americanae Sive Scriptores Septentrionales Rerum Ante-Columbianarum in America.* 1837.

REES, JAMES, *The Beauties of the Hon. Daniel Webster.* New York, 1839.

ROBERTS, CHRISTOPHER, *The Middlesex Canal.* Cambridge, 1938.

ROBINSON, CHARLES E., *A Concise History of the United Society of Believers Called Shakers.* East Canterbury, 1893.

RUSK, RALPH L., *The Life of Ralph Waldo Emerson.* New York, 1949.

SANBORN, EDWIN P., *History of New Hampshire.* From Its First Discovery to the Year 1830. Manchester, 1875.

SILVER, HELENETTE, *History of New Hampshire Game and Furbearers.* Concord, 1957.

SQUIRES, J. DUANE, *The Granite State of the United States.* A History of New Hampshire from 1623 to the Present. 4 vols. New York, 1956.

STARKEY, MARION L., *The Devil in Massachusetts.* A Modern Inquiry into the Salem Witch Trials. New York, 1949.

STRAW, WILLIAM PARKER, *Amoskeag in New Hampshire—an Epic in American Industry.* New York, 1948.

TAFT, H. C., *Early Days of Railroading.* Lowell, 1913.

TANNER, H. S., *A Description of the Canals and Railroads of the United States, Comprehending Notices of All the Works of Internal Improvement Throughout the Several States.* New York, 1840.

THOREAU, HENRY DAVID, *A Week on the Concord and Merrimack Rivers.* Boston and New York, 1894.

UNITED STATES. OFFICE OF CHIEF OF ENGINEERS, *Letter from the Secretary of War Transmitting, with a Letter from the Chief of Engineers, Reports of Examination and Survey of the Merrimack River, Massachusetts, from Its Mouth to Haverhill.* Washington, 1909.

VARNUM, ATKINSON, *Navigation on the Merrimack River.* Old Residents' Historical Association Contributions, Vol. 1. 1879.

VOSE, G. L., *A Sketch of the Life and Works of Loammi Baldwin, Civil Engineer.* Boston, 1885.

WALKER, JOSEPH BURBEEN, *Chronicles of an Old New England Farm: The House and Farm of the First Minister of Concord, N.H. 1728–1906.* Concord, 1908.

WALKER, JOSEPH BURBEEN, *Diaries of the Rev. Timothy Walker Nov. 18, 1730 to Sept. 1, 1782.* 1889.

WALKER, JOSEPH BURBEEN, *The Forests of New Hampshire.* Concord, 1883.

WALKER, JOSEPH BURBEEN, *Historical Sketch of the New Hampshire Asylum for the Insane.* Manchester, 1886.

WALKER, JOSEPH BURBEEN, *The New Hampshire Covenant of 1774.* Concord, 1903.

WALKER, JOSEPH B., *The Valley of the Merrimack.* Concord, 1863.

WEBSTER, DANIEL, *Correspondence Between Mr. Webster and His New Hampshire Neighbors.* Washington, 1850.

WEBSTER, DANIEL, *The Diplomatic and Official Papers of Daniel Webster, While Secretary of State.* New York, 1848.

WEBSTER, DANIEL, *The Letters of Daniel Webster,* C. H. Van Tyne, ed. New York, 1902.

WEBSTER, DANIEL, *The Private Correspondence of Daniel Webster,* Fletcher Webster, ed. Boston, 1857.

WHITTIER, JOHN GREENLEAF, *Works.* 7 vols. Boston and New York, 1892.

WILBUR, SIBYL, *The Life of Mary Baker Eddy.* New York, 1908.

WILSON, HAROLD FISHER, *The Hill Country of Northern New England. Its Social and Economic History, 1790–1830.* New York, 1936.

WINSOR, JUSTIN, *The Memorial History of Boston.* 4 vols. Boston, 1881–83.

WINSOR, JUSTIN, *Narrative and Critical History of America.* 8 vols. Boston, 1889.

WINTHROP, JOHN, *The History of New England from 1630–1649.* Boston, 1825–26.

WOODBURY, GEORGE, *John Goffe's Mill.* New York, 1948.

WORKERS OF THE FEDERAL WRITERS' PROJECT OF THE WORKS PROGRESS ADMINISTRATION FOR THE STATE OF NEW HAMPSHIRE, *American Guide Series. New Hampshire. A Guide to the Granite State.* Boston, 1938.

Index

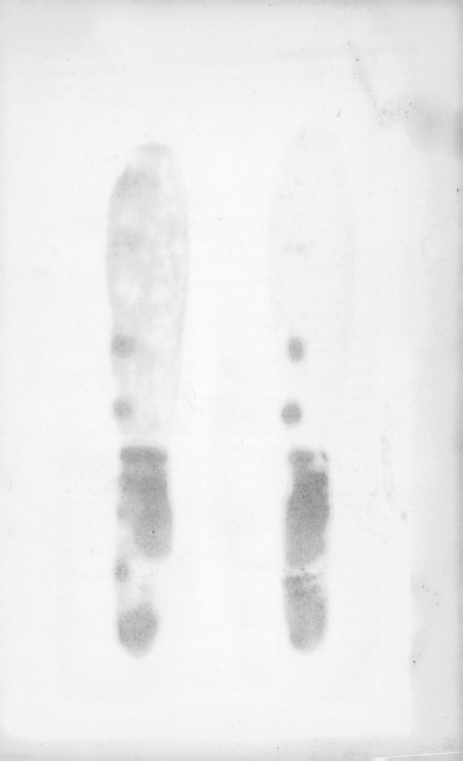

DATE DUE

JUN 07 1996	
NOV 28 2000	
8/30/04	